The County Court Practitioner 2000

AUSTRALIA
LBC Information Services
Sydney

CANADA AND USA
Carswell
Toronto

NEW ZEALAND
Brooker's
Auckland

SINGAPORE AND MALAYSIA
Sweet & Maxwell Asia
Singapore and Kuala Lumpur

The County Court Practitioner 2000

Fifteenth Edition

Stephen M. Gerlis

District Judge

Robert Blackford, LLB, FCI ARB

Barrister, Former Solicitor

Sweet & Maxwell

Published in 2000 by
Sweet & Maxwell Limited of
100 Avenue Road, Swiss Cottage, London NW3 3PF
(http://www.smlawpub.co.uk)
Typeset by Dataword Services Limited, Chilcompton
Printed and bound in Great Britain by
MPG Books Ltd, Bodmin, Cornwall.

No natural forests were destroyed to make this product;
only farmed timber was used and replanted

A CIP catalogue record for this book
is available from the British Library.

ISBN 0752 007 114

Preface

In the last couple of editions of this book we forecast the great changes that were to come affecting civil practice and procedure. Now they have arrived and are in place. The Woolf proposals have been transformed into the Civil Procedure Rules and mark the most radical change to civil practice and procedure for over a century. The poker game system of litigation has been replaced with its complete opposite — cards on the table. The adversarial system has been supplanted by a requirement of co-operation both with the court and between parties. The control of litigation is now firmly taken out of the hands of the parties and their lawyers and placed within the responsibility of the courts, who will be prepared to enforce case management by drastic sanctions if necessary. No longer will costs be allowed to total up like a taxi-meter, dependent on the amount of work done — proportionality applies throughout all of the new changes. No more making mountains out of molehills. This applies both subjectively and objectively — courts will look at cases not only within their own context but in relation to court resources generally, to see whether too many of these precious resources are being wasted on cases which do not merit it.

Those practitioners who thought that the new provisions were merely tinkering with the old have come in for a rude awakening. The changes have been described as the "litigation revolution" and that is not over-stating the position. Early indications are that the changes are working effectively — the only real difficulties being created by the necessity to get used to a changed regime. The introduction of pre-action protocols means that much of the work must be "front-loaded" with a definite view to settlement. Failure to go down this path could be very expensive for those who do not heed the warnings.

What we have endeavoured to do in this publication is not just slavishly to reproduce all the rules and practice directions, but to put them in their context from a practical point of view

PREFACE

— giving advice where necessary under the heading "Practical Points". The object of the exercise is that this book should be easily portable and usable for the busy practitioner, be they qualified or unqualified, student or trainee. In this we are following a successful tradition established not only for this book but for the whole of the Practitioner series. The work is up to date as of September 1999.

We would like to thank all the staff at Sweet & Maxwell for their encouragement and assistance and our families for all their support.

District Judge Stephen Gerlis   October 1999
Robert Blackford

Contents

CONTENTS

CONTENTS

CONTENTS

CONTENTS

CONTENTS

CONTENTS

CONTENTS

CONTENTS

Table of Cases

TABLE OF CASES

TABLE OF CASES

Table of Statutes

[Where legislation is reproduced in the test, the paragraph reference is **bold**]

Table of Statutory Instruments

[Where legislation is reproduced in the test, the paragraph reference is **bold***]*

TABLE OF STATUTORY INSTRUMENTS

Table of Civil Procedure Rules

[Where legislation is reproduced in the test, the paragraph reference is **bold***]*

TABLE OF CIVIL PROCEDURE RULES

TABLE OF CIVIL PROCEDURE RULES

TABLE OF CIVIL PROCEDURE RULES

TABLE OF CIVIL PROCEDURE RULES

TABLE OF CIVIL PROCEDURE RULES

TABLE OF CIVIL PROCEDURE RULES

TABLE OF CIVIL PROCEDURE RULES

Chapter 1

The New Scheme

Background to the Scheme

In July 1996 Lord Woolf presented his final report *Access to* **1.01**
Justice on a review of the current rules and procedures of the
civil courts in England and Wales. The aims of the review were:

- To improve access to justice and reduce the costs of litigation;

- To reduce the complexity of the rules and modernise terminology;

- To remove unnecessary distinctions of practice and procedure;

- To ensure that litigation is dealt with expeditiously.

In October 1996, the Lord Chancellor published his strategy
for implementing Lord Woolf's review with a target date for
implementation of the main elements of October 1998. This
date was pushed back to April 26, 1999.

The civil justice reforms are now in force as the Civil
Procedure Rules 1998 (CPR), and are based on the principles
contained in Lord Woolf's report. Various amendments to the
practice directions have been made since they came into force
and will no doubt be made in the future.

The Civil Procedure Rules and practice directions can be
found in the *Civil Procedure* (2nd ed., Sweet & Maxwell, 1999)
and on the Sweet & Maxwell website at: www.smlawpub.co.uk.

Design of the Scheme

The new arrangement consists of a set of Civil Procedure Rules **1.02**
("CPR") referred to in this work thus, *e.g.* "Pt. 3, r.3.4", two
Schedules, which list pre-existing Rules which have been modi-
fied, and Practice Directions referred to in this

1

work as, *e.g.* "Pt. 27, PD 3.4", and new forms. The Rules themselves are divided into "parts", *e.g.* "Part 27 — The Small Claims Track". A list of the Parts, Practice Directions and Schedules is at Appendix 1 to this book. Except where otherwise provided, these new provisions replace the existing rules in **both the County Court and the High Court and the Civil Division of the Court of Appeal (CPR, Pt. 2, r.2.1(1)).**

What is In and What is Not?

1.03   Enforcement has been left out of the new procedure and is the subject of a separate study, with a view to new proposals being brought in, probably after the millennium. Although, originally, possession cases were not to be included as part of the changes, a sort of hybrid has emerged whereby they come within the new Part 8 procedure but the existing claim forms are retained. This has led to a rather confused system which requires tidying up (see Chapter 5 — Starting a Case — Part 8).

The starting point from which to discover which procedures are within the new rules and which are not is Part 2. This states:

2.1—(1) Subject to paragraph (2), these Rules apply to all proceedings in —

(a) county courts;
(b) the High Court; and
(c) the Civil Division of the Court of Appeal.

(2) These Rules do not apply to proceedings of the kinds specified in the first column of the following Table (proceedings for which rules may be made under the enactments specified in the second column) —

Proceedings	Enactments
1. Insolvency proceedings	Insolvency Act 1986, ss.411 and 412
2. Non-contentious or common form probate proceedings	Supreme Court Act 1981, s.127
3. Proceedings in the High Court when acting as a Prize Court	Prize Courts Act, 1894, s.3

Proceedings	Enactments
4. Proceedings before the judge within the meaning of Part VII of the Mental Health Act 1983	Mental Health Act 1983, s.106
5. Family proceedings	Matrimonial and Family Proceedings Act 1984, s.40
6. Adoption Proceedings	Adoption Act 1976, s.66

Special rules will apply to "specialist proceedings" as defined by **1.04** Part 49:

49.—(1) These Rules shall apply to the proceedings listed in paragraph (2) subject to the provisions of the relevant practice direction which applies to those proceedings.

(2) The proceedings referred to in paragraph (1) are —

(a) admiralty proceedings;
(b) arbitration proceedings;
(c) commercial and mercantile actions;
(d) Patents Court business (as defined by the relevant practice direction) and proceedings under —

    (i) the Copyright, Designs and Patents Act 1988[1];
    (ii) the Trade Marks Act 1994[2]; and
    (iii) the Olympic Symbol etc Protection Act 1995[3] and Olympic Association Right (Infringement Proceeding) Regulations 1995[4];

(e) Technology and Construction Court Business (as defined by the relevant practice direction);
(f) proceedings under the Companies Act 1985[5] and the Companies Act 1989[6]; and
(g) contentious probate proceedings.

(1) 1988 c.48.
(2) 1994 c.26.
(3) 1995 c.32.
(4) S.I. 1995 No. 3325.
(5) 1985 c.6.
(6) 1989 c.40.

Commencement of proceedings for all those actions or matters outside the scope of the reforms will be governed by the existing procedures under the County Court Rules 1981 and the Rules of the Supreme Court 1965. These, however, have been revoked, adapted and re-enacted as schedules to the new rules, so that they fall within the "overriding objective" set out in CPR, Part 1.

Transitional Arrangements (CPR, Part 51 and Practice Direction)

1.05 The new rules apply to all cases issued from April 26, 1999, and will be applied at an appropriate stage to existing cases, with a long stop date of 12 months for application to all cases. Thus, if a file comes to the attention of the court, that will be an opportunity for the court to convert the file to a post-Woolf one, subject to the discretion of the judge (CPR, Pt. 51, PD 15(1), (2)). Order 17, r.11(9) — automatic strike out — ceased to apply on April 26, 1999.

Unless a trial date is fixed for pre-Woolf cases by April 25, 2000, or there is an outstanding prognosis in a personal injury case or trust case, there will be an automatic stay on cases. The stay can be lifted on application but it will be on terms that the case will continue under the CPR (Pt. 51, PD 19).

An application made to the court after April 26, 1999 must be made in accordance with the new rules and any assessment of costs that takes place after that date is also under the new rules. Summary assessment of costs in interlocutory matters lasting no longer than one day was introduced on the March 1, 1999 and in all relevant matters on April 26, 1999 (see Chapter 21 — Costs). The new costs rules have also now been applied to Family proceedings.

In relation to work done before April 26, 1999, the principle of proportionality (see para. 1.08, below) will not apply, but any work done before that date will not be disallowed if it would not have been disallowed under the new rules.

Practical point:

1.06 Practitioners will need to divide bills between work done pre- and post-April 26, 1999.

For judgment in default and on admissions in relation to cases commenced before April 26, 1999, see Part 51, PD 7 and 8.

The Overriding Objective (see above) applies to **all** cases as from April 26, 1999. The pre-action protocols (see Chapter 3 — Pre-action Disposal) apply after April 26, insofar as it has been possible to comply with them since publication date in January 1999.

Practical point:
Note *Shikari v. Malik*, *The Times*, May 20, 1999, in which the Court of Appeal said that litigants whose actions had commenced before the new rules came into force cannot rely on what had been tolerated in the past being tolerated in the future. A similar view was expressed by the Court of Appeal in *Biguzzi v. Rank Leisure plc* (1999) N.L.D., July 26.

The Overriding Objective

CPR, Part 1, r.1.1(1) states as follows: 1.07

> The Rules are a new procedural code with the overriding objective of enabling the court to deal with cases justly.

The net effect of this is that all existing case law relating to practice and procedure covered by the new rules and practice directions is now redundant and a new body of case law will no doubt be created in time, based on the new procedural code (see *Bank of England v. Vagliano Brothers* [1891] A.C. 107).

Practical points:
- Practitioners are advised to avoid referring to pre-April 26, 1999 cases when dealing with matters which come within the new "code".

- Expect the court to use the "overriding objective" as the basis for its decisions arising out of the Civil Procedure Rules.

- The Rules and practice directions have been written in "Plain English". Latin expressions will now be discouraged. Indeed, many common expressions are changed, as will be apparent from the rules and practice directions, *e.g.* "plaintiff" becomes "claimant"; "*ex parte*" becomes "without notice", "liquidated" and "unliquidated" become "specified" and "unspecified".

Proportionality

When exercising any power under the Civil Procedure Rules or   1.08
interpreting the Rules, the court must give effect to the overriding objective (Pt. 1, r.1.2) and are expected to be helped in this

by the parties (Pt. 1, r.1.3). In order to achieve the overriding objective as set out in Pt. 1, r.1.1 above, Pt. 1, r.1.1(2) states that this includes:

- (a) ensuring that the parties are on an equal footing;
- (b) saving expense;
- (c) dealing with the case in ways which are **proportionate**:

     (i) to the amount of money involved;
     (ii) to the importance of the case;
     (iii) to the complexity of the issues; and
     (iv) to the financial position of each party;

- (d) ensuring that it is dealt with expeditiously and fairly; and
- (e) allotting to it an appropriate share of the court's resources, while taking into account the need to allot resources to other cases.

Practical points:

- Proportionality applies throughout the proceedings and shows up specifically in the provisions relating to disclosure of documents (a further effort to move matters along search and disclosure must be proportionate — party may resist both on these grounds: see Chapter 16 — Disclosure) and costs (costs bearing some relationship to amount claimed/recovered: see Chapter 21 — Costs).

The "Tracks"

1.09 A three-tiered system has been introduced governed principally by monetary value. By far the largest number of cases fall into the small claims track which, broadly covers claims up to £5,000 (with the exception of personal injuries and housing disrepair cases where the limit is £1,000) (see Chapter 11 — Small Claims Track). The "fast track" deals with cases between £5–15,000 *where the time estimate is no longer than a day* (see Chapter 12 — Fast Track) and the multi-track is for cases above that level and any others which don't fall within the other two tracks (see Chapter 13 — Multi-track).

Cases can only be issued in the High Court if they have a value of £15,000 or more (other than personal injuries where the limit is £50,000 or more) (see Chapter 4 — Starting a Case). For the first time the High Court now has a filing system like the county courts.

Cases at all levels are now principally managed by the courts, not the lawyers, with controlled timetables and trial dates fixed at an early stage (see Chapter 10 — Case Management).

Part 1, r.1.4 provides that case management will also be used **1.10** to further the overriding objective. This includes (Pt. 1, r.1.4(2)):

(a) encouraging the parties to co-operate with each other in the conduct of the proceedings;
(b) identifying the issues at an early stage;
(c) deciding promptly which issues need full investigation and trial and accordingly disposing summarily of the others;
(d) deciding the order in which issues are to be resolved;
(e) encouraging the parties to use an alternative dispute resolution procedure if the court considers that appropriate and facilitating the use of such procedure;
(f) helping the parties to settle the whole or part of the case;
(g) fixing timetables or otherwise controlling the progress of the case;
(h) considering whether the likely benefits of taking a particular step justify the cost of taking it;
(i) dealing with as many aspects of the case as it can on the same occasion;
(j) dealing with the case without the parties needing to attend at court;
(k) making use of technology; and
(l) giving directions to ensure that the trial of a case proceeds quickly and efficiently.

Also note that:

The court may deal with a case at any place that it considers appropriate (Pt. 2, r.2.7).

Co-operation

CPR, Pt. 1, r.1.3:   **1.11**

1.3 The parties are expected to help the court to further the overriding objective.

Pt. 1, r.1.4(2)(a):

(2) Active case management includes —

      (a) encouraging the parties to co-operate with each other in the conduct of the proceedings;

Similarly, we see the introduction of "Pre-action Protocols" (see Chapter 3 — Pre-action Disposal) which are based on the notion of co-operation between parties before the commencement of proceedings.

Narrowing the Issues

1.12 Again we need only refer to Pt. 1, r.1.4(2) above. A number of the paragraphs clearly have this end in view. Pre-action protocols are also a tool to be used in this connection. The case management conference, particularly in the multi-track, is another tool, the object of which is to define the issues so that the evidence can be directed only at those issues which need to be tried.

Telephones, Video and Information Technology

1.13 The use of Information Technology is specifically referred to at Pt. 1, r.1.4(2)(k) (see above). A full computerised system of support for the new procedures is not likely to be in effect before the year 2000, although temporary measures are in force.

The Senior Master has tried to encourage the use of telephones to deal with short interlocutory matters at the RCJ, but with little response so far. This is an area where there will need to be a considerable cultural change before the use of the telephone in this way becomes widespread.

As for video links, see Chapter 17 — Evidence.

1.14 Part 2, r.2.3 contains the definition of various words and expressions:

"child" has the meaning given by rule 21.1(2) (*i.e.* "child" means a person under 18);

"claim for personal injuries" means proceedings in which there is a claim for damages in respect of personal injuries to the claimant or any other person or in respect of a person's death, and "personal injuries" includes any disease and any impairment of a person's physical or mental condition;

"claimant" means a person who makes a claim (*i.e.* the expression "plaintiff " has been replaced);

"CCR" is to be interpreted in accordance with Part 50 (*i.e.* A provision previously contained in the County Court Rules 1981);

"court officer" means a member of the court staff;

"defendant" means a person against whom a claim is made;

"defendant's home court" means —

(a) if the claim is proceeding in a county court, the county court for the district in which the defendant's address for service, as shown on the defence, is situated; and

(b) if the claim is proceeding in the High Court, the district registry for the district in which the defendant's address for service, as shown on the defence, is situated or, if there is no such district registry, the Royal Courts of Justice;

(Part 6, r.6.5 provides for a party to give an address for service — *see Chapter* 6)

"filing", in relation to a document, means delivering it, by post or otherwise, to the court office;

"judge" means, unless the context otherwise requires, a judge, Master or district judge or a person authorised to act as such;

"jurisdiction" means, unless the context requires otherwise, England and Wales and any part of the territorial waters of the United Kingdom adjoining England and Wales;

"legal representative" means a barrister or a solicitor, solicitor's employee or other authorised litigator (as defined in the Courts and Legal Services Act 1990) who has been instructed to act for a party in relation to a claim.

"litigation friend" has the meaning given by Part 21 (*see Chapter* 4);

"patient" has the meaning given by rule 21.1(2) (*i.e.* "patient" means a person who by reason of mental disorder within the meaning of the Mental Health Act 1983 is incapable of managing and administering his own affairs);

"RSC" is to be interpreted in accordance with Part 50 (*i.e.* A provision previously contained in the Rules of the Supreme Court 1965);

"statement of case" —

(a) means a claim form, particulars of claim where these are not included in a claim form, defence, Part 20 claim, or reply to defence; and

(b) includes any further information given in relation to them voluntarily or by court order under rule 18.1 (*see Chapter 15*) (*i.e.* the expressions "writ" and "pleading" have been replaced);

"statement of value" is to be interpreted in accordance with rule 16.3 (*see Chapter 4*);
"summary judgment" is to be interpreted in accordance with Part 24 (*see Chapter 6*).

(2) A reference to a "specialist list" is a reference to a list that has been designated as such by a relevant practice direction.

(3) Where the context requires, a reference to "the court" means a reference to a particular county court, a district registry, or the Royal Courts of Justice.

Computation of Time

1.15 Part 2, r.2.8 shows how to calculate any period of time for doing any act which is specified by the rules, practice directions or by a judgment or order of the court:

(2) A period of time expressed as a number of days shall be computed as clear days.

(3) In this rule "clear days" means that in computing the number of days —

(a) the day on which the period begins; and
(b) if the end of the period is defined by reference to an event, the day on which that event occurs is not included.

Examples:

(i) Notice of an application must be served at least three days before the hearing.
An application is to be heard on Friday, October 20.
The last date for service is Monday, October 16.

(ii) The court is to fix a date for a hearing. The hearing must be at least 28 days after the date of notice.
If the court gives notice of the date of the hearing on October 1, the earliest date for the hearing is October 30.

    (iii) Particulars of claim must be served within 14 days of service of the claim form.

        The claim form is served on October 2.

        The last day for service of the particulars of claim is October 16.

(4) Where the specified period —

    (a) is five days or less; and

    (b) includes —

        (i) a Saturday or Sunday; or

        (ii) a Bank Holiday, Christmas Day or Good Friday, that day does not count.

Example:

    Notice of an application must be served at least three days before the hearing.

    An application is to be heard on Monday, October 20.

    The last date for service is Tuesday, October 14.

(5) When the period specified —

    (a) by these Rules or a practice direction; or

    (b) by any judgment or court order,

for doing any act at the court office ends on a day on which the office is closed, that act shall be in time if done on the next day on which the court office is open.

    2.9—(1) Where the court gives a judgment, order or direction which imposes a time limit for doing any act, the last date for compliance must, wherever practicable —

    (a) be expressed as a calendar date; and

    (b) include the time of day by which the act must be done.

Practical points:
The requirement for a time of day in every such order is new **1.16** and should be noted. Part 2, r.2.9 states:

    (2) Where the date by which an act must be done is inserted in any document, the date must, wherever practicable, be expressed as a calendar date.

2.10—Where "month" occurs in any judgment, order, direction or other document, it means a calendar month.

Note that the time limits may be varied by parties:

2.11—Unless these Rules or a practice direction provide otherwise or the court orders otherwise, the time specified by a rule or by the court for a person to do any act may be varied by the written agreement of the parties.

See also: Pt. 3, r.3.8 (sanctions have effect unless defaulting party obtains relief), Pt. 28, r.28.4 (variation of case management timetable — fast track); Pt. 29, r.29.5 (variation of case management timetable — multi-track) and RSC Ord. 59, r.2C (appeals to the Court of Appeal) in Schedule 1, (provides for time limits that cannot be varied by agreement between the parties).

Forms (CPR, Part 4)

1.17 The forms set out in the practice directions must be used where required (Pt. 4, r.4(1) but may be varied if the circumstances warrant it (Pt. 4, r.4(2)). A full list of the forms is set out in the Practice Direction to Part 4 and is reproduced in Appendix 2 to this book.

Chapter 2

Officers of the Court: their Jurisdiction and Powers

General

The officers of the county court are the following: circuit judge **2.01**
and district judge comprising the judicial officers, and court
manager (formerly known as the "chief clerk") and staff who
are the administrative or court officers.

Circuit Judges

Circuit judges are assigned by section 5 of the County Court Act **2.02**
1984 ("the 1984 Act") to sit in county courts. Section 37 of the
1984 Act, set out below, vests them with their powers, and
gives them authority of jurisdiction:

37.—(1) Any jurisdiction and powers conferred by this or any
other Act:

  (a) on a county court; or
  (b) on the judge of a county court;

may be exercised by any judge of the court.
  (2) Subsection (1) applies to jurisdiction and power conferred on all county courts or judges of county courts or on
any particular county court or the judge of any particular
county court.

The judges also have a general ancillary jurisdiction as
provided in section 38 of the 1984 Act, set out below:

38.—(1) Subject to what follows, in any proceedings in a
county court the court may make any order which could be
made by the High Court if the proceedings were in the High
Court.

(2) Any order made by a county court may be —

(a) absolute or conditional;
(b) final or interlocutory.

(3) A county court shall not have power —

(a) to order freezing or search orders (*see Chapter 14 — Interim Remedies*); or
(b) to make any order of a prescribed kind. [However, there is an exception in the case of the Business List in the Central London County Court].

2.03   The procedure in cases before judges is as prescribed by those Rules made pursuant to section 75 of the 1984 Act and the new Civil Procedure Rules 1998. Where no specific procedure is provided by these rules, the general principles of practice in the High Court may be adopted (section 76) by the circuit judge or district judge. For proceedings under certain Acts, procedures may be prescribed by special rules, *e.g.* the Adoption Rules 1984. Note that the trial of a small claim may not be assigned to a circuit judge without that judge's consent.

The mode of address for circuit judges, recorders and assistant recorders sitting in court or in chambers is "Your Honour"; the correct method of describing them in the lists is given in *Practice Direction* [1982] 1 W.L.R. 101, CA.

District Judges

2.04 District judges are appointed by the Lord Chancellor pursuant to section 6 of the 1984 Act and are addressed as "Sir" or "Madam". Their jurisdiction according to the Practice Direction with Part 2 of the CPR is as follows:

(1) A district judge may make an injunction in proceedings which he or she otherwise has jurisdiction to hear. These include:

- Any claim allocated or allocatable to the small claims or fast track.
- Proceedings for the recovery of land.
- By consent of the parties — this includes making, varying and discharging an injunction.
- Ancillary to a charging order.
- Ancillary to an order appointing a receiver by way of equitable execution.
- Order restraining receipt of Crown debt (RSC, Ord. 77, r.16).

(2) A district judge may not commit a person to prison where a statute gives jurisdiction: Attachments of Earnings Act 1971, s.23, County Court Act 1984, s.14 (various contempts of court), Housing Act 1996, ss.152–157 (anti-social behaviour), Protection from Harassment Act 1997, s.3 and Part 4 of the Family Law Act 1996 (domestic violence proceedings).

(3) A district judge has jurisdiction to hear the following: **2.05**

- Any claim allocated to the small claims or the fast track.
- Any claim treated as being allocated to the multi-track under CPR, Pt. 8, r.8.9(c) and Table 2 of the practice direction to Part 8. Mortgagee's and landlord's claims for the recovery of land fall within this provision.
- The assessment of damages without financial limit.
- With the consent of the parties and the Designated Civil Judge (*see Chapter 13 — The Multi-track*), any other matter.

(4) The district judge will normally hear all applications in the course of proceedings whether made before or after judgment unless the circuit judge otherwise directs. Normally such hearings will be in chambers (*see CPR, Part 23 and Chapter 15 — Applications*).

Deputy District Judges

Deputy district judges (appointed under section 8 of the 1984 **2.06** Act) exercise the full jurisdiction and powers of a district judge except in relation to applications under the Children Act 1989, where the Family Proceedings (Allocation to Judiciary) Directions 1993 (amended 1994) restrict them to hearing interlocutory matters (other than without notice applications) and unopposed trials, nor in relation to committals under Part IV of the Family Act 1996 or the Protection from Harassment Act 1997. A deputy district judge may not (as may a full district judge) exercise the powers of a district judge when sitting in a court in a district to which he is not appointed (contrast sections 6(5) and 8(1) of the 1984 Act).

Court Manager and "Proper Officer"; Devolution to Administrative Staff

2.07 Section 75(3)(d) of the 1984 Act provides that the rules made thereunder may prescribe cases in which:

(a) the jurisdiction or powers of a county court or the judge of a county court may be exercised by a district judge or some other officer of the court; or

(b) the jurisdiction or powers of the district judge of a county court may be exercised by some other officer of the court.

The County Court Rules 1981 ("the 1981 Rules") recognise that the court manager performs most of the functions assigned by the former rules to the district judge, except those of a purely judicial nature. Accordingly, except in the judicial context, the term "district judge" is replaced in the 1981 Rules by "proper officer" which is defined (Ord. 1, r.3) as the district judge or in relation to any act of a formal or administrative nature, the chief clerk or any other officer of the court, acting on his behalf. There is a saving for acts which are by statute the responsibility of the district judge, such as the keeping of records under section 12 of the 1984 Act.

However, in some cases the 1981 Rules go beyond allowing officers of the court to perform acts of a formal or administrative nature, in particular with regard to the enforcement of judgments.

Solicitors

2.08 Solicitors advise and represent litigants before the court providing a channel of communication between the court and the parties to the proceedings as well as between the parties themselves. As for solicitors signing statements of case, see Chapter 4 — Starting a Case. For service on solicitors, see Chapter 6 — Service.

Change of solicitor

2.09 CPR, Pt. 42, r.42.1(1) applies where a party wants to change his solicitor, either appointing another or acting in person. In all such cases the party concerned must file a Notice of Change, serving it on every other party, including the previous solicitor, if there was one. A form is provided by the Practice Direction.

Note that a notice is required where a solicitor has been acting for an assisted person and the legal aid certificate has been revoked or discharged, his retainer terminated or the assisted person wishes someone else to act for them (Pt. 42, PD 2.2).

Former solicitors are considered as continuing to act unless and until the requisite notice has been served or an order has been made under Pt. 42, r.42.3(1) declaring that the solicitor has ceased to act. Such an order can be made following an application by the solicitor and has to be supported by evidence (r.42.3(2)). There is no indication in the Rules or practice directions as to what evidence is needed.

Rights of Audience

Sections 27 and 28 of the Courts and Legal Services Act 1990 **2.10** contain a comprehensive code relating to rights of audience. None of section 28 and only parts of section 27 have been brought into force and they are reproduced in *The County Court Practice* (Butterworths) in the note to section 60 of the 1984 Act. Suitably qualified and admitted solicitors and barristers have rights of audience and the right to conduct litigation, as do the parties themselves.

On April 11, 1995, the Lord Chancellor issued a Practice Direction which removed any objection to female advocates wearing trouser suits in court so long as they were of a dark colour, unobtrusive and compatible with the wearing of robes. Failure by qualified representatives to wear proper court dress in open court may result in the judge refusing to listen to the advocate. Therefore, if inadequately robed, the advocate should request leave of the judge to appear notwithstanding the deficiency.

Section 60(2) of the 1984 Act in relation to county courts **2.11** provides that in actions brought by local authorities for possession of a house and/or the recovery of rent or other sum claimed in respect of any persons in occupation of such house, then insofar as the proceedings are heard by the district judge, any authorised officer of the authority may address the district judge.

A Lord Chancellor's Practice Direction, dated January 27, 1978, provides that Fellows of the Institute of Legal Executives, employed in giving assistance in the conduct of litigation to solicitors, may address the court where those solicitors are acting in unopposed applications for an adjournment, or to obtain judgment by consent (unless, notwithstanding the consent, a question arises as to the applicant's entitlement to the judgment or its terms).

2.12   Solicitors' clerks are allowed to address the district judge on applications (section 27(2)(e) of the Courts and Legal Services Act 1990), and usually on small claims, in chambers.

It has been held that unrepresented litigants are entitled to an assistant in civil proceedings: *R. v. Leicester City Justices, ex p. Barrow* [1991] 3 All E.R. 935, on the understanding that the assistant is there to assist and not to address the court (*MacKenzie v. MacKenzie* [1970] 3 All E.R. 1034, CA). A litigant in person is entitled to have the proper assistance of a friend even if the hearing is in chambers (*Re H (A Minor) (Chambers proceedings: McKenzie friend), The Times*, May 6, 1997, CA) except in family matters (*R. v. Bow County Court, ex p. Pelling* (1999) N.L.D. March 1, Div.Ct.). Except in relation to the special rules applying to lay representatives in small claims matters (see Chapter 11 — Small Claims Track), an application for rights of audience by a lay person on behalf of a litigant in person should only be granted in exceptional circumstances (*D. v. S. (Rights of audience), The Times*, January 1, 1997, CA).

As for representation by a lay representative or on behalf of a company at a small claims hearing: see Chapter 11 — Small Claims Track. The court may allow an authorised employee of a company or corporation to address the court.

Chapter 3

Pre-action Disposal — Protocols and ADR

A. Pre-Action Protocols

Overview

- Personal injury protocol — in fast track cases particularly **3.01**
- Clinical disputes protocol
- Further protocols to come
- Set letters of claim and response
- Instruction of experts
- Sanctions for non-compliance

General

The introduction of pre-action protocols as part of the Woolf **3.02** reforms is a crucial element in the concept of quick and economic justice. They provide for much of the work involved in preparing cases to be done prior to the issue of proceedings, or "front-loaded" as it is otherwise known. This increases the possibility of settling cases without proceedings having to be taken at all or, at the very least, narrowing the issues and expediting the proceedings themselves.

The system operates by means of detailed set "letters of claim" followed by time-limited responses from the potential defendant. Bare denials will not be enough as reasons for denial will have to be given and vital documentation and information exchanged.

As yet, only two pre-action protocols exist, one for personal injuries and the other for clinical disputes (formerly known as "medical negligence"). Two others are in the course of preparation — debt recovery and professional negligence.

Practical point

3.03 Even if a protocol does not exist for the type of action in question, the Practice Direction to the Civil Procedure Rules on Protocols contains a form of protocol to cover those matters:

> 4. In cases not covered by any approved protocol, the court will expect the parties, in accordance with the overriding objective and the matters referred to in rule 1.1(2)(a), (b) and (c), to act reasonably in exchanging information and documents relevant to the claim and generally in trying to avoid the necessity for the start of proceedings.

In other words, even where no pre-action protocol exists, the parties are to act as though one were in force by, *e.g.*, co-operating with each other with regard to the exchange of information and the appointment of any relevant experts.

Personal Injury Protocol

3.04 Purpose (as stated in protocol):

- More pre-action contact between the parties

- Better exchange of information

- Better pre-action investigation

- To put the parties in a position to settle case fairly and early, without litigation. To enable proceedings to run to a timetable and efficiently if litigation does become necessary

The personal injury protocol is designed primarily for road traffic accidents, tripping and slipping accidents and accidents at work that are likely to be allocated to the fast track, because time is of the essence in these cases (Pre-Action Protocol, 2.3). As for multi-track cases, the spirit, if not the letter, of the protocol is to be followed, especially because of the "cards on the table" approach to litigation enshrined in the changes (Protocol, 2.4)

3.05 (1) Letter of claim (Specimen — Appendix A to Protocol and Appendix 3 to this book)

- Two copies to be sent to defendant "immediately sufficient information is available to substantiate a realistic claim and before issues of quantum are addressed in detail".

But note:

> **2.6** The claimant's legal representative may wish to notify the defendant and/or his insurer as soon as they know a claim is likely to be made, but before they are able to send a detailed letter of claim, particularly for instance, when the defendant has no or limited knowledge of the incident giving rise to the claim or where the claimant is incurring significant expenditure as a result of the accident which he hopes the defendant might pay for, in whole or in part. If the claimant's representative chooses to do this, it will not start the timetable for responding.

(2) Contents of letter of claim:

- clear summary of facts
- indication of nature of injuries
- indication of financial loss
- request for details
- sufficient information to enable defendant to commence investigations and put a broad valuation on the risk.

(3) After defendant has made clear his position on liability, then claimant must provide details of special damages as soon as possible.

(4) Letters of claim are not intended to have same status as pleading and sanctions should not apply (unless letter not sent at all!).

(5) Defendant's response:

- Defendant to reply and to identify insurer (if any) within 21 days.
- Insurers must reply within three months stating whether liability is denied, and if so, giving reasons for their denial of liability.
- Formal admissions will be binding in cases up to £15,000

(6) The documents:

- If the defendant denies liability this must be accompanied with documents in the defendants possession that are "material" to the issues. A list of specimen documents is given in the Personal Injury Protocol (Appendix B to Protocol).
- Where the defendant admits primary liability but alleges contributory negligence by the claimant, reasons and material documents must be supplied. The claimant should reply to the allegation before proceedings are issued.

(7) Instructing the expert:

- Before instructing claimant to send to defendant a list of experts
- Defendant has 14 days to object to any or all of them
- If object to some only, claimant should use mutually acceptable one
- If objection to all then claimant may instruct expert of their own choice **and the claimant doesn't have to disclose the report prior to proceedings, save where there is an admission** (see below)
- If defendant does not object, defendant loses the right to instruct own expert unless first party agrees; the court so directs or first party refuses to disclose original of report that has been amended
- Draft letter of instruction included with the protocol (Specimen letter of instruction to medical expert — Appendix C to Protocol and Appendix 5 to this book)
- Agreed questions may be sent to expert
- Cost of agreed expert's report borne by instructing first party; costs of answering questions borne by those asking them.

Note Protocol, 3.21:

Where the defendant admits liability in whole or in part before proceedings are issued, the medical report obtained by agreement should be disclosed. The claimant should then delay issuing proceedings for 21 days to enable parties to consider whether the claim is capable of settlement.

Stocktaking

Note Protocol, 2.12:   3.06

Where a claim is not resolved when the protocol has been followed, the parties might wish to carry out a stock-take of the issues in dispute, and the evidence that the court is likely to need to decide those issues, **before proceedings are started.** Where the defendant is insured and the pre-action steps have been conducted by the insurer, the insurer would normally be expected to nominate solicitors to act in the proceedings and the claimant's solicitor is recommended to invite the insurer to nominate solicitors to act in the proceedings and do so 7–14 days before the intended issue date.

Settling

Note Protocol, 2.13:   3.07

Parties and their legal representatives are encouraged to enter into discussions and/or negotiations prior to starting proceedings. The protocol does not specify when or how this might be done but parties should bear in mind that the courts increasingly take the view that litigation should be a last resort, and that claims should not be issued prematurely when a settlement is in reasonable prospect.

Protocol for Resolution of Clinical Disputes

(1) Purpose (as stated in Protocol):   3.08

- to maintain/restore the patient healthcare provider relationship;
- to resolve as many disputes as possible without litigation;
- to encourage openness and awareness of options;
- to reduce delay and costs.

The Clinical Negligence Protocol contains fairly detailed advice to healthcare providers and patients as to reporting procedures, the supply of hospital records and referral to ADR.

(2) Letter of claim (Appendix C1 to Protocol and Appendix 3 to this book):

- Clear summary of the facts
- Main allegation of negligence
- The patient's injuries
- Financial losses in outline
- Chronology of events in more complex cases
- Reference to any relevant documents plus copies if not in the defendant's possession
- Offer to settle if relevant

(3) Defendants' response (Appendix C2 to Protocol):

- Acknowledge within 14 days
- Reasoned answer within three months, with admission or part admission or specific denial together with documents relied on
- Response to offer to settle

(4) Experts:

- "It is recognised that in clinical negligence disputes the parties and their advisers will require flexibility in their approach to expert evidence".
- Expert opinions may be needed on breach of duty and causation; on patient's condition and prognosis; to assist in valuing the claim.

(5) Alternative Dispute Resolution:

- Protocol refers to NHS complaints procedure, mediation and arbitration
- There is an existing protocol for obtaining hospital medical records for medical negligence and personal injury claims (The Law Society, revised ed., June 1998)

Compliance with the Protocols

3.09 The standards set in the protocols will be "the normal reasonable approach to pre-action conduct"

The Practice Direction on Protocols contains guidance as to compliance:

2.1 The Civil Procedure Rules enable the court to take into account compliance or non-compliance with an applicable protocol when giving directions for the management of proceedings (see rules 3.1(4) and (5) and 3.9(e)) and when making orders for costs (see rule 44.3(5)(a)).
2.2 The court will expect all parties to have complied in substance with the terms of an approved protocol.

2.3 If, in the opinion of the court, non-compliance has led to the commencement of proceedings which might otherwise not have needed to be commenced, or has led to costs being incurred in the proceedings that might otherwise not have been incurred, the orders the court may make include:

(1) an order that the party at fault pay the costs of the proceedings, or part of those costs, of the other party or parties;

(2) an order that the party at fault pay those costs on an **indemnity** basis;

(3) if the party at fault is a claimant in whose favour an order for the payment of damages or some specified sum is subsequently made, an order depriving that party of interest on such sum and in respect of such period as may be specified, and/or awarding interest at a lower rate than that at which interest would otherwise have been awarded;

(4) if the party at fault is a defendant and an order for the payment of damages or some specified sum is subsequently made in favour of the claimant, an order awarding **interest** on such sum and in respect of such period as may be specified at a higher rate, not exceeding **10 per cent** above base rate (*cf.* Pt. 36, r.36.21(2)), than the rate at which interest would otherwise have been awarded.

2.4 The court will exercise its powers under paragraphs 2.1 and 2.3 with the object of placing the innocent party in no worse a position than he would have been in if the protocol had been complied with.

As to non-compliance: 3.10

3.1 A claimant may be found to have failed to comply with a protocol by, for example:

(a) not having provided sufficient information to the defendant; or

(b) not having followed the procedure required by the protocol to be followed
(*e.g.* not having followed the medical expert instruction procedure set out in the Personal Injury Protocol).

3.2 A defendant may be found to have failed to comply with a protocol by, for example:

(a) not making a preliminary response to the letter of
claim within the time fixed for that purpose by the
relevant protocol (21 days under the Personal Injury
Protocol, 14 days under the Clinical Negligence
Protocol);

(b) not making a full response within three months of the
letter of claim, as required by the relevant protocol;
or

(c) not disclosing documents required to be disclosed by
the relevant protocol,

When it comes to assessment of costs, the costs rules also
provide in addition that in deciding whether costs were reasonably incurred or are proportionate the court may take into
account the efforts made if any before and during the proceedings in order to try to resolve the dispute. Both sides may make
offers to settle at the pre-proceedings stage with consequent
sanctions for failure to accept if the case is unnecessarily
prolonged.

Commencement

3.11 Note Practice Direction — Protocols:

5.1 Compliance or non-compliance, as the case may be,
with the protocols specified in the Schedule will be taken into
account by the court in dealing with any proceedings commenced after April 26, 1999 but will not be taken into
account by the court in dealing with proceedings started
before that date.

5.2 Where, in respect of proceedings commenced after
April 26, 1999, the parties have by work done before that
date substantially achieved the object designed to be achieved
by steps to be taken under a protocol, the parties need not
take those steps and their failure to do so will not be treated,
for the purposes of paragraphs 2 and 3, as non-compliance.

5.3 Where, in respect of proceedings commenced after
April 26, 1999, the parties have not had time since the
publication of the protocols in January 1999 to comply with
the applicable provisions, their failure to have done so will
not be treated, for the purposes of paragraphs 2 and 3, as
non-compliance.

5.4 As and when an additional protocol is approved, a
Practice Direction will specify the date after which compliance or non-compliance with that protocol will be taken
into account by the court.

Practical points:

- Nothing in the new Civil Procedures Rules changes the limitation period for the issue of proceedings. As practitioners must now do more work before proceedings are started it is important that they do not lose sight of the limitation date.   3.12

- It is important that the contents of the letter of claim and response comply with the provisions of the protocol so these should be checked carefully before being sent out.

- Selecting and getting reports from impartial experts is an important element of the protocols as is agreeing the expert with the other side. Practitioners are reminded of the exhortation in the Overriding Objective to co-operation between the parties.

- It is important that claimant's representatives remember to include costs as part of the settlement. If costs are not agreed then there is no settlement at all and any subsequent proceedings issued just to recover costs are likely to be struck out as an abuse of process.

B. Alternative Dispute Resolution ("ADR")

CPR, Pt. 1, r.1.4 provides that the court must further the overriding objective by actively managing cases. Active case management includes: 3.13

(2)(e) Encouraging the parties to use an alternative dispute resolution procedure if the court considers that appropriate and facilitating the use of such procedure;

The court will do this by either setting up its own schemes where the budget permits (Central London County Court has a fast track (£5,000–15,000) scheme) or providing information as to where such schemes are available. Part 26, r.26.4(1) enables the court to stay the proceedings for a month (or longer if the parties agree) while such alternative methods of settling the matter are explored and an invitation to do this is in the Allocation Questionnaire (see Chapter 10 — Case Management). Failure to take advantage of such schemes where they are available may be condemned in costs. Legal Aid is now available to cover mediation.

ADR is still in its infancy and judges have been told not to put too much pressure on parties at the present moment to go   3.14

3.14 THE COUNTY COURT PRACTITIONER 2000

to ADR if there is clear reluctance — even though there are costs sanctions available against parties who fail to go to ADR.

However, once more schemes become available, such encouragement is likely to become more positive. Some matters, especially commercial, building and neighbour disputes are certainly prime candidates for ADR.

Chapter 4

Starting a Case — General Procedure

Overview

- A new claim form for use in county court and high court **4.01**
- Detailed provisions for the contents of particulars of claim

Which Court?

The following must be issued in the High Court: **4.02**

- any claim where the High Court has exclusive jurisdiction by statute (these include a claim for damages or other remedy for libel or slander);
- claims for *habeas corpus* and judicial review;
- claims needing to be heard in a High Court specialist list.

The following must be issued in a county court:

- personal injury claims where the claimant does not expect to recover £50,000 or more;
- other claims where the claimant does not expect to recover £15,000 or more;
- any claim where the county court has exclusive jurisdiction by statute.

Otherwise a claim may be issued in either court but if the claimant believes that it should be dealt with by a High Court judge by reason of its value, complexity or general importance, it should be started in that court.

Chancery business

4.03 Notwithstanding the general financial restrictions on making use of the High Court by CPR, Pt. 7, PD 2.5, Chancery business may be commenced in the High Court or the county court, but the upper limit for Chancery business in the county court referred to in section 23 of the County Courts Act 1984 as "Equity Jurisdiction" remains at a maximum figure of value of the Estate or Trust of £30,000. When the county court is used for Chancery business, the claim form should be marked on the top right hand corner "Chancery business".

Complex cases; special enactments

4.04 Regardless of value, claims may be started in the High Court if the claimant believes the claim should be dealt with by a High Court judge by reason of complexity of facts, legal remedies or procedures involved and/or importance to the public (Pt. 7, PD 2.4).

Some enactments specifically require commencement in the High Court or in a county court, when the claim must be issued in the court which the enactment specifies.

The proceedings are started when the court issues the claim form but for the purposes of the Limitation Act 1980 the claim is "brought" when the completed claim form is received at the court office if that is earlier.

Statements of Case (CPR, Part 16)

4.05 "Statement of case" is the new term for a pleading and includes:

- claim form (see para. 4.12, below);
- particulars of claim where these are not included in a claim form (see para. 4.19, below);
- defence;
- Part 20 claim;
- reply to defence; and

any further information given in relation to them voluntarily or by court order.

Subsequent statements of case

A subsequent statement of case must not contradict or be **4.06** inconsistent with an earlier one; for example a reply to a defence must not bring in a new claim. Where new matters have come to light, the appropriate course may be to seek the court's permission to amend the statement of case.

Amending the statement of case

The previous, rather lax, system in the county court of allowing **4.07** amendments without leave up to a return day has been tightened up.

A statement of case **which has not yet been served**, may always be amended, and no permission is required (Pt. 17, r.17.1(1)). But note Pt. 17, r.17.2:

> 17.2—(1) If a party has amended his statement of case where permission of the court was not required, the court may disallow the amendment.
> (2) A party may apply to the court for an order under paragraph (1) within 14 days of service of a copy of the amended statement of case on him.

If an amendment is required **after service**, an application must **4.08** be filed accompanied by the proposed amendment. The application may be dealt with at a hearing, but not if the Court considers a hearing would not be appropriate, or where the parties themselves agree that a hearing is unnecessary, or simply agree the amendment, although this would be subject to scrutiny by the court (Pt. 23, r.23.8 and Pt. 17, PD 1.1) Any party who seeks permission will find that permission is given subject to directions as to amendments made as to any other statements of case, and as to service. A party applying for an amendment will usually be responsible for the costs of and arising from the amendment. If a statement of case is amended the statement of truth should be re-verified (Pt. 17, PD 1.4) As to amendments made after a limitation period has expired, Pt. 17, r.17.4 confirms the previous practice of the court to allow amendments only if there is a new claim arising out of the same facts. An amendment to correct the name of a party after a genuine mistake is allowable, if the court permits, under Pt. 17, r.17.4(3).

Statements of Truth (CPR, Part 22)

What is it? **4.09**

A statement that the party putting forward a document believes it to be true.

Which documents?

- statement of case, *i.e.* formerly known as a "pleading"
- response to order for further information (which, by virtue of Pt. 2, r.2.3(1) **is** a statement of case)
- a witness statement

To be signed by:

- maker of statement if witness statement
- party or litigation friend or legal representative if a statement of case or response.

(Pt. 22, r.22.1(6))

Failure:

- contents cannot be relied on document as evidence of any of the matters set out in it until verified
- statement of case not so verified *may* be struck out

(Pt. 22, PD 4)

Form of statement (Pt. 22, PD 2)

4.10   "I believe [or as the case may be, 'the claimant believes'] that the facts in this [name of document being verified] are true".

If it is a witness statement which is being verified, the wording should be:

"I believe that the facts stated in this witness statement are true".

In the case of experts, the form is:

"I believe that the facts I have stated in this report are true and that the opinions I have expressed are correct." (Pt. 35, PD 1.5)

Practical points:
4.11   - A false statement amounts to a contempt (Pt. 32, r.32.14) so practitioners are advised that only those with direct knowledge of the facts should actually sign the

statement of truth, although the form of the statement of truth does allow the signatory to say that "the claimant believes it to be true". Practitioners cannot sign a witness statement other than their own.

- Where a party is legally represented, and the legal representative signs the document, it will be assumed that he did explain to the client beforehand the possible consequences if the statement turns out not to be true (Pt. 22, PD 3.8)

- Where a company or corporation is involved, the statement should be signed by a person holding a senior position; as to what is meant by "a senior position", see Pt. 22, PD 3.5, 3.11. In the case of a partnership, a partner or person having control of the business should sign (Pt. 22, PD 3.6).

- Note Pt. 22, PD 3.6A:

    An insurer or the Motor Insurers' Bureau may sign a statement of truth in a statement of case on behalf of a party where the insurer or the Motor Insurers' Bureau has a financial interest in the result of proceedings brought wholly or partially by or against that party.

- For further guidance as to who may or may not sign a statement of truth, see Pt. 22, PD 3.11:

    Managing agent — An agent who manages property or investments for the party cannot sign a statement of truth. It must be signed by the party or by the legal representative of the party.

    Trusts — Where some or all of the trustees comprise a single party one, some or all of the trustees comprising the party may sign a statement of truth. The legal representative of the trustees may sign it.

    In-house legal representatives — Legal representative is defined in rule 2.3(1). A legal representative employed by a party may sign a statement of truth. However a person who is not a solicitor, barrister or other authorised litigator, but who is employed by the company and is managed by such a person, is not employed by that person and so cannot sign a statement of truth. However, such a person may be a manager and able to sign the statement on behalf of the company in that capacity.

- Note that the cost of using an affidavit instead of a statement verified under Part 22 can only be recovered if the rule or practice direction requires an affidavit. The net result of this is that affidavits are now much less likely to be used.

The Claim Form

4.12 Subject to an alternative procedure of limited application (Part 8 in the Civil Procedures Rules: see Chapter 5 — Starting a Case — Part 8 Alternative Procedure), all proceedings are now started in all Courts by a **claim form** which may set out the particulars of claim in the space provided on the form. A copy of the claim form appears at Appendix 6 to this book. If there is insufficient room on the claim form to set out all the details of the claim, the claimant may use a supplementary document called "particulars of claim". If the claimant intends to use particulars of claim, this must be stated on the claim form.

4.13 Note the provisions of Pt. 7, r.7.5:

- The particulars of claim must be served on the defendant within 14 days of the service of the claim form but, in any event, no later than the last day for service of the claim form.
- Within seven days of service of the particulars of claim, the claimant must file a copy of the particulars and a certificate of service (Pt. 6, r.6.10 makes provision for certificates of service).

The Particulars of Claim must, if not accompanying the claim form, be served no later than the latest time for serving the claim form, *i.e.* within four months after the date of issue (Pt. 7, r.7.5(1)). Six months is allowed for service out of the jurisdiction wherever that may be (Pt. 7, r.7.5(3)). Application can be made to extend time for service if made **before** the four months (or six months) has expired (Pt. 7, r.7.6(2)), but any application for an Order to extend time for service *"must be supported by evidence"* (Pt. 7, r.7.6(4)). Where there is to be service out of the jurisdiction, an endorsement is required (Pt. 7, PD 3.5).

The required contents of the claim form are apparent from the form itself, Practice Form N1, and are given below. The claim form is very similar to the previous form of summons, and gives about two-thirds of an A4 page in which to set out the details of the claim. The claim form for use in the Summons Production Centre is virtually unchanged in layout from the N1 previously in use there.

The claim form must: 4.14

- contain a concise statement of the nature of the claim;
- specify the remedy which the claimant seeks;
- in a money claim, state the value which the claimant places on the claim; and;
- contain such other matters as may be set out in a practice direction. (Pt. 16, r.16.2(1))

In a claim for money, the claim form must also **specify** the amount of money claimed, or, if the claimant is unable to do so, he must state in the claim form that he expects to recover:

- not more than £5,000;
- more than £5,000 but not more than £15,000; or
- more than £15,000. (Pt. 16, r.16.3(2))

Alternatively the claimant may state that he does not know how much he expects to recover. This is likely to be an unattractive option, as such a statement will almost inevitably lead to the charging of the maximum court fee!

In a claim which does not exceed £5,000 in value for, or 4.15 which includes a claim for, personal injury, the claimant must also state whether the amount he expects to recover as general damages for pain, suffering and loss of amenity (Pt. 16, r.16.3(3)). This is relevant on allocation of the claim to track should it become defended. If the pain suffering and loss of amenity element of the claim exceeds £1,000, the claim will not be allocated to the small claims track.

Similarly, in a claim which includes a claim by a tenant of residential premises against his landlord where the tenant is seeking an order that the landlord carry out repairs or other work to the premises, the claimant must state whether the amount of damages he expects to recover for this part of the claim, or any resulting damages claim, exceeds or does not exceed £1,000. Again, if such a claim or resulting claim is expected to exceed £1,000, it will not be allocated to the small claims track should it become defended (Pt. 16, r.16.3(4)).

Issuing in the High Court

Where the claim form is issued in the High Court, the claimant 4.16 must either state that he expects to recover more than £15,000, or else he must show by naming it, an enactment which provides that the claim may be commenced only in the High Court, or otherwise he must state that the claim is one of those on the Specialist Jurisdiction lists (Pt. 16, r.16.3(5)), see Parts 49, 50 and 51 and Chapter 1 — The New Scheme.

Specified/unspecified claims

4.17   The distinction has now gone, for the purposes of claims brought under the new Rules, between "liquidated" and "unliquidated" claims. The distinction now is between a claim for "a specified sum" and a claim for "an unspecified sum". The importance of the distinction is in how admissions are dealt with (see Chapter 7 — Responses to proceedings), and also in connection with the new rules for automatic transfer (see Chapter 10 — Case Management).

Practical points:

4.18

- It should be borne in mind by defendants that there may be judgment for more than initially claimed — the old position that the claim was limited to the amount which the plaintiff had claimed, does not now apply. Furthermore, the court is now expressly empowered to grant any remedy to which the claimant may be entitled whether or not the claimant has sought it. Claimants may still seek "such further or other relief as the court deems appropriate" — the previous practice.

- It is worth noting that a claimant is not bound to only make an unspecified claim in cases where there has previously been an assessment, *e.g.* for personal injuries ("damages not exceeding £x") but can elect to make a specified claim ("damages in the sum of £x") and claim a default judgment (see Chapter 7—Responses to Claim) for that sum.

Contents of Particulars of Claim (CPR, Part 16, r.16.4)

4.19   16.4—(1) Particulars of claim must include:

    (a) a concise statement of the facts on which the claimant relies;

    (b) if the claimant's seeking interest, a statement to that effect and the details set out in paragraph (2);

    (c) if the claimant's seeking aggravated damages or exemplary damages, a statement to that effect and his grounds for claiming them;

(d) if the claimant is seeking provisional damages, a statement to that effect and his grounds for claiming them, and

(e) such other matters as may be set out in a practice direction.

(2) If the claimant is seeking interest he must:

(a) state whether he is doing so —

    (i) under the terms of a contract,

    (ii) under an enactment and if so which, or

    (iii) on some other basis and if so what that basis is; and

(b) if the claim is for a specified amount of money, state —

    (i) the percentage rate at which interest is claimed;

    (ii) the date from which it is claimed;

    (iii) the date to which it is calculated, which must not be later than the date on which the claim form is issued;

    (iv) the total amount of interest claimed to the date of calculation; and

    (v) the daily rate at which interest accrues after that date.

Where a claim is made for an **injunction or declaration in respect of or relating to any land or the possession, occupation, use or enjoyment of any land,** the particulars of claim must:

(1) State whether or not the injunction or declaration relates to residential premises, and

(2) Identify the land by reference to a plan where necessary.

Where a claim is brought to enforce a right to recover **possession of goods,** the particulars of claim must contain a statement showing the value of the goods.

Where a claim is based upon a **written agreement:**

(1) A copy of the contract or documents constituting the agreement should be attached to or served with the particulars of claim and the original(s) should be available at the hearing, and

(2) Any general conditions of sale incorporated in the contract is or the documents constituting the agreement are

bulky this Practice Direction is complied with by attaching or serving only the relevant parts of the contract or documents).

Where a claim is based upon an **oral agreement**, the particulars of claim should set out the contractual words used and state by whom, to whom, when and where they were spoken.

Where a claim is based upon an **agreement by conduct**, the particulars of claim must specify the conduct relied on and state by whom, when and where the acts constituting the conduct were done.

Matters Relied on which must be Specifically set out in the Particulars of Claim

4.20 Practice Direction to Part 16:

> 11.1 A claimant who wishes to rely on evidence:
>
> (1) under section 11 of the Civil Evidence Act 1968 of a conviction of an offence, or
> (2) under section 12 of the above-mentioned Act of a finding or adjudication of adultery or paternity, must include in his particulars of claim a statement to that effect and give the following details:
>
>> (1) the type of conviction, finding or adjudication and its date,
>> (2) the Court or Court Martial which made the conviction, finding or adjudication, and
>> (3) the issue in the claim to which it relates.
>
> 11.2 The claimant must specifically set out the following matters in his particulars of claim where he wishes to rely on them in support of his claim:
>
> (1) any allegation of fraud,
> (2) the fact of any illegality,
> (3) details of any misrepresentation,
> (4) details of all breaches of trust,
> (5) notice or knowledge of a fact,
> (6) details of unsoundness or mind or undue influence,
> (7) details of wilful default, and
> (8) any facts relating to mitigation of loss or damage.

Practical points:

4.21
- In pleading **misrepresentation** it is always necessary to allege that the party alleging them has relied on this misrepresentation to his detriment. Precedent books should be consulted.

- New is the requirement to *"deal with any facts relating to mitigation"*, meaning the extent to which the claimant has mitigated or endeavoured to mitigate his loss. Curiously there is no such requirement on a defendant.

Any party may:

(1) refer in his statement of case to any point of law on which his claim is based,
(2) give in his statement of case the name of any witness whom he proposes to call, and
(3) attach to or serve with the statement of case a copy of any document which he considers is necessary to his claim (including any expert's report to be filed in accordance with Part 35).

Where the Claim is in respect of personal injuries (Pt. 16, PD 4)

The Practice Direction to Part 16 provides that the Particulars **4.22** must contain:

(1) The claimant's date of birth, and
(2) Brief details of the claimant's personal injuries.

The claimant must attach to his particulars of claim a schedule of details of any past and future expenses and losses which he claims.

Where the claimant is relying on the evidence of a medical practitioner, the claimant must attach to or serve with his particulars of claim a report from a medical practitioner about the personal injuries which he alleges in his claim.

In a provisional damages claim, the claimant must state in his particulars of claim:

(1) That he is seeking an award of provisional damages **4.23** under either section 32A of the Supreme Court Act 1981 or section 51 of the County Courts Act 1984.
(2) That there is a chance that at some future time the claimant will develop some serious disease or suffer some serious deterioration in his physical or mental condition, and

(3) Specify the disease or type of deterioration in respect of which an application may be made at a future date.

Practical point:
Formerly the medical report was required *"to substantiate the injuries alleged"*. Presumably the changed wording is only so as to reduce this wording to basic English, but the new wording seems less stringent than before.

In a fatal accident claim, the claimant must state in his particulars of claim (Part 16, PD 5):

4.24   (1) that it is brought under the Fatal Accidents Act 1976,
(2) the dependants on whose behalf the claim is made,
(3) the date of birth of each dependant, and
(4) details of the nature of the dependency claim.

A fatal accident claim may include a claim for damages for bereavement
    In a fatal accident claim, the claimant may also bring a claim under the Law Reform (Miscellaneous Provisions) Act 1934 on behalf of the Estate of the deceased.
(For information on apportionment under the Law Reform (Miscellaneous Provisions) Act 1934 and the Fatal Accidents Act 1976 or between dependants, see Pt.37 and the Practice Direction which supplements it).

In a claim for recovery of land (see also Chapter 5 — Part 8 alternative procedure), the particulars of claim must (Part 16, PD 6):

4.25   (1) Identify the land sought to be recovered.
(2) State whether the claim relates to residential premises.
(3) If the claim relates to residential premises, state whether the rateable value of the premises on every day specified by section 4(2) of the Rent Act 1977 in relation to the premises exceeds the sum so specified or whether the rent for the time being payable in respect of the premises exceeds the sum specified in section 4(4)(b) of the Act.
(4) Where the claim relates to residential premises and is for non-payment of rent, state:

  (a) the amount due at the start of the proceedings,
  (b) details of all payments which have been missed,
  (c) details of any history of late or under payment,

  (d) any previous steps taken to recover the arrears of rent with full details of any Court proceedings, and

  (e) any relevant information about the Defendant's circumstances, in particular whether any payments are made on his behalf directly to the claimant under the Social Security Contributions and Benefits Act 1992.

(5) Give details about the agreement or tenancy, if answer which the land was held, stating when it determined and the amount of money payable by way of rent or licence fee.

(6) In a case to which section 138 of the County Courts Act 1984 applies (forfeiture for non-payment), state the daily rate at which the rent in arrear is to be calculated.

(7) State the ground on which possession is claimed whether statutory or otherwise, and

(8) In a case where the claimant knows of any person entitled to claim relief against forfeiture as under-lessee (including a mortgagee) under Section 146(4) of the Law of Property Act 1925 (or in accordance with Section 38 of the Supreme Court Act 1981), give the name and address of that person.

(See also further rules about recovery of land in RSC Orders 88 and 113 (Schedule 1 to the CPR) and CCR Orders 6 and 24 (Schedule 2 to the CPR).

*Where the claim is for the delivery of goods let under a **hire purchase agreement** to a person other than a company or other corporation, the claimant must state in the particulars of claim (Part 16, PD 7.1):*

7.1 (1) the date of the Agreement,   4.26

  (2) the parties to the Agreement,

  (3) the number or other identification of the Agreement,

  (4) where the claimant was not one of the original parties to the Agreement, the means by which the rights and duties of the creditor passed to him,

  (5) whether the Agreement is a regulated agreement and if it is not a regulated agreement, the reason why,

  (6) the place where the Agreement was signed by the defendant,

(7) the goods claimed,
(8) the total price of the goods,
(9) the paid-up sum,
(10) the unpaid balance of the total price,
(11) whether a Default Notice or a Notice under Section 76(1) or 98(1) of the Consumer Credit Act 1974 has been served on the defendant, and if it has, the date and method of service,
(12) the date when the right to demand delivery of the goods accrued,
(13) the amount (if any) claimed as an alternative to the delivery of goods, and
(14) the amount (if any) claimed in addition to:-

   (a) the delivery of the goods, or
   (b) any claim under (13) above, with the grounds of each claim.

Where the claim is not for the delivery of goods, the claimant must state in his Particulars of Claim (Pt. 16, PD 7.2):

- the matters set out in paragraph 8.19(1) to (6) above,
- the goods let under the Agreement,
- the amount of the total price,
- the paid up sum,
- the amount (if any) claimed as being due and unpaid in respect of any instalment or instalments of the total price, and
- the nature and amount of any other claim and hot it arises.

Defamation

4.27 As before, proceedings for defamation may not be started, nor transferred, to the county court save by agreement in writing between the parties. Part 16, PD 8 contains the requirements for the contents of the particulars of claim.

Specialist Proceedings

(For definition see Part 49 and Chapter 1 — The New Scheme)
4.28   The Claim Form N1 cannot always be used, as *"it may be necessary"* to follow the relevant Practice Direction and use the Practice Form approved for issue of the particular specialist proceedings, that is one of those proceedings listed in Parts 49 and 50. The Civil Procedure Rules will apply only to the extent

that they are not inconsistent with rules and practice directions which apply to these specialist claims.

Children and patients (CPR, Part 21)

Once proceedings are started, there must be a "litigation **4.29** friend", the new expression for a "next friend"; or "guardian *ad litem*" (Pt. 21, r.21.2). A "child", in the Rules means a person under 18, referred to in other enactments as "a minor". A "patient" means a person who by reason of mental disorder within the meaning of the Mental Health Act 1983 is incapable of managing and administering his own affairs (Pt. 21, r.21.1). There is a proviso that the court may make an Order permitting a "child" to conduct proceedings by itself (Pt. 21, r.21.2(3)).

A litigation friend must file the following (Pt. 21, r.21.5):

- his/her authorisation,
- certificate of suitability, *i.e.* can fairly and competently conduct the proceedings and no adverse interest,
- undertaking of claimant to pay costs ordered.

The court's approval of **settlements** is necessary wherever claimant or any party is a patient or child (Pt. 21, r.21.10). All money is to be paid into court and will become subject to directions (Pt. 21, r.21.11).

Addresses and Titles

Claimant's address

If not represented by a solicitor, the claimant must give his **4.30** residence or business address as his address for service (Pt. 6, r.6.5(3)(a)). If represented, the solicitor's address will be his address for service (but the claim form itself requires his personal address also to be given) (Pt. 6, r.6.5(4)). The address for service must be within England or Wales (Pt. 6, r.6.5(2)).

Children and patients

A child's name should be followed by "(a child by . . . his **4.31** litigation friend)" or, if a litigation friend is dispensed with, then simply "(a child)" (Pt. 21, PD 1.5). The name of a party suffering mental disorder should be followed by "(by . . . his litigation friend)" (Pt. 21, PD 1.3).

Firms and other unincorporated bodies

4.32 In the county court, the names of individuals and partners suing or sued in their own names may be followed by "trading as (*firm name*) and when suing or sued in the names of the firm or body, the name may be followed by "(*a trading name*)" (CCR, Ord. 5, r.10(1)). In the High Court it will be convenient to follow a similar practice, as hitherto

Failure to comply with these requirements may result in sanctions.

Discontinuing a Claim (CPR, Part 38)

4.33 To discontinue a claim or part of a claim a claimant must:

- File a notice of discontinuance
- Serve a copy on every other party

Pt. 38, r.38.3(1))

The Notice of Discontinuance must state that notice on every other party has been served and, where consent of some other party is needed, a copy of that consent must be attached (Pt. 38, r.38.3(2), (3)). The notice must make it clear that, if there is more than one defendant, which one is the claim discontinued against (Pt. 38, r.38.3(4).

Liability for costs

4.34 Unless the court orders otherwise, a claimant who discontinues is liable for the costs of the defendant up to the date of service of the notice (Pt. 38, r.38.6(1)). Part 44, r.44.12 provides for the basis of assessment of costs where a claim has been discontinued — basically this will be on the standard basis. These provisions as to costs do not apply to small claims (Pt. 38, r.38.6(3)).

Stay of proceedings

4.35 Where the action has only been partly discontinued, the court may order that the rest of the action remains stayed until the costs are paid (Pt. 38, r.38.8).

Chapter 5

Starting a Case — Part 8
Alternative Procedure

General

Here the claimant states on the claim form that Part 8 applies, **5.01**
and that he seeks a decision not involving a substantial dispute
of fact; or a practice direction permits, or requires, "Part 8
Procedure". A copy of the Part 8 Claim Form is at Appendix 7
to this book.
Note the provisions of Pt. 8, r.8.1(6):

> (6) A rule or practice direction may, in relation to a
> specified type of proceedings —
>
>> (a) require or permit the use of the Part 8 pro-
>> cedure; and
>> (b) disapply or modify any of the rules set out in
>> this Part as they apply to those proceedings.

The claimant must specify (Pt. 8, r.8.2):

- the question to be decided; or
- the remedy sought; and
- the enactment, if any, under which the claim is made.

Which Matters?

The Practice Direction to Part 8, which was originally published **5.02**
with the CPR in January 1999, gives examples of where the
procedure may be used:

> **1.4** The types of claim for which the Part 8 procedure may
> be used include:
>
>> (1) a claim by or against a child or patient which has been
>> settled before the commencement of proceedings and

45

the sole purpose of the claim is to obtain the approval of the court to the settlement,

(2) a claim for provisional damages which has been settled before the commencement of proceedings and the sole purpose of the claim is to obtain a consent judgment,

(3) an application for a deposition to be taken abroad under Part 34, made other than in existing proceedings,

(4) an application for a deposition to be taken in England and Wales for use before courts abroad, and

(5) provided there is unlikely to be a substantial dispute of fact, a claim for a summary order for possession against named or unnamed defendants occupying land or premises without the licence or consent of the person claiming possession.

5.03 Practice Direction 8B was issued in late March 1999 and sets out a list of all those proceedings where the Part 8 procedure **must** be used. The Practice Direction is divided into three sections, A, B, and C.

Section A applies to:

- all claims listed in Table 1 to the Practice Direction;

- claims where an Act provides that an application of claim is to be brought by originating summons; and

- claims or applications that before April 26, 1999 would have been brought by originating summons, but only if such claim or application is not listed in section C to the Practice Direction

provided that no other method of bringing the claim after April 26, 1999 is prescribed in a Schedule rule or practice direction.

5.04 The matters listed in Table 1 are all **High Court** matters and include:

- enforcement of charging orders;

- some applications for reciprocal enforcement of judgments;

- some proceedings by and against the Crown;

- mortgage possession actions;

- proceedings under the Landlord and Tenant Acts 1927, 1954 and 1987;

- applications for possession under RSC, Ord. 113 (squatters).

Section B applies to: 5.05

- all claims listed in Table 2 to the Practice Direction;

- in the **county court**, claims for:

  — the recovery of possession of land; or
  — damages for harassment under section 3 of the Protection from Harassment Act 1997.

- claims that before April 26, 1999 would have been brought:

  — in the High Court by originating motion, but only if not included in section C to the Practice Direction;
  — in the county court, by originating application or petition.

provided that no other procedure is prescribed in an act, Schedule rule or practice direction.

The matters listed in Table 2 include: 5.06

- in the **High Court**:

  — appeals by case stated under RSC, Ord. 56, rr.8 and 10
  — various other appeals under RSC, Ord. 94
  — references to the European Court

- in the **county court**

  — summary possession proceedings under CCR, Ord. 24
  — enforcement of charging orders by sale
  — applications under the Landlord and Tenant Acts 1927, 1954, 1985 and 1987, including, importantantly, applications for a new tenancy under section 24 of the 1954 Act (although it looks as though the old type of claim form can be used for the latter.)
  — certain applications under the Consumer Credit Act 1974

— accelerated possession order applications
— injunction applications under section 152 of the Housing Act 1996.

Contents of Claim

5.07 County Court Rules ("CCR"), Ords 6 and 7 make special provision for the contents of the particulars of claim in certain types of claim and for service of them, and there are also to be found in the CCR further special provisions relating to the venue for bringing proceedings and for periods of notice for hearings. Paragraphs B2 and B3 of the Practice Direction make it clear that such special provisions continue to apply in precedence to the general provisions of this Practice Direction 8B.

Section C applies to certain appeals in the High Court.

The Procedure

High Court

5.08 The main differences between the general procedure under Part 7 (see Chapter 4 — Starting a case) and the Part 8 (High Court) procedure are:

- the claimant must file and serve any evidence on which he wishes to rely with the claim form;

- an acknowledgement of service **must** be filed;

- the defendant must file and serve any evidence on which he wishes to rely when he files and serves his acknowledgement of service;

- the acknowledgement is served by the defendant;

- a defence is not required;

- default judgment is not available;

- the claim is treated as allocated to the multi track;

- the claimant must file and serve any evidence in reply within 14 days of service of the defendant's evidence; and

- the court may require or permit any party or witness to attend to give oral evidence or to be cross-examined.

The Part 20 (Third Party and Counterclaims) procedure (see Chapter 8 — Part 20 Claims) applies to Part 8 claims, save that leave is always required to issue.

A defendant may object to the use of the Part 8 procedure and the court has power, whether of its own motion or otherwise, to order that the procedure should cease to apply.

County Court

Section B of Practice Direction 8B (county court procedure) 5.09 varies the general Part 8 procedure described above. The "variant" element of the procedure is that a date for hearing will be fixed on issue, at least 21 days notice of which will be required to be given. Section B also provides that an Acknowledgement of Service is not required to be served, but it would appear that Pt. 8, r.8.4(2) will still apply. This provides that a defendant who has not filed an acknowledgement may attend the hearing but may not take any part in it without the court's permission.

Otherwise the Part 8 procedure will apply, which includes the filing of evidence on issue for the claimant, and with the acknowledgement of service for the defendant. This could have serious repercussions for commercial landlords with large portfolios.

Practical points:

- Claimants must use the not very user-friendly pre-April 5.10 26 forms (N5, N119, N120 — see Part 4 (Forms) and Part 8, PD 8B, B.8(2)). There is no change in the information that must be included in particulars of claim (see CCR, Ord. 6, rr.3 and 5 which are retained in CPR, Sched. 2) notwithstanding Pt. 16, PD 6, 7 which appear to be redundant. As before, on issue the court fixes a date for the hearing (PD 8B, para. B.9) and, except in cases where other rules provide for a shorter period, 21 days' notice of the hearing must be given. At the hearing the court may hear the case or give directions.

- Does a mortgagee/landlord have to complete a statement of truth? None of the forms prescribed for possession proceedings includes a statement of truth. However Pt. 22, r.22.1(1) provides that a statement of case must be verified by a statement of truth. Part 2, r.2.3(1) provides that 'statement of case' means ". . . particulars of claim where these are not included in a claim form . . .". Part

22, r.22.1(7) and the Practice Direction to Part 22, para 2.3 both envisage situations where the statement of truth is included in a separate document. The better view is that a statement of truth in the form of wording given by r.22.1(7) should be prepared and filed with the claim form. Note that by Pt. 22, PD 1.6 where a form has a jurat for an affidavit then a statement of truth is not required in addition. This would apply, *e.g.* to Form N5B — application for accelerated possession order, which has a jurat already endorsed.

- Careful thought needs to be given by mortgagees/landlords and their advisors as to whether statements of truth should be completed by housing officers, managing agents, or solicitors (see para. 4.11, above). However failure to comply with Pt. 22, r.22.1(1) is not necessarily fatal to proceedings. Rule 22.2(1) provides that proceedings remain effective but the claimant cannot rely upon the contents as proof of the facts alleged without calling evidence and the court may strike out the statement of case.

- As for which track possession matters should be allocated to: see Chapter 10 — Case Management.

Chapter 6

Service

Overview

General

This is covered in Part 6 and the practice direction which 6.02 supplements it.

The court has a general power to dispense altogether with service of any document "if it is appropriate to do so" (Pt. 6, r.6.9) and application may be made for such an order, without notice. The Court may also make an order authorising service by some method not of itself authorised by the Rules; an application for such an order can also be made without notice, supported by evidence (Pt. 6, PD 9). An order permitting an alternative method of service will specify the method and will state the date when the document will be deemed served (Pt. 6, r.6.8).

When solicitors are authorised by their clients to accept service, or hold themselves out as accepting service, then, except in cases where personal service on a party is required by some enactment, by court order, or by a practice direction, the document must be served on those solicitors.

An enactment, a rule within the Civil Procedure Rules, or a 6.03 practice direction, may make a specific provision and requirement for service, or in any case at all, the Court can order service as it thinks fit. Subject to this, the five methods of service are given under Pt. 6, r.6.2(1):

- Personal service
- First class post
- Leaving the document at the party's address for service, namely his residence or place of business within the jurisdiction, or else the business address of his solicitors

51

- Through a document exchange in accordance with Pt. 6, PD 2

- By fax (Pt. 6, PD 3).

Personal Service (CPR, Part 6, r.6.4)

6.04   (a) On individuals is by leaving the document with that individual.

(b) On companies or other corporations, by leaving the document with a person holding a "senior position", as defined by practice direction, within the company or corporation.

(c) On a partnership, provided partnerships are being sued in the name of their firm, by leaving it with any of the partners, or else, on a person having at the time of service "the control or management of the partnership business at the principal place of business" of the partnership.

Service by the Court

6.05   As provided in Pt. 6, r.6.3(1), documents issued, or prepared by the court, are served by the court; but this is subject to exceptions, namely it does not apply wherever:

- A Rule provides that a party themselves must serve.

- The party on whose behalf the document is to be served informs the court in writing, that they wish to serve themselves.

- The court itself orders otherwise.

- The court has sent a Notice of Non-Service.

- There is a Practice Direction.

Service will normally be by first-class post (Pt. 6, PD 8.1).

Service on Companies

6.06   Whilst the Pt. 6, r.6.4(4) provide that service on a company may be by leaving it with the person holding "a senior position" within the company or corporation, the existing Rules in the Companies Act 1985 remain intact, so that as an alternative,

service may be made by leaving the document at, or posting it
to, an "authorised place", pursuant to section 725 of the
Companies Act 1985; section 694A (Service of Documents on
Companies incorporated outside the United Kingdom and
Gibraltar and having a branch in Great Britain) and section 695
(see also Pt. 6, PD 6). Similar provisions apply to corporations,
service to be wherever the corporation carries on its activities or
has its principal office.

Address for Service (CPR, Part 6, r.6.5)

Documents to be served outside the jurisdiction are not dealt 6.07
with in the Civil Procedure Rules but continue to be governed
by RSC, Ord. 11.

A party must give an address for service within England and
Wales. If he is represented, his address for service is his
solicitor's address (except, usually, as to service of a claim form
— see para. 6.14, below). If not, he must give his residence or
place of business (unless he does not reside or carry on business
in England and Wales, when he may give any address within
England and Wales).

If an unrepresented party has not given an address for service, 6.08
the document must be sent as follows (Pt. 6, r.6.5(6)):

(1) Individual:

  • Usual or last known residence

(2) Proprietor of a business:

  • Usual or last known residence; or
  • Place of business or last known place of business.

(3) Individual suing or sued in name of firm (see also Pt. 6,
    PD 4):

  • Usual or last known residence or
  • Principal or last known place of business

(4) Corporation incorporated in England and Wales (other
    than a company):

  • Principal office; or
  • Any place within the jurisdiction where it carries
    on its activities and which has a real connection
    with the claim

(5) Company registered in England and Wales:

- Principal office; or
- Any place of business of the company within the jurisdiction which has a real connection with the claim.

(6) Any other company or corporation:

- Any place within the jurisdiction where the corporation carries on its activities
- Any place of business of the company within the jurisdiction

This is all to be found in Pt. 6, r.6.5.

Deemed Service (CPR, Part 6, r.6.7)

First class post:
6.09 Deemed effective the second day after the document was posted to the address for service (see below) of the person to be served.

Leaving the document:
6.10 Deemed effective the day **after** the document was left at the address for service (see para. 6.17 below) of the person to be served. This might be a trap for the unwary and is something that is being looked into by the rules committee as it seems unfair when compared with the immediate effect of service by fax (see para. 6.12, below).

Through a document exchange (Part 6, PD 2):
6.11 Deemed effective the second day after it was left at the document exchange. The address for service of the party to be served must include a document exchange box number or his writing paper or that of his solicitor must set one out. This method of service cannot be used if the party has indicated in writing that he is unwilling to be served by it.

By fax (Part 6, PD 3):
6.12 Deemed effective the day of transmission if transmitted before 4.00 p.m. on a business day (or the next business day if transmitted otherwise) to a fax number indicated in writing for the purpose by the party to be served or his solicitor. A fax number set out on solicitors' writing paper is assumed to be so indicated, as is one set out on a statement of case or a response to a claim filed with the court. It is not mandatory also to send a

hard copy but it is advisable to do so in case the fax was not received. Some courts have been refusing to accept service of documents at the court by fax — this is contrary to the rules.

By other electronic means:
Permitted only when both the party serving and the party to be 6.13
served are legally represented and the latter's solicitors have agreed in writing to the method of service and have provided an email address or other electronic identification. Effective the second day after the day on which it was transmitted. It is not mandatory also to send a hard copy but it is advisable to do so in case the transmission was not received.

When documents are served after 5.00 pm on a business day, or on the weekend or a Bank Holiday, the document shall be deemed served as having been served on the next business day.

Service of the Claim Form

The general rule is that the claim form must be served on the 6.14
defendant within four months from issue (six months where service is out of the jurisdiction (Pt. 7, r.7.5). An order may be made extending time (Pt. 7, r.7.6), application to be supported by evidence.

Proof of service

A rule, practice direction or order may require a certificate of 6.15
service to be filed.

Non-service by court (Pt. 6, r.6.11)

The court will only try to effect service at the address initially 6.16
given by the claimant. Where this fails, the court will give notice to that effect. It then becomes the party's responsibility to effect service (Pt. 6, PD 8.2).

Address for service of claim form (Pt. 6, r.6.13)

The defendant's address for service must be given in the claim 6.17
form if he is to be served by the court. His solicitor's address should be given as his address for service only if the solicitor is authorised to accept service. When a claim form is or particulars of claim are served on a partner or person having control or management of a partnership business at its principal place of

business, notice must also be served as to the capacity in which the person is served. If the court effects service, it will provide a notice to this effect. If the party effects service, he must file a certificate of service within seven days.

Certificate of service (Pt. 6, r.6.10)

6.18 A certificate of service must state that a document has not been returned undelivered and, where the method of service was:

- by post, the date of posting;
- personal, the date of personal service;
- through a document exchange, the date of delivery to it;
- by delivery to or leaving at a permitted place, the date of delivery or leaving;
- by fax, the date and time of transmission;
- by other electronic means, the date of transmission details of the means of transmission;
- by alternative method permitted by the court, the details required by the court.

Where a contract makes provision for service and the claim is in respect only of that contract, it may be served in accordance with that provision (Pt. 6, r.6.15). The court may in some circumstances by order authorise service on the agent of a defendant who is abroad (Pt. 6, r.6.16). The application must be supported by evidence and may be made without notice.

Service Personnel

6.19 Guidance notes as to service on members of H.M. Forces and members of the United States Air Force are annexed to the Practice Direction to Part 6.

Service on Children and Patients (Pt. 6, r.6.6)

6.20 The person who must be served with the claim form where the child is not also a patient, is the child's parents or guardians, or if none, the person with whom the child resides, or in whose care the child is. Claim forms where the person to be served is a "patient" is — or if there is one — the person authorised under Part VII of the Mental Health Act 1983 to conduct proceedings in the name of the patient — or the person with whom the patient resides, or in whose care the patient is. With regard to any other document, after the claim form, service will be on "the litigation friend".

Chapter 7

Responses to Claim

Overview

7.01   ● High Court system of acknowledgements of service applied to county court.

    ● Specific requirements for defences.

    ● New provisions for admissions

General

7.02 A copy of the particulars of claim or the claim form if it contains the particulars of claim, is sent to defendants accompanied by a "response pack" (CPR, Part 7, r.7.8(1)).
The pack includes:

    ● an Admission Form (N9A);

    ● a Defence and Counterclaim Form (N90) (A copy of this is at Appendix 8 to this book);

    ● an Acknowledgement of Service (N9).

Options for Defendant

7.03 To complete:

    (a) The admission form if the claim, or the amount claimed is admitted, or

    (b) The admission form and the defence form, if part claim is admitted (see para. 7.14, below), or

    (c) The defence form if whole claim is disputed, or a claim is made against the claimant, or

(d) The acknowledgement of service where defendant needs 28 days rather than 14 to prepare his defence or where he contests the court's jurisdiction (Part 10, r.10.1(3) and see Part 11 generally).

The Acknowledgement of Service

Acknowledgements of Service are to be filed within 14 days 7.04 after the date of service of the particulars of claim, or within 14 days of the date of service of the claim form if it contains the particulars of claim (Pt. 10, r.10.3(1)). The above time limit will not apply where different and longer periods are specified for claim forms served out of the jurisdiction (Pt. 10, r.10.3(2)).

The court informs claimants of receipt of an Acknowledgement of Service, which itself has to provide an address to which documents for the defendant are to be sent.

Default Judgments

A default judgment may be entered whenever a defendant fails 7.05 to file an acknowledgement of service within the specified period or does not within that period, file a defence (see para. 7.25, below), or serve an admission (Pt. 12, r.12.1). However, where the claim form states that particulars of claim are to follow, the defendant need not respond until the particulars of claim have been served upon him.

But there are prohibited cases, such as:

- Those for delivery of goods under the Consumer Credit Act 1974 (Pt. 12, r.12.2).

- Where the Part 8 procedure (see Chapter 5) is used.

- By the claimant where the defendant has applied for summary judgment.

- In Part 20 claims (see Chapter 8) other than counterclaims, *i.e.* it does apply to counterclaims but not to others.

- Where a Practice Direction so provides.
(Part 12)

Where Part 8 procedure is being used, if defendant fails to file 7.06 an acknowledgement, he will be unable to take any active part in the hearing without the leave of the court (Pt. 8, r.8.4) (see Chapter 5 — Starting a Case — Part 8 Alternative Procedure).

Where there is a Part 20 claim, a default judgment can now be obtained in the county court on a counterclaim. If the counterclaim is for money or delivery of goods where the defendant to the counterclaim is given the alternative of paying the value of the goods, this can be done administratively but at the moment is problematical, see para. 8.15, below. This is new in the county court.

For other types of Part 20 claims, except for contribution or indemnity between defendants to the claim (where a default judgment cannot be obtained), there are special rules where the Part 20 defendant has failed to file an acknowledgement or defence and in such cases:

- Defendant is deemed to admit the Part 20 claim.

- Defendant is bound by any judgment in the main pro-ceedings so far as it is relevant to the Part 20 claim.

- Claimant may obtain judgment by filing a request in the relevant practice form provided:

  - default judgment has been taken against that Part 20 claimant, and
  - he has satisfied that default judgment, and
  - the remedy he seeks is limited to contribution or indemnity.

If any of these conditions is not met, the Part 20 claimant may only enter default judgment if he obtains the Court's permission.

The mechanisms for obtaining a default judgment

7.07 There are two mechanisms in place for obtaining default judgments, depending on the nature of the claim:

   (a) Firstly, a simple request for judgment under Part 12 is available for money claims (Pt. 12, r.12.4(1)). A money claim will include both one for specified sums, and one which is in respect of unspecified damages. The pro-cedure is that judgment is entered simply on filing a request for default judgment, and this of course without any consideration of the claim's merits (Pt. 12, r.12.4(2)).

(b) The second case, is where the claim is for a remedy other than a money claim, or is a claim only for costs other than fixed costs, and also in certain other cases which are set out in Pt. 12, r.12.10 — in all of these an application must be made for judgment using the Part 23 application procedure (see Chapter 15 — Applications). On such an Application a hearing will be given, and the court will give "such judgment as it appears to the court that the claimant is entitled to on his statement of case" (Pt. 12, r.12.11(1)). Under this procedure, that is an application for judgment, the Court will consider the merits.

Most default judgments are likely to be entered simply from filing a request in the appropriate form (see para. 7.11, below).

Conditions for entering judgments in default

In all cases whether by way of a request for judgment or an 7.08 application for a default judgment, the court must be satisfied that:

(a) The particulars of claim have been served — this is likely to appear from the certificate of service on the court file.

(b) The defendant has not filed an acknowledgement of service, or has not filed a defence, and in either case the time for doing so has expired.

(c) The defendant has not satisfied the claim.

(d) The defendant has not filed or served an admission together with a request for time to pay, and

(e) The defendant has not made an application for summary judgment which has not been disposed of.

(Pt. 12, r.12.3 and PD 4.1).

Special cases requiring an application (Pt. 12, r.12.10)

These are: 7.09

(a) against children and patients;

(b) for costs other than fixed costs only;

(c) by one spouse against the other on a claim in tort;

(d) for delivery up of goods where the defendant will not be allowed the alternative of paying their value;

(e) against the Crown; or

(f) against persons or organisations who enjoy immunity from civil jurisdiction under the provisions of the International Organisations Acts 1968 and 1981.

Interest

7.10 When applying for default judgment the claimant may also apply under Pt. 12, r.12.6 for interest to the date of judgment, but only if:

(a) the particulars of claim include the details required by rule 16.4;

(b) where interest is claimed under section 35A of the Supreme Court Act 1981 or section 69 of the County Courts Act 1984, the rate is no higher than the rate of interest payable on judgment debts at the date when the claim form was issued; and

(c) the claimant's request for judgment includes a calculation of the interest claimed for the period from the date up to which interest was stated to be calculated in the claim form to the date of the request for judgment.

In any other case, where interest is claimed, the amount will be decided by the court (Pt. 12, r.12.6(2)). Part 12, r.12.7 sets out the procedure for deciding the amount of interest.

Forms

7.11 For default judgments by request, use Forms N205A or N255, or where the amount is to be decided by the court, N225B.

Admissions (CPR, Part 14)

7.12   14.1

(1) A party may admit the truth of the whole or any part of another party's case.

(2) He may do this by giving notice in writing (such as in a statement of case or-by letter).

(3) Where the only remedy which the claimant is seeking is the payment of money, the defendant may also make an admission in accordance with—

(a) rule 14.4 (admission of whole claim for specified amount of money);

    (b) rule 14.5 (admission of part of claim for specified amount of money);

    (c) rule 14.6 (admission of liability to pay whole of claim for unspecified amount of money); or

    (d) rule 14.7 (admission of liability to pay claim for unspecified amount of money where defendant offers a sum in satisfaction of the claim).

Admission of whole of claim for specified sum

In this case, the defendant must serve the admission direct on the claimant. The claimant then files it with his request for judgment using Form 205A (Pt. 14, r.14.4(4)).   **7.13**

Admission of part of claim for specified sum

The defendant files the admission with the court which then serves a copy on the claimant. The claimant has 14 days in which to notify the court whether he accepts the offer or not (Pt. 14, r.14.5(3)–(5)). If he does not do so the claim is stayed until the claimant does. If the defendant accepts the offer, he obtains judgment by filing a request, but if he does not, then the claim is treated as defended (Pt. 26, r.26.3(4)(a)).   **7.14**

Admission of claim for unspecified sum

Again the admission is filed in court and the court serves a copy on the claimant. Again the claimant has 14 days to respond (by filing a request for judgment) or the claim is stayed until he does (Pt. 14, r.14.6(1)–(5)). When the claimant files the request for judgment, judgment is entered "for an amount to be determined by the court", and the file is referred to the judge for him to give management directions (Pt. 14, rr.14.6(7) and 14.8).   **7.15**

Admission of claim for unspecified sum coupled with offer in satisfaction

This is a new concept. Where such an admission is made, once again it is filed in court and the court serves a copy on the claimant, who has 14 days in which to respond (Pt. 14, r.14.7(2)-(3)). If he does not respond, the claim is stayed until he does. If the claimant accepts the offer, he may obtain judgment for the amount offered by filing a request (Pt. 14, r.14.7(4)).   **7.16**

Practical point:

7.17 Unfortunately there is something of a lacuna in the costs rules at the moment, because fixed costs only apply to claims for a specified sum, and there is nothing at present in the rules which provides for the court to assess costs where this type of admission is made.

Requests for time to pay

7.18 If a defendant makes an admission under Pt. 14, rr.14.4, 14.5 or 14.7, he may request time to pay (Pt. 14, r.14.9(1)–(6)). The claimant may agree the request or reject it. If he rejects it, the court will determine the time or rate of payment (Pt. 14, r.14.10(4)).

Contents of Defence

Address for service

7.19 At the foot of the Defence Form a space is provided for the address for service. This must be within the jurisdiction and will be that of the legal representative if he has signed the acknowledgement of service (Pt. 10, r.10.5).

In response, a "defence" must (Pt. 16, r.16.5):

   a. State:

      (i) which parts of the claim the defendant admits
      (ii) which parts he denies;
      (iii) which parts he neither admits nor denies, because he does not know whether they are true, but which he wishes the claimant to prove;

   b. Give the defendant's version of the facts in so far as they differ from those in the statement of claim;
   c. Say why the defendant disputes the claimant's entitlement to any, or to a particular, remedy or the value of the claim or assessment of damages; and
   d. Specify any document vital to the defence.

Practical point:

7.20 Note that the requirement to specify a document is mandatory as compared to the discretionary requirement to attach a document to a claim: see Chapter 4 — Starting a Case.

Damages can be admitted, if desired for the purpose of the action whichever way it goes, but otherwise a Defendant shall not be taken to admit damages unless he does expressly admit them.

Practical point:
A defence which admits liability but which denies damage may 7.21
well be treated by the court as an admission of an unspecified
claim and judgment may be entered with damages to be assessed
at a disposal hearing (see Chapter 10 — Case Management).
The fact that an issue as to quantum is not raised in a "defence"
or that there has been a default judgment does not necessarily
mean that issue cannot be raised at a hearing on quantum
(*Lunnun v. Singh and Others, The Times*, July 19, 1999, CA).
Statements of value (see Chapter 4 — Starting a case) can be
disputed, in which the Defendant must say why and if able, give
his own (Pt. 16, r.16(6)). Representative capacities must be
stated in a defence, and if an acknowledgement of service has
not been given, an address for service must be supplied (r.16(7)
and (8)).

Verification of Truth

Part 15, PD 2.1: 7.22

Part 22 requires a defence to be verified by a statement of
truth) (as it is a "statement of case": *see Chapter 4 — Starting
a case*).

2.2 The form of the statement of truth is as follows: "[I
believe] [the defendant believes] that the facts stated in this
defence are true."

The Statement of Truth is in fact printed on Form N90 (above
the space for signatures).

Note Part 10, PD 4:

4.2 Where the defendant is a company or other corporation,
a person holding a senior position in the company or
corporation may sign the acknowledgement of service on the
defendant's behalf, but must state the position he holds.
4.3 Each of the following persons is a person holding a
senior position:

1. in respect of a registered company or corporation, a
   director, the treasurer, secretary, chief executive,
   manager or other officer of the company or corporation, and

> 2. in respect of a corporation which is not a registered company, in addition to those persons set out in (1), the mayor, chairman, president, town clerk or similar officer of the corporation.

4.4 Where the defendant is a partnership, the acknowledgement of service may be signed by:

> 1. any of the partners, or
> 2. a person having the control or management of the partnership business.

4.5 Children and patients may acknowledge service only by their litigation friend or his legal representative unless the court otherwise orders

Defence: Details

7.23 Part 16, r.16.5

> (3) A defendant who:
>
> > (a) fails to deal with an allegation; and
> > (b) has set out in his defence the nature of his case in relation to the issue to which that allegation is relevant, shall be taken to require that allegation to be proved.
>
> (4) Where the claim includes a money claim, a defendant shall be taken to require that any allegation relating to the amount of money claimed be proved unless he expressly admits the allegation.
>
> (5) Subject to paragraphs (3) and (4), a defendant who fails to deal with an allegation shall be taken to admit that allegation.
>
> (6) If the Defendant disputes the claimant's statement of value under rule 16.3 (*in relation to a claim for personal injuries*) he must:—
>
> > (a) state why he disputes it; and
> > (b) if he is able, give his own statement of the value of the claim.

7.24 Additionally, by Part 16, PD 14.1:

where the claim is for personal injuries and the claimant has attached a medical report in respect of his alleged injuries, the defendant should;

(1) state in his defence whether he
  (a) agrees,
  (b) disputes, or
  (c) neither agrees nor disputes but has no knowledge of
the matters contained in the medical report,
(2) where he disputes any part of the medical report, give in his defence his reasons for doing so, and
(3) where he has obtained his own medical report on which he intends to rely, attach it to his defence.

14.2 Where the claim is for personal injuries and the claimant has included a schedule of past and future expenses and losses, the defendant should include in or attach to his defence a counter-schedule stating;

(1) which of those items he:
  (a) agrees,
  (b) disputes, or
  (c) neither agrees nor disputes but has no knowledge of, and
(2) where any items are disputed, supplying alternative figures where appropriate.

For special requirements for defences in defamation cases, see Pt. 16, PD 15.

Time for Filing Defence

The period for filing a defence is 14 days after service of the particulars of claim, or 28 days after service where the defendant has filed an Acknowledgement of Service (Pt. 15, r.15(4)(1)). These periods will not apply where different and longer periods are specified where claim forms are served out of the jurisdiction; nor where the defendant has made an application disputing the court's jurisdiction; nor in those cases where the claimant has applied for summary judgment before a defence has been filed, in which case the defendant need not file his defence until the summary judgment hearing (Pt. 15, r.15.4(2)) (see Chapter 9 — Summary Judgment and Disposal). 7.25

Extension by Agreement

The parties can agree for an extension, but not beyond 28 days further and beyond what is specified in the Civil Procedure Rules (Pt. 15, r.15.5(1)). Both parties must in such cases notify the Court of the agreed extension (Pt. 15, r.15.5(2)). 7.26

Service

7.27 The same rules apply as with any other document, namely that they will be served by the court save where a rule says otherwise or a party wishes to serve himself and so notifies the court, or there is a Practice Direction as to service, or the court otherwise orders or those cases in which Notice of Non-Service has been sent out by the court (Pt. 6, r.6.3) (see Chapter 6 — Service).

Defence of Set-Off

7.28 Part 16, r.16.6:

> 16.6—Where a defendant —
>
> (a) contends he is entitled to money from the claimant; and
> (b) relies on this as a defence to the whole of part of the claim,
>
> the contention may be included in the defence and set off against the claim.

Defence of Payment in Money Claims (Pt. 15, r.15.10)

7.29 If this is the defence, to shorten matters, the claimant will receive a Notice from the court asking him, the complainant, to state whether he wishes to proceed, and if he does so, send a copy of that response to the defendant; the proceedings will be stayed in any event within 28 days after service of the court's Notice, if the claimant fails at all to respond to it; application can then be made by any party to restore.

Stay of proceedings where six months has elapsed (Pt. 15, r.15.11)

7.30 Where six months has expired since the end of the period for filing a defence, and neither a defence, an admission or a counterclaim has been filed, nor an admittance, and the claimant has not entered or applied for judgment, then the claim is automatically stayed; parties may apply for the stay to be lifted.

Practical point:
7.31 This staying of proceedings after six months is new.

Reply (Pt. 16, r.16.7)

A Reply, as before the county court, is optional; if the claimant 7.32
does wish to file a reply in response to the defence, he should
do so when he files his Allocation Questionnaire. There are to
be no further "statements of case" after a reply without the
permission of the court (Pt. 15, r.15.9).

16.7—(1) A Claimant who does not file a reply to the
defence shall not be taken to admit the matters raised in the
defence.
(2) A claimant who—

(a) files a reply to a defence, but
(b) fails to deal with a matter raised in the defence, shall
be taken to require that matter to be proved.

Practical point:
It may be that eventually replies will become less common save 7.33
in those cases where there is a positive assertion by the
defendant which is not covered by the particulars of claim or
which the claimant wishes to meet by himself raising a positive
case.

Chapter 8

Part 20 Claims

Overview

8.01 Any claim other than a claim by a claimant against a defendant, is called a "**Part 20 claim**". The old reference to "Third Party" has gone.

Part 20 claims fall into four categories:

- counterclaims against claimant(s);
- counterclaims against claimant(s) and a non-party;
- claims for contribution or indemnity made between defendants to the claim;
- any other claim made by a defendant against a non-party.

Any person who becomes a defendant to a Part 20 claim may himself bring a similar claim against another (whether or not already a party), and this, too, will be a Part 20 claim.

Procedure Rules applying to Part 20 Claims

8.02 See Pt. 20, PD 3:

The Civil Procedure Rules apply generally to Part 20 Claims as if they were claims. However, by Part 20, r.20.2, the following Rules do NOT apply to Part 20 Claims:

(a) Pt. 7, rr.7.5 and 7.6 (time within which a claim form may be served);
(b) Pt. 16, r.16.3(5) (statement of value where claim to be issued in the High Court); and
(c) Pt. 26 (case management — preliminary stage).

and by Part 20, r.20.3:

(a) Part 12 (default judgment); and
(b) Part 14 (admissions) except Rules 14.1(1) and (2) (which provide that a party may admit in writing the truth of another party's case) and 14.3 (admission by notice in writing — application for judgment).

Counterclaims (CPR, Part 20, rr.20.4(2) and 20.5(1), (2) and (3))

A counterclaim may be made without permission where: 8.03

- it is brought against the claimant or one or more of them; and

- it is filed with the defence.

Thus leave will be required to commence a counterclaim:

- before or after filing of the counterclaimant's defence

- where no defence is filed.

Form of Counterclaim and the Reply

See (Pt. 20, PD 6.1 and 6.2):   8.04

1.6: Where a defendant to a claim serves A COUN-TERCLAIM under this Part, the defence and counterclaim should normally form one document with the counterclaim following on from the defence.
2.6: Where a claimant serves A REPLY and a defence to counterclaim, the reply and the defence to counterclaim should normally form one document with the defence to counterclaim following on from the reply.

A blank form for a Part 20 claim is part of "the response pack" sent out by the court with the claim form to a defendant. Note Pt. 4, r.4(1), (2) and (3):

4.1 The contents of a Part 20 claim should be verified by a STATEMENT OF TRUTH. Part 22 requires a statement of case to be verified by a statement of truth.
4.2 The form of the statement of truth should be as follows:

'[I believe] [Part 20 claimant]' believes that the facts stated in this statement of case are true'.

4.3 Attention is drawn to Pt. 32, r.32.14 which sets out the consequences of verifying a statement of case containing a false statement without an honest belief in its truth.

Filing and service

8.05 The counterclaim is made by filing particulars of the counterclaim and must be served with the defence. Time for defence to counterclaim is 14 days. Acknowledgement of Service may not be filed in relation to a counterclaim, which is anomalous because it may be used for every other form of Part 20 claim, thereby giving the defendant to the Part 20 claim an additional 14 days in which to file a defence.

A counter-claimant may thus be in the position of having to file his allocation questionnaire before he knows how the claimant (defendant to counterclaim) pleads to the counterclaim. However, Pt. 3, r.3.1(2) provides:

> (2) Except where these Rules provide otherwise, the court may:
>
> (a) extend or shorten the time for compliance with any rule, practice direction or court order (even if an application for extension is made after the time for compliance has expired);

8.06 Part 20, r.20.12(1) provides that where a Part 20 claim form is served on a person who is not already a party it must be accompanied by:

> (a) a form for defending the claim;
> (b) a form for admitting the claim;
> (c) a form for acknowledging service; and
> (d) a copy of:
>> (i) every statement of case which has already been served in the proceedings; and
>> (ii) such other documents as the court may direct.

See also Pt. 20, r.20.8:

> 20.8—(1) Where a Part 20 claim may be made without the court's permission, the Part 20 claim form must —
>> (a) in the case of a counterclaim, be served on every other party when a copy of the defence is served;

    (b) in the case of any other Part 20 claim, be served on the person against whom it is made within 14 days after the date on which the party making the Part 20 claim files his defence.

(2) Paragraph (1) does not apply to a claim for contribution or indemnity made in accordance with Rule 20.6.

(3) Where the court gives permission to make a Part 20 claim, it will at the same time give directions as to the service of the Part 20 claim.

Note also Pt. 20, PD 7.1 to 7.5:

7.1 The title of every Part 20 claim should contain: 8.07

(1) the full name of each party, and
(2) his status in the proceedings (*e.g.* claimant, defendant, Part 20 claimant, Part 20 defendant), for example:

> AB Claimant
> CD Defendant/Part 20 Claimant
> EF Part 20 Defendant.

7.2 Where a defendant makes a counterclaim not only against the claimant but also against a non-party the title should show this as follows:

> AB Claimant/Part 20 Defendant
> CD Defendant/Part 20 Claimant and
> XY Part 20 Defendant.

7.3 Where there is more than one Part 20 claim, the parties to the first Part 20 claim should be described as 'Part 20 Claimant (1st claim)' and 'Part 20 Defendant (1st claim)', the parties to the second Part 20 claim should be described as 'Part 20 Claimant (2nd claim)' and 'Part 20 Defendant (2nd claim)', and so on. For example:

> AB Claimant and Part 20 Defendant (2nd claim)
> CD Defendant and Part 20 Claimant (1st claim)
> EF Part 20 Defendant (1st claim) and Part 20 Claimant (2nd claim)
> GH Part 20 Defendant (2nd claim).

7.4 Where the full name of a party is lengthy it must appear in the title but thereafter in the statement of case it may be identified by an abbreviation such as initials or a recognised shortened name.

7.5 Where a party to the proceedings has more than one status *e.g.* Claimant and Part 20 Defendant (2nd claim) or Part 20 Defendant (1st claim) and Part 20 Claimant (2nd claim) the combined status must appear in the title but thereafter it may be convenient to refer to the party by name, *e.g.* Mr. Smith, or, if paragraph 7.4 applies, by initials or a shortened name.

Counterclaims Against Non-party

8.08 Leave is always required to bring a new party into the proceedings and thus is required to make this type of Part 20 claim.

Contribution and Indemnity

8.09 This type of Part 20 claim may be brought without leave at any time by a defendant who has acknowledged service or filed a defence. The claim is made by filing a notice and serving it on the defendant to the Part 20 claim. The Part 20 claim must be served within 14 days of issue. The rules about filing defence and acknowledgement of service are the same as for a claim.
See Pt. 20, r.20.6:

20.6 A defendant who has filed an acknowledgement of service or a defence may make a Part 20 claim for Contributions or Indemnity against another defendant by —

(a) filing a notice containing a statement of the nature and grounds of his claim; and
(b) serving that notice on the other defendant.

Other Part 20 Claims

8.10 This is any claim brought by a defendant against any person who is not already a party for contribution or indemnity or some other remedy (Pt. 20, r.20.7).
This type of Part 20 claim may be made without leave, (now referred to as "permission") where it is issued before or at the same time as the defence of the defendant making the Part 20 claim and is made by filing a Part 20 claim form. The Part 20 claim must be served within 14 days after the party making the Part 20 claim files his defence and the rules as to acknowledgement of service and defence apply.
An application for permission to make a Part 20 claim may be made without notice. If permission is given, the judge must at

the same time give directions for the filing of defence to the Part 20 claim.

Applications for Permission, Where Counterclaim, or Other Part 20 Claim is not Served with Defence

See Pt. 20, PD 2:   8.11

2.1 An application for permission to make a Part 20 claim must be supported by EVIDENCE stating:

(1) the state which the action has reached;
(2) the nature of the claim to be made by the Part 20 claimant or details of the question or issue which needs to be decided;
(3) a summary of the facts on which the Part 20 Claim is based, and
(4) the name and address of the proposed Part 20 defendant.

(For further information regarding evidence see the Practice Direction which supplements Part 32).
2.2 Where delay has been a factor contributing to the need to apply for permission to make a Part 20 claim an explanation of the delay should be given in evidence.
2.3 Where possible the applicant should provide a timetable of the action to date.
2.4 Rules 20.5(2) and 20.7(5) allow applications to be made to the court without notice unless the court otherwise directs.

Where the Court gives permission to make a Part 20 claim later, after defence has been served, directions will be given as to service (Pt. 20, r.20.8).

Practical point:
Permission to make a Part 20 claim involves an application 8.12
supported by elaborate evidence, and accordingly it is obviously
very advisable to serve all Part 20 claims with the defence if at
all possible.

Case Management under Part 20 (r.20.13)

If a defence to a Part 20 claim is filed, the case will be referred 8.13
to the procedural judge to consider giving management

directions. Note that Part 26 (allocation) (see Chapter 10 — Case Management) does not apply to Part 20 claims but the judge:

- must, so far as possible, manage the Part 20 claim(s) with the claim; and

- may order that a Part 20 claim be managed separately from the claim.

For the court's powers at the case management hearing, see Pt. 20, PD 5.3 and 5.4:

5.3 At the hearing the Court may:
- (1) treat the hearing as a summary judgment hearing;
- (2) order that the Part 20 proceedings be dismissed;
- (3) give directions about the way any claim, question or issue set out in or arising from the Part 20 Claim should be dealt with;
- (4) give directions as to the part, if any, the Part 20 defendant will take at the trial of the claim;
- (5) give directions about the extent to which the Part 20 defendant is to be bound by any judgment or decision to be made in the claim.

5.4 The court may make any of the orders in 5.3(1) to (5) either before or after any judgment in the claim has been entered by the claimant against the defendant.

8.14   Part 20, r.20.9 applies whenever the court is considering whether to permit a Part 20 Claim, dismiss it, or require it to be dealt with separately.

The matters to which the court may have regard include (Pt. 20, r.20.9(2)):

- (a) the connection between the Part 20 claim and the claim made by the claimant against the defendant;
- (b) whether the Part 20 claimant is seeking substantially the same remedy which some other party is claiming from him; and
- (c) whether the Part 20 claimant wants the court to decide any question connected with the subject matter of the proceedings: —

> (i) not only between existing parties but also between existing parties and a person not already a party; or
>
> (ii) against an existing party not only in a capacity in which he is already a party but also in some further capacity.

Default Judgment in Part 20 claims (Pt. 20, r.20.11)

Note that default judgment can now, *in theory,* be obtained in 8.15 the county court on a counterclaim. If the counterclaim is for money, or delivery of goods where the defendant (to the counterclaim) is given the alternative of paying the value of the goods, this can be done administratively. This is completely new for the county court. It will be particularly important in road traffic accident cases where, traditionally, defences to counterclaims are often overlooked.

For the moment, however, there appears to be a conflict with Part 12 which may, strictly speaking, prevent judgment being obtained on a counterclaim:

> 12.3—(1) The claimant may obtain judgment in default of an acknowledgement of service only if —
>
> (a) the defendant has not filed an acknowledgement of service or a defence to
> the claim (or any part of the claim); and
>
> (b) the relevant time for doing so has expired.
>
> (2) The claimant may obtain judgment in default of defence only if —
>
> (a) the defendant has filed an acknowledgement of service but has not filed a defence; and
>
> (b) the relevant time for doing so has expired.

As there is no provision for acknowledgements of service of a counterclaim, it follows that the rule permitting default judgment to be obtained does not apply. This anomalous situation is likely to be changed by a rule amendment. Some courts *may,* however, in the interim allow default judgments on counterclaims.

For other types of Part 20 claim, except claims for contribu- 8.16 tion or indemnity between defendants to the claim (where you cannot obtain a default judgment at all), there are special rules where the Part 20 defendant has failed to file an acknowledgement of service or defence. In such cases the Part 20:

- defendant is deemed to admit the Part 20 claim;

- defendant is bound by any judgment in the main proceedings so far as it is relevant to the Part 20 claim;

- claimant may obtain judgment by filing a request in the relevant practice form provided;

- default judgment has been taken against that Part 20 claimant; and

- he has satisfied that default judgment; and

- the remedy he seeks is limited to contribution or indemnity.

If any of those conditions is not met, the Part 20 claimant may only enter default judgment if he obtains the court's permission.

Chapter 9

Summary Judgment and Disposal

A. SUMMARY JUDGMENT (CPR, PART 24)

Overview

- Available to both claimant **and** defendant   9.01
- Court may instigate on own initiative
- New basis for order
- New provisions for evidence
- Goodbye "Conditional leave", hello "Conditional orders"
- Available for small claims

General

Part 24 makes broad provision for deciding claims or issues 9.02 without a trial, replaces the old RSC, Ord. 14 and CCR, Ord. 9, r.14 and is available to both claimants and defendants. Except with permission, claimants must wait until a defendant has filed an acknowledgement of service or a defence before applying for summary judgment (Pt. 24, r.24.4(1)). If a defendant does neither, then a claimant can proceed by way of a default judgment: see Chapter 7 — Responses to Claim). Where the application is made before a defence is filed, the defendant against whom it is made need not file a defence (Pt. 24, r.24.4(2)). **However, where the defendant is seeking summary judgment against the claimant, it does not appear that the defendant is relieved from having to file a defence.** Summary judgment is now available in small claims matters from which it was previously disallowed.

The Allocation Questionnaire asks the parties if they intend to make an application for summary judgment. As the notes to the questionnaire do not give any indication as to what exactly this means, this may cause some confusion for litigants in person. The Part 24 procedure can also be used where just a point of law is involved (Pt. 24, PD 1.3(1))

Proceedings Excluded from Part 24

9.03 Summary judgment **cannot** be given against:

- a defendant in proceedings for possession of residential property,
- a mortgagor in mortgage possession proceedings,
- a former tenant holding over.

Nor can a summary judgment be given in proceedings for an admiralty claim *in rem*, nor in contentious probate (Pt. 24, r.24.3). For applications against claimants, there are not any excluded proceedings (Pt. 24, r.24.3(1)).

Certain claims in respect of mortgages and tenancy agreements

9.04 An application can be made under Part 24 if it is a claim for specific performance of an agreement for the sale, purchase, exchange, mortgage or charge on any property, or for the grant or assignment of a lease or tenancy. Similarly there may be an application for rescission of such an agreement, or for the forfeiture or return of any deposit made under such agreement. The application notice, evidence in support, and a draft order must be served no less than four clear days before the hearing of any such application (Pt. 24, PD 7).

Claims for an Order for Accounts and Inquiries

9.05 Whenever the claim form expressly or by implication involves accounts and inquiries, an application may be made under Part 24 for a summary order so directing (Pt. 24, PD 6).

Procedure

The Application

9.06 The court is expressly empowered to fix a summary judgment hearing of its own initiative (Pt. 24, r.24.4(3)), particularly to further the "objective" of deciding which issues need investigation and which can be dealt with summarily. However, normally, a file will not come to the judge's attention until allocation, unless a vigilant clerk spots something amiss, but on allocation, or possibly earlier, the court will always consider its powers under Pt. 3, r.3.4(1) to consider sanctions or summary disposal (see "Summary Disposal", para. 9.15, below).

Where the court is considering making an order for summary judgment of its own initiative it must give each party likely to be affected by the order at least three days notice of the hearing (Pt. 24, r.24.4(3)), extending the three-day period provided for in Pt. 3, r.3.3(3).

Applications by a party under Part 24 may be based on a point of law, the evidence which can reasonably be expected, or lack of it, or a combination of both (Pt. 24, r.24.2).

No particular form is prescribed but Form N244 may be used 9.07 (see Part 23 and Chapter 15 — Applications). It must contain a statement that it is an application for summary judgment (Pt. 24, PD 2(2)), identify concisely the point of law or provision in a document on which the applicant relies, and/or state that the applicant believes that the respondent has no real prospect of succeeding and that there is no other reason why the matter should go to trial (Pt. 24, r.24.2(3)). Non-compliance with these technicalities is likely to be fatal to the application (see *Barclays Bank v. Piper, The Times*, May 31, 1995, CA). The application notice should draw the attention of the respondent to Pt. 24, r.24.5(1) (Pt. 24, PD 2(5)), *i.e.*:

(1)   If the respondent to an application for summary judgment wishes to rely on written evidence at the hearing, he must —

(a) file the written evidence; and
(b) serve copies on every other party to the application,

at least seven days before the summary judgment hearing.

The respondent is entitled to 14 days notice of the application, setting out the issues the court has to decide (Pt. 24, r.24.4(3)). Notice must be given, either by the party who brings the application, or by the court if the hearing is fixed of the court's own motion.

The hearing

9.08 Witness statements may be used at the hearing of the application but, curiously, there is no requirement for them (because the statement of case and/or application notice when verified by the statement of truth can stand as evidence). The application will normally be heard by a district judge or Master (Pt. 24, PD 3.1) although either of them could direct that it is heard by a circuit judge (Pt. 24, PD 3.2).

The Principles

9.09 The test is now based on that for setting aside judgment as discussed in *Alpine Bulk Transport Co. Inc. v. Saudi Eagle Shipping Co. Inc. (The Saudi Eagle)* [1986] 2 Lloyd's Rep. 221, CA. This test differs fairly significantly from the previous test, basically described as "no arguable defence". It mitigates against weak defences and is extended to claims, replacing applications to strike out statements of case for disclosing no reasonable grounds as an alternative or in addition to making an application for summary disposal (see Pt. 3, r.3.4 and below). Indeed, this can the implied by the reference to r.3.4 in this r.and it would be sensible for practitioners to consider including an application under Part 24 as an alternative to an application under r.3.4.

A case that is merely "arguable", as under the old Rules, will not suffice now to resist applications if:

    (a) [the Court] considers —

        (i) that the claimant has no real prospect of succeeding on the claim or issue; or
        (ii) that the defendant has no real prospect of successfully defending the claim or issue; and

    (b) there is no other reason why the case or issue should be disposed of at a trial.

(Pt, 24, r.24.2)

9.10 Part 24 throws no burden onto the respondent to show that he has a defence or a claim as the case may be — *cf.* RSC Ord. 14, rr.3(1) and 4(1). The burden of proving that the other side dos not have a claim or defence is on the applicant.

Conditional Orders (CPR, Part. 24, PD 4.3)

Where it appears to the court possible that a claim or defence 9.11
may succeed but improbable that it will do so, the court may
make a Conditional Order. A conditional order may require a
party to pay into court and/or take some further step in the
action against the sanction of dismissal or strike out, at the same
time further Directions are likely to be made (Pt. 24, PD 5(1)).
Part 3, r.3.1(5) provides:

> (5) The court may order a party to pay a sum of money into
> court
> (6) When exercising its power under paragraph (5) the court
> must have regard to —
>
>   (a) the amount in dispute; and
>   (b) the costs which the parties have incurred or which
>   they may incur."

See also Pt. 37, r.37.2:

> 37.2—(1) This rule applies where the court makes an
> order permitting a defendant to defend or to continue to
> defend on condition that he makes a payment into court.
> (2) Where a defendant to a money claim makes such a
> payment into court he may choose to treat the whole or any
> part of the money paid into court as a Part 36 payment."

Practical points:
  • The old-style order of 'Unconditional leave to defend' 9.12
    has gone.

  • Part of a claim only may be the subject of a Part 24
    Application.

  • The court may consider the issue on which the claim, or
    part of the claim, depends.

Final Orders

Subject to the question of conditional orders (see para. 9.11, 9.13
above) these may be:

  (a) Judgment on the claim.
  (b) Striking out, or dismissal of claim.
  (c) Application dismissed.

If the claim proceeds directions will be given as on a case management conference. Fixed costs may be awarded on an application for summary judgment (Pt. 45, r.45.1(2)). This will be dependant on the amount awarded. For details see Pt. 45, r.45.4, Table 2.

B. Summary Disposal (CPR, Part 1, r.1.4(2)(c), Part 3, PD 1.1)

Overview

9.14   Part 1, r.1.4(2)(b) includes as an example of active case management the summary disposal of issues which do not need full investigation at a trial. The Rules give distinct powers which may be used to achieve this. Part 3, r.3.4 provides:

(1) In this rule and rule 3.5, reference to a statement of case includes reference to part of a statement of case.
(2) The court may strike out a statement of case if it appears to the court —

(a) that the statement of case discloses no reasonable grounds for bringing or defending the claim;
(b) that the statement of case is an abuse of the court's process or is otherwise likely to obstruct the just disposal of the proceedings; or
(c) that there has been a failure to comply with a rule, practice direction or court order.

9.15   The Practice Direction (Part 3, r.3.4 and PD 1.4) gives examples of the type of claim that should be struck out:

(1) those which set out no facts indicating what the claim is about, for example "Money owed £5,000",
(2) those which are incoherent and make no sense,
(3) those which contain a coherent set of facts but those facts, even if true, do not disclose any legally recognisable claim against the defendant.

This includes claims which are "vexatious, scurrilous or obviously ill-founded". As far as defences are concerned, included in those that should be considered for strike-out are a defence if (Pt. 3, r.3.4 and PD 1.6):

(1) it consists of a bare denial or otherwise sets out no coherent statement of facts, or

(2) the facts it sets out, while coherent, would not even if true amount in law to a defence to the claim.

A court officer has power to refer a claim or defence to a 9.16 judge at any time if he considers that it may fall within the above criteria (Pt. 3, r.3.4 and PD 2–3). Note also Pt. 3, r.3.4(4):

Where:

(a) the court has struck out a claimant's statement of case;

(b) the claimant has been ordered to pay costs to the defendant; and

(c) before the claimant pays those costs, he starts another claim against the same defendant, arising out of facts which are the same or substantially the same as those relating to the claim in which the statement of case was struck out,

the court may, on the application of the defendant, **stay** that other claim until the costs of the first claim have been paid.

Practical points:

9.17

• The message is, therefore, that a clear and concise statement of the facts is what is needed.

• It may well be worth adding an application for summary judgment under Part 24 (see above) as an alternative to an application to strike out under Pt. 3, r.3.4 as if one fails on the strike out one may succeed on the application for summary judgment where the burden on the respondent is heavier. Indeed, Pt. 24, r.24.2 specifically refers to r.3.4.

Chapter 10

Case Management by the Court

A. CASE MANAGEMENT

Overview

10.01
- Duty to case manage is mandatory
- New provisions for automatic transfer
- Court monitors "milestone" dates
- Court is responsible for allocating cases
- Specific criteria for allocation
- "Disposal hearings" replace assessments of damages
- Court has wide power to impose sanctions

General

10.02 The court's duty to manage cases is set out at Pt. 1, r.1.4:

1.4—(1) The court must further the overriding objective by actively managing cases.
(2) Active case management includes —

  (a) encouraging the parties to co-operate with each other in the conduct of the proceedings;
  (b) identifying the issues at an early stage;
  (c) deciding promptly which issues need full investigation and trial and accordingly disposing summarily of the others;
  (d) deciding the order in which issues are to be resolved;
  (e) encouraging the parties to use an alternative dispute resolution procedure if the court considers that appropriate and facilitating the use of such procedure;

(f) helping the parties to settle the whole or part of the case;
(g) fixing timetables or otherwise controlling the progress of the case;
(h) considering whether the likely benefits of taking a particular step justify the cost of taking it;
(i) dealing with as many aspects of the case as it can on the same occasion;
(j) dealing with the case without the parties needing to attend at court;
(k) making use of technology; and
(l) giving directions to ensure that the trial of a case proceeds quickly and efficiently.

This is expanded upon by Pt. 3, r.3.1(2):   10.03

(2) Except where these Rules provide otherwise, the court may —

(a) extend or shorten the time for compliance with any rule, practice direction or court order (even if an application for extension is made after the time for compliance has expired);
(b) adjourn or bring forward a hearing;
(c) require a party or a party's legal representative to attend the court;
(d) hold a hearing and receive evidence by telephone or by using any other method of direct oral communication;
(e) direct that part of any proceedings (such as a counterclaim) be dealt with as separate proceedings;
(f) stay the whole or part of any proceedings or judgment either generally or until a specified date or event;
(g) consolidate proceedings;
(h) try two or more claims on the same occasion;
(i) direct a separate trial of any issue;
(j) decide the order in which issues are to be tried;
(k) exclude an issue from consideration;
(l) dismiss or give judgment on a claim after a decision on a preliminary issue;
(m) take any other step or make any other order for the purpose of managing the case and furthering the overriding objective.

Automatic Transfer (CPR, Part 26, r.26.2)

10.04 Where:

- the claim is for a specified sum of money; and
- the claim was commenced in a court which is not the defendant's home court; and
- the defendant is an individual

the claim will be automatically transferred to the defendant's home court unless:

- the claim was commenced in a specialist list (Part 49 and see Chapter 1 — The New Scheme); or
- the claim has already been transferred to the home court of another defendant under Pt. 13, r.13.4 (application to set judgment aside) or Pt. 14, r.14.12 (admission — determination of rate of payment); or
- Pt. 15, r.15.10 ("states paid" defence) or Pt. 14, r.14.5 (part admission of claim for specified sum) applies, in which case the transfer will not take place until the claimant responds to the notice from the court as to whether he wishes the claim to proceed.

Where there is more than one defendant, the home court of the defendant who filed his defence first will determine whether, and if so to which home court, the case will be transferred. At the moment, this is true even if the first defendant has filed a "states paid" defence, and the claimant says he does not wish to proceed against that defendant!

Monitoring "Milestone" Dates

10.05 In order for the court to be pro-active in managing cases the court is now required to specifically monitor certain important or "milestone" dates and take action if requirements of the court have not been complied with by those dates.

The dates are the dates for return of the Allocation Questionnaire (see para. 10.07, below) and the Listing Questionnaire (see Chapter 12 — Fast Track). The court is assisted by a computerised diary system which produces a daily report of cases where the milestone dates have occurred following which the file can be placed before the judge to decide what action may be necessary.

One other aspect of "milestone" dates is the importance of the trial date. This is likely to be fixed at an early stage in the proceedings and the parties must work towards that date. The importance of maintaining the trial date is paramount and is reflected in the Practice Directions relating to the trial date set out in the chapters on fast track and multi-track.

Allocation (CPR, Part 26)

This is at the core of the new powers given to the court for case 10.06 management and is based on information provided to the court by the parties in Allocation Questionnaires. It provides for the court to allocate cases to a track suitable for the particular case, subject also to a monetary jurisdiction. On filing of defence, or, in the case of multiple defendants, where at least one defence has been filed and the time for filing the other defences has expired, the court will issue allocation questionnaires to all parties.

Allocation questionnaire (Pt. 26, r.26.5) (see Appendix 9 in this book for form)

This is a brand new procedure. Once a defence is filed the court 10.07 will send to each party who has filed a claim or defence a form of questionnaire. This is a comprehensive document requiring detailed information concerning the case. The first part of the form deals with the possibility of settlement; the second part invites representations as to track; the third part deals with pre-action protocols; the fourth part covers applications, the fifth part deals with witnesses; the sixth part covers experts; the seventh part covers location of trial and the last parts deal with representation and estimates of length of hearing, costs and other information.

The questionnaire must be filed no later than the date specified in it, which shall be at least 14 days after the date when it is deemed served on the party in question (Pt. 26, r.26.4(6)). Failure by any party to respond to the questionnaire will result in the papers been put before the court. Thus it will be necessary for the court to specifically note when the receipt of the replies are expected and act accordingly (see para. 10.05, above). Part 26, PD 2.5 suggests that if neither side file the questionnaire the court may make an order requiring return of the questionnaire within three days of service of the order in default of which the court may strike out the claim or counterclaim, but if only one side fails to return the questionnaire the court should either allocate or fix an allocation hearing.

10.08   Where all parties request a stay to explore settlement (Pt. 1, r.1.4(2)(e)), or the court considers that such a stay would be desirable, one of parties having requested it, the court will direct that the proceedings be stayed for a month (Pt. 26, r.26.5(2)). This date may be extended. The claimant must tell the court if settlement has been reached in default of which the court will proceed as if it had not (Pt. 26, r.26.5(5)).

When every defendant has filed a questionnaire, or the time for doing so has expired (whichever is the sooner), and there is no stay for settlement (see above), the court will consider whether to allocate to track or request further information, either in writing or at an allocation hearing. Depending on the responses, the court may decide to allocate the case to one of three "tracks".

Scope of each track (Pt. 26, r.26.6)

10.09   26.6—(1) Subject to paragraphs (2) and (3) , the small claims track is the normal track for any claim which has a financial value of not more than £5,000.

(2) The small claims track is the normal track for —

(a) any claim for personal injuries where—

  (i) the financial value of the claim is not more than £5,000; and
  (ii) the financial value of any claim for damages for personal injuries is not more than £1,000;

(b) any claim which includes a claim by a tenant of residential premises against his landlord where—

  (i) the tenant is seeking an order requiring the landlord to carry out repairs or other work to the premises (whether or not the tenant is also seeking some other remedy);
  (ii) the cost of the repairs or other work to the premises is estimated to be not more than £1,000, and
  (iii) the financial value of any other claim for damages is not more than £1,000.

(Rule 2.3 defines 'claim for personal injuries' as proceedings in which there is a claim for damages in respect of personal injuries to the claimant or any other person or in respect of a person's death.)

(3) For the purposes of paragraph (2) "damages for personal injuries" means damages claimed as compensation for pain, suffering, and loss of amenity and does not include any other damages which are claimed.

(4) The small claims track is not the normal track for a claim which includes a claim by a tenant of residential premises against his landlord for damages for harassment or unlawful eviction.

(5) Subject to paragraph (6), the fast track is the normal track for any claim-

(a) for which the small claims track is not the normal track; and
(b) which has a financial value of not more than £15,000.

(6) The fast track is the normal track for the claims referred to in paragraph (5) only if the court considers that—

(a) the trial is likely to last for no longer than one day; and
(b) oral expert evidence at trial will be limited to—

(i) one expert per party in relation to any expert field; and
(ii) expert evidence in two expert fields.

(7) The multi-track is the normal track for any claim for which the small claims track or the fast track is not the normal track.

General rules for allocation

Part 26, r.26.7:   10.10

26.7—(1) In considering whether to allocate a claim to the normal track for that claim under rule 26.6, the court will have regard to the matters mentioned in rule 26.8(1) (see below).

(2) The court will allocate a claim which has no financial value to the track which it considers most suitable having regard to the matters mentioned in rule 26.8(1).

(3) The court will not allocate a claim to a track if the financial value of the claim, assessed by the court under rule 26.8, exceeds the limit for that track unless all the parties consent to the allocation of the claim to that track.

Claims which have no financial value will be allocated by the court to the most appropriate track having regard to the considerations set out below (Pt. 26, r.26.7(2)). Note that liability cannot be allocated to one track and quantum to another. The court does have power at any stage to re-allocate a case to a different track (Pt. 26, r.26.10)

Part 26, r.26.8(1):

26.8—(1) When deciding the track for a claim, the matters to which the court shall have regard include —

(a) the financial value, if any, of the claim;
(b) the nature of the remedy sought;
(c) the likely complexity of the facts, law or evidence;
(d) the number of parties or likely parties;
(e) the value of any counterclaim or other Part 20 claim and the complexity of any matters relating to it;
(f) the amount of oral evidence which may be required;
(g) the importance of the claim to persons who are not parties to the proceedings;
(h) the views expressed by the parties; and
(i) the circumstances of the parties.

10.11   The court disregards any amount not in dispute and any claim for interest, costs and contributory negligence when assessing the financial value of the claim (Pt. 26, r.26.8(2)). So if the claim is for £6,000 and there is an admission of liability and damages in, say, £1,500, this would bring the case into the small claims track. For further guidance on the considerations see Pt. 26, PD 7.

The parties will be served with notice of allocation, together with a copy of the allocation questionnaire served by other parties and any further information provided. Having allocated a case, the court can always re-allocate it to a different track. Note that there is power to allocate to a track of a higher value than the claim without the consent of the parties, but not to a track of a lower value (see Pt. 26, r.26.7(3) above).

Allocation of Possession Proceedings

10.12 At the hearing of a possession case the court may proceed to hear the case and dispose of the claim or give case management directions, including allocation to track (Pt. 8, 8BPD B.13).

However, this does leave open the questions as to which is the appropriate track for possession proceedings. Although Pt. 26 (allocation to track) is disapplied by Pt. 8, r.8.9(c), it is reapplied by Pt. 8, 8BPD B.15 and r.8.1(6)(b). Accordingly the normal principles apply — see Pt. 26, rr.26.6 to 26.10 and above. In addition to the financial value of the claim, consideration should be given to the importance of a borrower/tenant preserving his or her home and whether the loan was to secure a domestic or commercial loan and the amount of the arrears. Where it is just the amount of arrears which is being challenged there may be some argument that this may conveniently be resolved in the small claims or fast track.

Defended mortgage possession claims are relatively rare but there is no guidance in the Rules or any Practice Direction as to how the court should assess the financial value of such a case. In view of rule Pt. 26, r.26.8(2)(a) it could be argued that the amount in dispute is that matters, but the potential loss of a borrower's home which will inevitably be worth more than £15,000 and Pt. 26, r.26.8(1)(b) are strong pointers towards allocation to multi-track. There can be little doubt that undue influence cases, where the whole of the outstanding balance is in issue will be allocated to multi-track.

Disposal Hearings

This is the new term for assessment of damages. The procedure **10.13** is to be found at paragraphs 12 of the practice direction to Part 26. The need for such a hearing will arise on:

- the taking of default judgment on a claim for an unspecified sum, admission of a claim for an unspecified sum

- the entry of judgment for an unspecified sum following an admission or order.

The procedure provides a discretionary power for the judge to allocate the assessment to a suitable track with the consequent costs implications and, in the case of a potential small claims matter, Pt. 12, r.12.8(2) (see para. 10.14, below) provides that allocation to the small claims track is normally to be expected. Even if the assessment is not allocated, the judge will have to bear in mind the principle of proportionality when considering the costs to be awarded on the hearing to ensure that the costs are reasonable in relation to the amount recovered.

10.14   Note Pt. 26, PD 12.8:

(1) At a disposal hearing the Court may give directions or decide the amount payable in accordance with this sub-paragraph.

(2) If the financial value of the claim (determined in accordance with Part 26) is such that the claim would, if defended, be allocated to the Small Claims Track, the Court will normally allocate it to that track and may treat the disposal hearing as a final hearing in accordance with Part 27.

(3) If the Court does not give directions and does not allocate the claim to the Small Claims Track, it may nonetheless order that the amount payable is to be decided there and then without allocating the claim to another track.

(4) Rule 32.6 applies to evidence at a disposal hearing unless the court otherwise directs.

(5) The Court will not exercise its powers under sub-paragraph 12.8(3) unless any written evidence on which the claimant relies has been served on the defendant at least 3 days before the disposal hearing.

Note Pt. 26, PD 12.9 as to costs in disposal hearings:

(1) Attention is drawn to the Costs Practice Directions and in particular to the Court's power to make a summary assessment of costs.

(2) Attention is drawn to Rule 44.13(1) which provides that if an order makes no mention of costs, none are payable in respect of the proceedings to which it relates.

(3) Attention is drawn to Rule 27.14 (special rules about costs in cases allocated to the Small Claims Track).

(4) Attention is drawn to Part 45 (fixed trial costs in cases which have been allocated to the Fast Track). Part 45 will not apply to a case dealt with at a disposal hearing whatever the financial value of the claim. So the costs of a disposal hearing will be in the discretion of the Court.

Note Pt. 26, PD 12.10 as to the jurisdiction of Masters and district judges on disposal hearings:

Unless the Court otherwise directs a Master or a district judge may decide the amount payable under a relevant order irrespective of the financial value of the claim and of the track to which the claim may have been allocated.

B. Sanctions

Overview

Although automatic sanctions were recommended in *Access to*   10.15
Justice, the Civil Procedure Rules and Practice Directions have
shied away from these and opted instead for the court to have
general powers to impose sanctions whenever they are
necessary.

General

Part 3, r.3.1 states as follows: 10.16

> (3) When the court makes an order, it may —
>
>   (a) make it subject to conditions, including a condition to
>   pay a sum of money into court; and
>   (b) specify the consequence of failure to comply with the
>   order or a condition.
>
> (4) Where the court gives directions it may take into
> account whether or not a party has complied with any
> relevant pre-action protocol.
> (5) The court may order a party to pay a sum of money
> into court if that party has, without good reason, failed to
> comply with a rule, practice direction or a relevant pre-action
> protocol.
> (6) When exercising its power under paragraph (5) the
> court must have regard to—
>
>   (a) the amount in dispute; and
>   (b) the costs which the parties have incurred or which
>   they may incur.

In making orders, the court does not have to wait for an
application. Part 3, r.3.3 makes it clear that it can make orders
of its own initiative subject to the right to the parties to apply to
set it aside.

This power extends to striking out a statement of case (Pt. 3,
r.3.4) (see Chapter 9 — Summary Judgment and Disposal).
Sanctions are also available for non-payment of fees and this
includes striking out (Pt. 3, r.3.7)

Relief from Sanctions

10.17 Pt. 3, r.3.9(1) states:

> On an application for relief from any sanction imposed for a failure to comply with any rule, practice direction or court order the court will consider all the circumstances including —
>
> (a) the interests of the administration of justice;
> (b) whether the application for relief has been made promptly;
> (c) whether the failure to comply was intentional;
> (d) whether there is a good explanation for the failure;
> (e) the extent to which the party in default has complied with other rules, practice directions, court orders and any relevant pre-action protocol (i.e. a party can develop a record for default in the action which will mitigate against them on any further application for relief);
> (f) whether the failure to comply was caused by the party or his legal representative;
> (g) whether the trial date or the likely trial date can still be met if relief is granted;
> (h) the effect which the failure to comply had on each party; and
> (i) the effect which the granting of relief would have on each party.
>
> (2) An application for relief must be supported by evidence.

Costs as a Sanction

10.18 Costs are widely seen as an important sanction to be imposed for default. As will be seen later in this book (see Chapter 21 — Costs), costs can be a sanction for, among other things, failure to observe a pre-action protocol, failure to take up Alternative Dispute Resolution (see Chapter 3 — Pre-action Disposal), or failure to conduct the case properly. To this is added the stricture that solicitors must notify their clients when a costs order is made against them (Pt. 44, r.44.2).

Note, however, Pt. 3, r.3.8(2):

Where the sanction is the payment of costs, the party in default may only obtain relief by appealing against the order for costs.

Chapter 11

The Small Claims Track (Part 27)

Overview

11.01   `   • The basic jurisdiction is increased

• The term "arbitration" no longer used

• Specialised directions in certain cases, *e.g.* dry cleaning, road traffic accidents, holidays, building disputes

• Paper disposal if both parties agree

• Limits on evidence

• Proper appeal system with slightly altered grounds

• Proceedings may be tape-recorded

• Summary judgment possible

As to Allocation see Chapter 10 — Case Management.

Unavailability of Small Claims Track

11.02 A claim for a remedy for harassment or unlawful eviction relating to residential premises may not be allocated to the small claims track whatever the financial value of the claim (CPR, Pt. 26, r.26.7(4)).

Otherwise, the small claims track will be the normal track for:

• any claim which has a financial value of not more than £5,000 subject to the special provisions about claims for personal injuries and housing disrepair claims (Pt. 26, r.26.6(1));

- any claim for personal injuries which has a total financial value of not more than £5,000 where the claim for damages for personal injuries (*i.e.* pain suffering and loss of amenity (Pt. 2, r.2.3) is not more than £1,000; and

- any claim which includes a claim by a tenant of residential premises against his landlord for repairs or other work to the premises where the estimated cost of the repairs or other work is not more than £1,000 and the financial value of any claim for damages in respect of those repairs or other work is not more than £1,000).

Unavailability of Procedures to Small Claims Track (Part 27, r.27.2)

The following rules will not apply to the small claims track: **11.03**

- Interim remedies, except interim injunctions (Part 25);

- Disclosure and inspection (Part 31) but see para. 11.05, below for provision of copy documents;

- Evidence (Part 32) except r.32.1 (power of court to control evidence);

- Miscellaneous rules about evidence (Part 33);

- Experts and assessors (Part 35) except rr.35.1 (duty to restrict expert evidence), 35.3 (experts — overriding duty to the court) and 35.8 (instructions to a single joint expert);

- Further information (Part 18) (formerly request for further and better particulars and interrogatories);

- Offers to settle and payments into court (Part 36)

- Hearings (Part 39) except r.39.2 (general rule — hearing to be in public).

Note that these rules are only dis-applied **after** allocation. At allocation stage, the procedural judge may: **11.04**

- give standard directions and fix a date for the final hearing which will be set out in the Notice of Allocation (Pt. 26, PD 8.2(1));

- give special directions (see para. 11.06, below) in the Notice and fix a date for the final hearing;

- give special directions in the Notice and direct that the court will consider what further directions are to be given no later that 28 days after the date the special directions were given;

- fix a date for a preliminary hearing under Pt. 27, r.27.6; or

- give notice that it proposes to deal with the claim without a hearing under Pt. 27, r.27.10 and invite the parties to notify the court by a specified date if they agree the proposal (see para. 11.06, below).

11.05   Standard directions are:

- a direction that each party shall, at least 14 days before the date fixed for the final hearing, file and serve on every other party copies of all documents (including any expert's report) on which he intends to rely at the hearing; and

- any other standard directions set out in the relevant practice direction (Pt. 27, PD, Appendix A, Form A); and

11.06   "Special directions" are:

- directions given in addition to or instead of the standard directions (Pt. 27, r.27.4(1)(b)) details of which are set out in Appendix A to the Practice Direction and include a direction to provide further information; to allow inspection of a document or object; permitting expert evidence and dealing with the instruction of the expert; requiring witness statements to be filed and served; as to the arrangements for video evidence and; that a party's statement of case be struck out if he fails to comply with a direction.

- In addition the court will have the power to order special directions tailored to the type of case (Pt. 27, r.27.4(1)(a)). These are set out in Appendix A to the Practice Direction (Pt. 27, PD 2.2) and at present cover the following cases — road traffic accidents (Form B), building, vehicle repair and other similar contractual claims (Form C), return of tenancy deposits and claims for damage caused (Form D) holiday and wedding claims (Form E).

If the court gives special directions, it may (before fixing a hearing) review the position after 28 days in case further directions are needed (Pt. 27, r.27.4(1)(c)). The court may add to, vary or revoke directions given (Pt. 27, r.27.7).

Perhaps more significantly, the procedural judge will have power to propose that the case is dealt with on paper only, *i.e.* without a hearing, subject to the agreement of the parties (Pt. 27, r.27.4(e)), although it is difficult to envisage many cases in which this will be used.

Summary Judgment

Under the old rules, summary judgment was not available in **11.07** small claims cases but now Pt. 24, r.24.3(1) says:

> The court may give summary judgment against a claimant in **any type** of proceedings.

For more information see Chapter 9 — Summary Judgment and Disposal, and see para. 11.08, below.

Preliminary Hearing

Part 27, r.27.6(1) provides: **11.08**

27.6—(1) The court may hold a preliminary hearing for the consideration of the claim, but only —

  (a) where —

      (i) it considers that special directions, as defined in rule 27.4, are needed to ensure a fair hearing; and

      (ii) it appears necessary for a party to attend at court to ensure that he understands what he must do to comply with the special directions; or

  (b) to enable it to dispose of the claim on the basis that one or other of the parties has no real prospect of success at a final hearing; or

  (c) to enable it to strike out a statement of case or part of a statement of case on the basis that the statement of case, or the part to be struck out, discloses no reasonable grounds for bringing or defending the claim.

Although Pt. 27, r.27.6(4) enables the court to treat the preliminary hearing as the hearing of the claim if the parties agree, time constraints and the availability of evidence are likely to mitigate against such action. If there is a preliminary hearing the parties will be given at least 21 days notice of the final hearing unless the parties agree to a shorter period (Pt. 27, r.27.6(5)), although pressure on lists is likely to ensure that the return date will not be before 21 days.

Conduct of the Hearing

11.09   Although district judges will be principally dealing with small claims track cases, there is nothing in the rules to prevent a circuit judge hearing cases (Pt. 27, PD 1). It will normally take place in the district judge's chambers, though it may be held in a courtroom and can be held at any place the court considers appropriate. It will usually be open to the public to attend (Pt. 27, PD 4.1(3)) but not if held away from the court or if the judge decides to hold it in private, which he may do if the parties agree; publicity would defeat the object of the hearing; it involves matters relating to national security; it involves confidential information; the interests of a child or patient need to be protected; or the judge considers it necessary in the interests of justice (Pt. 39, r.39.2(3)).

The case may be presented by the parties, lawyers or lay representatives (if the party is present) on their behalf, an employee (with the court's permission) or, in the case of a company, one of the officers or employees of the company and any other person with leave of the court (Pt. 27, PD 3.1).

Conduct is the same as before, *i.e.* the proceedings will be informal (Pt. 27, r.27.8(2)) save that the judge may limit cross-examination, *cf. Chilton v. Saga Holidays* [1986] 1 All E.R. 841, to be ignored (Pt. 27, r.27.8(5)).

Pt. 27, PD 4.3 — r.27.8 allows the court to adopt any method of proceeding that it considers to be fair and to limit cross-examination. The judge may in particular —

(1) ask questions of any witness himself before allowing any other person to do so,

(2) ask questions of **all** or any of the witnesses himself before allowing any other person to ask questions of any witnesses,

(3) refuse to allow cross-examination of any witness until all the witnesses have given evidence in chief,

(4) limit cross-examination of a witness to a fixed time or to a particular subject or issue, or both.

The strict rules of evidence do not apply, so that evidence **11.10** which would otherwise be inadmissible may be admitted (Pt. 27, r.27.8(3)). Evidence need not be on oath (Pt. 27, r.27.8(4)). Thus a party may rely on a witness statement in the absence of the witness (Pt. 22, r.22.1(1)(c)), though it must be verified by a statement of truth or it may be excluded (Pt. 22, r.22.3). Expert evidence, oral or written, may not be given without permission (Pt. 27, r.27.5). The usual direction permitting it will provide for a single expert jointly instructed (Pt. 27, PD, Appendix A) (see Chapter 18 — Experts).

The judge may decide to tape record the proceedings. In any event, he will be required to make a note of the central reasons for his judgment unless it is tape-recorded (Pt. 27, PD 5.4). This is new — previously there was no such requirement. A party will be entitled to a copy of such transcript or note of judgment on payment of the transcription charges or court fee for the note (Pt. 27, PD 5.1 and 5.7).

Non-attendance at Hearing

Non-attendance of a party may result in that party's claim or **11.11** defence being struck out unless they have previously notified the court (giving at least seven days' notice) that they will not be attending and given reasons. In that instance, their claim or defence will be considered (Pt. 27, r.27.9).

Note the provisions of Pt. 27, r.27.9:

27.9—(1) If a party who does not attend a final hearing —

(a) has given the court written notice at least 7 days before the date of the hearing that he will not attend; and

(b) has, in that notice, requested the court to decide the claim in his absence,

the court will take into account that party's statement of case and any other
documents he has filed when it decides the claim.

(2) If a claimant does not —

(a) attend the hearing; and
(b) give the notice referred to in paragraph (1)

the court may strike out the claim.

(3) If —

   (a) a defendant does not

      (i) attend the hearing; or

      (ii) give the notice referred to in paragraph (1); and

   (b) the claimant either —

      (i) does attend the hearing; or

      (ii) gives the notice referred to in paragraph (1), the court may decide the claim on the basis of the evidence of the claimant alone.

(4) If neither party attends or gives the notice referred to in paragraph (1), the court may strike out the claim and any defence and counterclaim.

In any case, the court has power to adjourn to another day and may do so if a party wishes to attend but cannot do so for good reason (Pt. 27, PD 6.2)

Setting Judgment aside for Non-attendance

11.12 Application within 14 days of receipt of the judgement can be made by any party who was not present when the judgment was made (Pt. 27, r.27.11) unless it was granted without a hearing (see Pt. 27, r.27.10 above) when no application can be made (Pt. 27, r.27.11(5)). The court will grant the application only if the applicant had a good reason for not attending or being represented or giving the notice **and** has a reasonable prospect of success at the rehearing (Pt. 27, r.27.11(3)). If set aside, the case may be immediately heard again (Pt. 27, r.27.11(4)) but time and listing constraints may mitigate against this and a rehearing may have to be ordered instead.

Appeals (Part 27, r.27.12)

11.13 Not to be confused with setting aside judgment above. The previous awkward definition of "setting award aside" has been replaced with a proper appeal. The grounds differ slightly from those previously and now must allege that (Pt. 27, r.27.12(1)):

- there was serious irregularity affecting the proceedings or judgment; and/or

- the court made a mistake of law.

Rule 27.12 provides—

(2) On an appeal the court may make any order it considers appropriate.

(3) The court may dismiss an appeal without a hearing.

(4) This r.does not limit any right of appeal arising under any Act.

Procedure for making an appeal

27.13—(1) A party who wishes to appeal must file a notice   **11.14**
of appeal not more than 14 days after the day on which
notice of the order was served on him.

(2) Notice of appeal —

(a) must be filed at the court which made the order; and

(b) must set out the grounds for the appeal with particulars of the serious irregularity or mistake of law alleged.

The practice direction to Part 27 adds more detail:

8.1 An appeal from a decision of a district judge under Part 27 will be dealt with by a Circuit Judge.

8.2 Attention is drawn to Rule 27.12 and 13 and in particular to the limited grounds of appeal and the time limits for giving notice of appeal.

8.3 A notice of appeal must set out particulars of the serious irregularity or mistake of law relied on.

8.4 When a notice of appeal is filed it will be put before a Circuit Judge as soon as possible after it is filed and he will decide how to deal with the appeal.

8.5 The court will serve a copy of the notice on all other parties.

8.6 The Circuit Judge may either:

(1) dismiss the appeal without a hearing if no sufficient ground is shown in the notice of appeal, or

(2) order that the appeal is to be listed for hearing.

8.7 The Circuit Judge will give any necessary directions:

(1) about the filing of any evidence concerning any allegation of serious irregularity, and

(2) about the supply to the parties of copies of any document (including any note made by the

judge who heard the case) which he has taken or may taken into account in dealing with the appeal.

8.8 Where the Circuit Judge dismisses the appeal without a hearing his order will contain brief reasons for his decision.

8.9 Where the Circuit Judge directs that the appeal is to be listed for hearing the court will give at least seven days notice of the hearing to all parties.

8.10 If the appeal is allowed, the Circuit Judge will if possible dispose of the case at the same time without ordering the claim to be reheard. He may do so without hearing further evidence.

There is a suggestion that leave may be required for the appeal. This is still just a proposal, and we will have to await legislation for this to happen.

Costs

11.15 The limit on costs recoverable in small claims remains. In the small claims track, these are governed by Pt. 27, r.27.14, which provides:

27.14—(1) This rule applies to any case which has been allocated to the small claims track unless paragraph (5) applies.

(Rules 43.10 and 43.11 make provision in relation to orders for costs made before a claim has been allocated to the small claims track.)

(2) The court may not order a party to pay a sum to another party in respect of that other party's costs except —

(a) the fixed costs payable under Part 44 attributable to issuing the claim;

(b) in proceedings which included a claim for an injunction or an order for specific performance a sum not exceeding the amount specified in the relevant practice direction (£260) for legal advice and assistance relating to that claim;

(c) costs assessed by the summary procedure in relation to an appeal under r.27.12; and

(d) such further costs as the court may assess by the summary procedure and order to be paid by a party who has behaved unreasonably.

(3) The court may also order a party to pay all or part of —

    (a) any court fees paid by another party;

    (b) expenses which a party or witness has reasonably incurred in travelling to and from a hearing or in staying away from home for the purposes of attending a hearing;

    (c) a sum not exceeding the amount specified in the relevant practice direction (£50) for any loss of earnings by a party or witness due to attending a hearing or to staying away from home for the purpose of attending a hearing;

    (d) a sum not exceeding the amount specified in the relevant practice direction (£200) for an expert's fees.

(4) The limits on costs imposed by this rule also apply to any fee or reward for acting on behalf of a party to the proceedings charged by a person exercising a right of audience by virtue of an order under section 11 of the Courts and Legal Services Act 1990 (a lay representative).

(5) Where —

    (a) the financial value of a claim exceeds the limit for the small claims track; but

    (b) the claim has been allocated to the small claims track in accordance with r.26.7(3),

the claim shall be treated, for the purposes of costs, as if it were proceeding on the fast track.

(Rule 26.7(3) allows the parties to consent to a claim being allocated to a track where the financial value of the claim exceeds the limit for that track)

Costs on claim re-allocated from the small claims track to another track

27.15 Where a claim is allocated to the small claims track **11.16** and subsequently re-allocated to another track, r.27.14 (costs on the small claims track) will cease to apply after the claim has been re-allocated, and the fast track or multi-track costs rules will apply from the date of re-allocation.

Chapter 12

Fast Track (Part 28)

Overview

12.01
- Cases between £5,000–£15,000 not lasting longer than a day
- Brand new concept
- Limited expert evidence
- Guaranteed and virtually immovable trial date within 30 weeks of allocation
- Strictly time-tabled trial
- Fixed costs for trial

Essential References

12.02
- CPR, Part 26, rr.26.6, 26.7, 26.8 (allocation)
- Part 28 (The Fast Track)
- Part 44, rr.44.9, 44.10 (costs)
- Part 46 (Fast Track Trial Costs)
- Practice Direction — The Fast Track

For Allocation see Chapter 10 — Case Management

Features

12.03 Cases exceeding £5,000 and not exceeding £15,000 in value where the trial will last no longer than a day. The objective is a trial date 20-30 weeks from issue. The rules and practice directions make it clear that adherence to the timetable and the preservation of the set trial date are an essential feature of fast track and that failure to comply with the requirements of the court by specified dates will result in sanctions being imposed unless an extension has been previously granted by way of a prospective application. Sanctions may include striking out, debarring evidence, and various costs orders. The judge can lay down a strict timetable for the hearing itself which is also expected to be adhered to. As there are fixed costs for the hearing any adjournment from one day to another means that there will be no extra costs for any subsequent day. Advocates should bear this in mind. There are also limits on the amount of expert evidence where allowed (see para. 12.04 below)

District judges and circuit judges are to have concurrent jurisdiction in fast track, with district judges eventually having sole jurisdiction.

Allocation

Part 26, r.26.6(5) and (6) provides: 12.04

(5) Subject to paragraph (6), the fast track is the normal track for any claim —
  (a) for which the small claims track is not the normal track; and
  (b) which has a financial value of not more than £15,000.

(6) The fast track is the normal track for the claims referred to in paragraph (5) only if the court considers that —
  (a) the trial is likely to last for **no longer than one day**; and
  (b) oral expert evidence at trial *(where allowed)* will be limited to —

      (i) one expert per party in relation to any expert field; and
      (ii) expert evidence in two expert fields

The claim will **not** be allocated to this track if the court considers that the trial is likely to last longer than five hours (Pt. 26, PD 9.1(3)(a)), taking account of the likely case management directions (see para. 12.05, below), the court's powers to control evidence and limit cross-examination (see para. 12.16, below) (Pt. 26, PD 9.1(3)(b)) and whether any Part 20 claim is involved (see Chapter 8) as the time for this will be included in the estimate (Pt. 26, PD 9.1(3)(e)). The **mere possibility** that the trial may last longer than five hours or the fact that there is to be a split trial will not prevent allocation to this track (Pt. 26, PD 9.1(3)(c) and (d)). However, if a case is **likely** to last more than one day, then the judge will consider allocating it to the multi-track even though it is within the financial value for the fast track limit.

Directions (CPR, Part 28, r.28.2(1))

12.05 Once a defence has been filed and the matter allocated to the fast track, the district judge will scrutinise the papers to consider the following:

- whether further details of the claim or defence are necessary;

- whether the matter can be disposed of summarily (where the test will be whether the claimant has a case which has a real prospect of being successful);

- whether a preliminary hearing is necessary (at least three day's notice) (Pt. 28, PD 3.10(1), r.3.10(2)); and

- The question of venue.

The judge will take account of steps already taken by the parties and their compliance or non-compliance with any relevant pre-action protocol (Pt. 28, PD 3.2; r.28.2(1)).

In addition, the district judge will be responsible for:

- Setting a timetable for the preparation and hearing of the case (see Listing Questionnaire para. 12.07, below). The timetable can include strict limits on amounts of time for evidence, cross-examination and speeches;

- Determining interlocutory applications;

- Exercising discipline for failure to comply with procedural directions.

- Local practice directions will cease in an effort to ensure uniformity.

"Typical" standard timetable (Part. 28, PD 3.12)

12.06 This will start from the date of service of the order for directions and provide for:

(a) Disclosure (see Chapter 16) — four weeks (Pt. 28, r.28.3);

(b) Exchange of witness statements — 10 weeks (Pt. 32, r.32.4, Pt. 28, PD 3.9(3));

(c) Exchange of experts' reports — 14 weeks;

(d) Dispatch of a listing questionnaire by the court (see para. 12.07, below) — 20 weeks;

(e) Return of questionnaire by parties (Pt. 28, r.28.5(1), Pt. 26, PD 9.2(1)) — 22 weeks;

(f) Trial listed **30 weeks maximum** from the start date (Pt. 28, r.28.2(3) and (4)), with notification of the trial "window" on allocation of not more than three weeks.

(g) Trial date fixed not less than three weeks from notice to parties (Pt. 28, r.28.6(2)) unless the parties have agreed to accept shorter notice or, exceptionally, the court has ordered that shorter notice be given (Pt. 28, PD 7.1(2)).

The parties must strive to co-operate with each other (Pt. 28, PD 2.2) and may agree directions provided they comply with Pt. 28, PD 3.6 and 3.7 (Pt. 28, PD 3.5) which broadly mirror the "typical" timetable above.

Any party may apply either for an order compelling another to comply with a direction or for a sanction to be imposed or for both (Pt. 28, PD 5.1). The application must be made without delay but the other party should first be given a warning (Pt. 28, PD 5.2).

The Listing Questionnaire (CPR, Part 28, r.28.5)

(See Appendix 10 of this book for form)

28.5—(1) The court will send the parties a listing question-   **12.07**
naire for completion and return by the date specified in the notice of allocation unless it considers that the claim can be listed for trial without the need for a listing questionnaire.

(2) The date specified for filing a listing questionnaire will not be more than 8 weeks before the trial date or the beginning of the trial period.

A fee of £200 is payable by the claimant on filing the listing questionnaire.

The listing questionnaire requires the parties to provide the following information (Pt. 28, PD 6.1(4)):

Directions

12.08 Whether:

- the party has complied with previous directions, and if not why and to what extent;
- further directions are required and if so which and why.

Experts

12.09 Whether:

- the court has already given permission for the use of written expert evidence, and if so for which experts and in which fields;
- reports have been agreed;
- the experts have met;
- the court has already given permission for the use of oral expert evidence and if so for which experts and in which fields;
- such permission is sought, and if so for which experts and in which fields;
- there are dates **within the trial window** when the experts are not available.

Other witnesses

12.10
- How many?
- Names and addresses
- Availability details **within the trial window**
- whether:
  — any statements are agreed
  — special facilities or an interpreter are required and if so what

Legal representation

12.11 Whether, and if so by whom, the party is to be represented together with availability details.

Other matters

The estimated: 12.12

- length of the case; and
- number of pages of evidence in the trial bundle

If neither party returns the listing questionnaire within 14 days of service, then, according to Pt. 28, PD 6.5(1), the court may make an order requiring return of the questionnaire within three days in default of which the claim will be struck out. If only one party returns the listing questionnaire then Pt. 28, PD 6.5(2) provides that the judge shall usually give listing directions or fix a listing hearing. If a listing hearing is directed, the court will fix a date which is as early as possible, giving the parties at least three days' notice (Pt. 28, PD 6.3).

The court may give directions as to the issues on which evidence is to be given, the nature of the evidence it requires on those issues and the way in which it is to be placed before the court, and may thereby exclude evidence which would otherwise be admissible (Pt. 32, r.32.1). A direction giving permission to use expert evidence will say whether it is to be by report or oral and will name the experts whose evidence is permitted (Pt. 28, PD 7.2(4)). Permission may be made conditional on the experts discussing their differences and filing a report on the discussion.

Interlocutory hearings

These will where possible, be avoided, but hearings will be   12.13
needed in these cases:

- where the court proposes to appoint an assessor (Pt. 28, PD 3.11); (not so, where proposal is for single joint expert) (see Chapter 18 — Experts);
- where a party is dissatisfied with directions (Pt. 28, PD 4.3);
- usually, on an application to enforce compliance (Pt. 28, PD 5.1);

The importance of keeping the trial date

It is essential to note the following: 12.14

Pt. 28, PD 5.4:

1. The court will not allow a failure to comply with directions to lead to the postponement of the trial unless the circumstances of the case are exceptional.
2. If it is practicable to do so the court will exercise its powers in a manner that enables the case to come on for trial on the date or within the period previously set.
3. In particular the court will assess what steps each party should take to prepare the case for trial, direct that those steps are taken in the shortest possible time and impose a sanction for non-compliance. Such a sanction may, for example, deprive a party of the right to raise or contest an issue or to rely on evidence to which the direction relates.
4. Where it appears that one or more issues are or can be made ready for trial at the time fixed while others cannot, the court may direct that the trial will proceed on the issues which are or will then be ready, and order that no costs will be allowed for any later trial of the remaining issues or that those costs will be paid by the party in default.
5. Where the court has no option but to postpone the trial it will do so for the shortest possible time and will give directions for the taking of the necessary steps in the meantime as rapidly as possible.
6. **Litigants and lawyers must be in no doubt that the court will regard the postponement of a trial as an order of last resort. The court may exercise its power to require a party as well as his legal representative to attend court at a hearing where such an order is to be sought.**

An agreement between the parties to adjourn the trial date is not likely by itself to be enough to secure an adjournment.

Trial

12.15 The trial will normally take place at the court where the case is being managed but it may be at another court if appropriate having regard to the needs of the parties and the availability of court resources. It may be held away from court if need be (Pt. 28, PD 8.1, r.2.7).

Preparation is two-sided:

- All judges must properly have digested the papers **before trial** (Pt. 28, PD 8.2).

- the trial bundle must be so put together as to assist such preparation (Pt. 28, PD 7.2(2)(c) and see Pt. 39, PD 3):

  — no more photocopying anything that does not move, but actual thought by the lawyer in charge put into what is really required.
  — There should be no unnecessary copies made. Complete bundle delivered on time (at least seven days before trial).

- The parties should attend all hearings with updated costs details, both of costs expended and those likely to be expended.

The court may set a timetable for the trial and will confirm or **12.16** vary the time estimate for the trial (Pt. 28, r.28.6(1)(b); and PD 7.2(2)(b)). No "typical" timetable is suggested by the rules or practice directions but a possible trial timetable for a one-day Fast Track case may look something like this:
(NB: a court day should normally be regarded as five hours (see Pt. 26, PD 9.1(1)(3)(a))

• judge's reading time	30 mins.
• opening (may be dispensed with — Pt. 28, PD 8.2)	10 mins.
• Cross examination and re-examination of claimant's witness(s)	90 mins.
• Cross examination and re-examination of defendants' witness(s)	90 mins.
• defendant's submissions	15 mins.
• claimant's submissions	15 mins.
• judge's "thinking time" and judgment	30 mins.
• Summary assessment of costs and consequential orders	20 mins.
Total:	5 hours

If the case has to go over from one day it should, if possible, be heard the next day (Pt. 28, PD 8.6).

As can be seen from the above, evidence in chief is not included because it is expected to be provided by witness statement (Pt. 32, r.32.5(2)) and cross-examination can be curtailed (Pt. 32, r.32.1(3)). The strict time-tabling of the trial and the lack of refresher fee (see para. 12.17, below) or additional costs make it clear that it is incumbent on the parties or their legal representatives to ensure that the timetable is kept to by proper preparation prior to trial taking into account the imposed constraints. The judge is likely to cut off a party if their time is being exceeded and will be watching for deliberate prevarication.

Fast track cases are likely to be "block listed" among a number of judges and courts, therefore last minute changes of venue are possible.

Costs

12.17 The costs of fast track proceedings will usually be summarily assessed at the conclusion of the trial (Pt. 28, PD 8.5). Thus the parties will have been required to exchange costs details on the suggested form (see Chapter 21 — Costs) at least 24 hours before the hearing. There are fixed costs for the advocate on the trial varying between £350 and £750 depending on the amount awarded in relation to the claimant and the amount claimed in relation to defendant but this is not dependent on the length of the trial (Pt. 46, r.46.2; see Chapter 21 — Costs).

Amount recovered (claimant) or claimed (defendant)	Fee
Up to £3000	£350
£3–10,000	£500
£10,000+	£750

A legal representative attending with counsel will be allowed £250 if his attendance was considered necessary (Pt. 46, r.46.3). However, should the case last longer than a day, no refresher is available — a clear incentive to finish within the time estimated. As to fast track costs generally: see Chapter 21 — Costs.

Chapter 13

Multi-track

Overview

- Cases over £15,000 not otherwise allocated to small 13.01
  claims or fast track (Pt. 26, r.26.6(6))
- Customised case management by court
- Pre-trial review by trial judge
- Early fixing of trial window

For Allocation see Chapter 10 — Case management.

Venue

The court normally gives any directions appropriate upon 13.02
allocation and then transfer the case to a Civil Trial Centre;
though it may either transfer to such a Centre to deal with
allocation directions or, with the consent of the Designated
Civil Judge for the Centre, or retain the case for the time being
for further management if it seems that there will be more than
one case management conference and the parties' representatives are an inconvenient distance from the court (Pt. 26, PD
10.2).

Civil Trial Centres are regionally situated and are supplemented by "feeder", usually smaller, local county courts who
transfer multi-track cases to the Centres. The Centres are
presided over by Designated Civil Judges who give guidance to
the courts within their responsibility as to the application of the
CPR and oversee their operation.

Steps on Allocation

The procedural judge, on allocation, may do any or all of the 13.03
following:

- issue written directions (Pt. 29, r.29.2(1)(a))

- set a timetable to fix, as appropriate:

    — a Case Management Conference (CMC)
    — a Pre-Trial Review (PTR) (Pt. 29, r.29.2(1)(b)) (Pt. 29, PD 4.5)
    — a date for the filing of a completed Listing Questionnaire (Pt. 29, r.29.2(3)(b))
    — set a trial date or a window for trial as soon as practicable (Pt. 29, r.29.2(2) and (3)(a)).

Directions

13.04   Directions, given at or without a hearing, will be tailored to the needs of the case and the steps already taken by the parties. The court will have regard to their compliance or non-compliance with any relevant pre-action protocol (Pt. 29, PD 4.2). Its concern will be to ensure that the issues are identified and that the necessary evidence is prepared and disclosed (Pt. 29, PD 4.3).

The court will expect the parties to co-operate in the giving of directions and may approve agreed directions which they submit (Pt. 29, PD 4.6). See Pt. 29, PD 4.7, 4.8 for guidance on the agreed directions which may be approved.

13.05   The directions will deal with disclosure of documents (see Chapter 16 — Disclosure), service of witness statements and expert evidence and may regulate amendments of statements of case (see Chapter 4 — Starting a Case) and the provision of further information. They should form a timetable for the steps to be taken through to the trial and make provision for the trial date or trial period (if not already fixed). In the absence of indications to the contrary, the court's general approach will be to direct (Pt. 29, PD 4.10):

- filing and service of any further information need to clarify a party's case

- standard disclosure

- simultaneous exchange of witness statements

- the instruction of a single joint expert on any appropriate issue; otherwise, simultaneous exchange of experts' reports (unless it is appropriate for reports on the amount of damages to be disclosed subsequently to those on liability); the court will not however (save by agreement) require instruction of a single expert nor appoint

an assessor without fixing a Case Management
Conference

- discussion between experts and a statement thereon, if
  they are not agreed

- a case management conference after the time for compliance and

- the fixing of a trial period.

Practical point:
Parties are advised to consider agreeing directions, although 13.06
these will be subject to the scrutiny of the court.

Case Management Conference ("CMC")

The purpose of the CMC is to set the agenda for the case at the 13.07
earliest possible stage to ensure that the procedures followed
and costs incurred are proportionate to the case. The court will
fix a Case Management Conference if it appears that it cannot
properly give directions on it own initiative and no agreed
directions have been filed which it can approve. It will be listed
as promptly as possible and at least three days' notice will be
given. This is likely to include:

- giving the parties directions on the future conduct of the
  case, including issues such as disclosure

- establishing the likely timescale of the case, and may
  include setting dates for the milestone events, *e.g.* a
  listing hearing, any further CMC, the return of the
  listing questionnaire, or any pre-trial review

- setting the trial date or trial window (if this has not
  already been done)

- agreeing a case summary (Pt. 29, PD 5.7) (see para.
  13.08, below)

- exploring with the parties:

    — the scope for settlement at this stage or the
      possibility of disposing of any particular issues
    — the extent to which experts will be needed,
      including the scope for using a single or joint
      expert and the need for oral evidence
    — the extent to which non-experts will be needed,
      and the need for oral evidence

119

— whether there should be a split trial or trial of a preliminary issue (in which case any directions would need to indicate to which aspect of the case they referred) (Pt. 29, PD 5.3(7)); and whether the case should be tried by a High Court Judge or a specialist judge (Pt. 29, PD 5.9).

Attendance

13.08 If a party intends to apply for a particular direction which may be opposed, he should serve notice and, if the time allowed for the hearing may thus be insufficient, warn the court accordingly (Pt. 29, PD 5.8). If a party has legal representation, a representative familiar with the case and with sufficient authority to deal with any issues which may arise must attend (Pt. 29, r.29.3(2)). That must be someone personally involved with the conduct of the case, able to deal with fixing the timetable, identification of issues and matters of evidence (Pt. 29, PD 5.2(2)). A wasted costs order or an order for indemnity costs against a litigant will usually be made if the inadequacy of the person attending or his instructions leads to an adjournment (Pt. 29, PD 5.3) (see *Baron v. Lovell, The Times,* September 14, 1999, CA) (see also Chapter 21 — Costs).

Parties must ensure that all relevant documents (including witness statements and experts' reports) are available to the judge and that all of them know what directions each of them seeks (Pt. 29, PD 5.6). They should consider whether parties personally should attend and whether it would be useful to provide a **case summary** (prepared by the claimant and agreed with the other parties if possible) setting out in 500 words a brief chronology, facts agreed and in dispute and evidence needed (Pt. 29, PD 5.7).

Time for compliance

13.09 The time by which something is directed to be done may be varied by written agreement (Pt. 2, r.2.11) but this does not apply to (Pt. 29, r.29.5):

- the date fixed for a Case Management Conference or Pre-trial Review;

- the date fixed for a Case Management Conference or Pre-trial Review;

- the date for return of the listing questionnaire;

- the trial date or trial period; or

- any date the variation of which would make it necessary to vary any of the above.

Preserving the Trial Date

Note Pt. 29, PD 7.4:   13.10

1. The court will not allow a failure to comply with directions to lead to the postponement of the trial unless the circumstances are exceptional.
2. If it is practical to do so the court will exercise its powers in a manner that enables the case to come on for trial on the date or within the period previously set.
3. In particular the court will assess what steps each party should take to prepare the case for trial, direct that those steps are taken in the shortest possible time and impose a sanction for non-compliance. Such a sanction may, for example, deprive a party of the right to raise or contest an issue or to rely on evidence to which the direction relates.
4. Where it appears that one or more issues are or can be made ready for trial at the time fixed while others cannot, the court may direct that the trial will proceed on the issues which are then ready, and direct that no costs will be allowed for any later trial of the remaining issues or that those costs will be paid by the party in default.
5. Where the court has no option but to postpone the trial it will do so for the shortest possible time and will give directions for the taking of the necessary steps in the meantime as rapidly as possible.
6. **Litigants and lawyers must be in no doubt that the court will regard the postponement of a trial as an order of last resort. Where it appears inevitable the court may exercise its power to require a party as well as his legal representative to attend court at the hearing where such an order is to be sought.**
7. The court will not postpone any other hearing without a very good reason, and for that purpose the failure of a party to comply on time with directions previously given will not be treated as a good reason.

Listing Questionnaire

(See Appendix 10 to this book for the relevant form)

13.11 The court will, (unless it considers them unnecessary), in accordance with the procedural judge's directions, send a Listing Questionnaire to the parties (Pt. 29, r.29.6(1)) no later than two weeks before they are to be returned (Pt. 29, PD 8.1(4)), which will be no later than eight weeks before the trial date or trial period (Pt. 29, PD 8.1(3)).The parties are encouraged to exchange copies of their questionnaires before filing them, to avoid the court being given conflicting or incomplete information (Pt. 29, PD 8.1(5)).

The Listing Questionnaire will help the court in deciding whether to fix a PTR (Pt. 29, r.29.7) (see para. 13.15, below). Where such a hearing has already been fixed, it will inform as to whether that hearing is still required.

Contents

13.12 The listing questionnaire will take on once again, very great significance. They will require to be filed at some stage in the directions process, but in any case it is intended that they should be filed at least 10 weeks before the intended trial (Pt. 29, r.29.2(2)).

The form of questionnaire is the same as for Fast Track (see Chapter 12). Thus, the Listing Questionnaire should ask for:

- confirmation that:
  — directions with regard to disclosure have been complied with;
  — witness statements and expert reports have been exchanged;
  — any other directions have been complied with. If directions have not been complied with, the parties will be required to give reasons why,
- confirmation of the remaining issues outstanding to be tried
- an estimate of the length of trial
- details of:
  — witnesses who will be attending to give evidence;
  — any special needs of anyone involved with the trial;

— any other information which the court should know at this stage.

Decisions after return of questionnaire

On the basis of the information provided, the court will: 13.13

- fix a Pre-trial Review (giving at least seven days notice)
- cancel a previously fixed Pre-trial Review (Pt. 29, r.29.7)
- give listing directions
- fix or confirm the trial date and/or
- give any directions for the trial itself (including a trial timetable) which it considers appropriate

(Pt. 28, r.29.8 and PD 8.2).

Failure to respond

Where no party files a questionnaire, the court will normally   13.14
order that if none is filed within three days, the claim and any counterclaim be struck out (Pt. 29, PD 8.3(1). Otherwise, if a party fails to file his questionnaire the court will fix a listing hearing on a date which is as early as possible (Pt. 29, PD 8.3(2)), giving the parties at least three days' notice (Pt. 29, PD 8.4). It will then normally fix or confirm the trial date and make other orders about steps to be taken to prepare the case for trial whether or not the defaulting party attends (Pt. 29, PD 8.3(2)).

Pre-trial Review

This may be held by the eventual trial judge about eight to 10   13.15
weeks (variable) before the trial itself in order to:

- resolve any discrepancies between the Listing Questionnaires;
- check that directions have been complied with;
- finalise the statement of issues to be tried. At the CMC the court will already have endeavoured to narrow the issues to those relevant to be tried (see Pt. 1, r.1.4);
- confirm the hearing date;

- set the parameters for the trial including:
  - to confirm which documents and case summaries need to be produced for the trial;
  - where appropriate, to fix the date by which any trial bundles should be lodged (usually seven days before the trial);
  - its length and budget.

The eventual advocates should attend together with their lay clients or persons authorised on their behalf. The dates for the case management conference, pre-trial review and the trial date will not be capable of alteration without leave of the court (see para. 13.09, below). Sanctions for failure to comply with directions, orders or timetables will apply as with fast-track, para. 12.03, above.

Listing Directions

13.16 The court may give directions as follows:

- As to the issues on which evidence is to be given, the nature of the evidence it requires on those issues and the way in which it is to be placed before the court, and may thereby exclude evidence which would otherwise be admissible (Pt. 32, r.32.1)

- A direction giving permission to use expert evidence will say whether it is to be by report or oral and will name the experts whose evidence is permitted (Pt. 29, PD 9.2(4))

- Setting a timetable for the trial and will confirm or vary trial date or week, the time estimate for the trial and the place of trial (Pt. 29, r.29.8(c)(i), and PD 9.1)

- For the preparation of a trial bundle (Pt. 29, PD 9.2(2)(c)).

The parties should seek to agree the directions and file the proposed order (which will not bind the court) (Pt. 29, PD 9.2(1)), making provision for the matters referred to above and any other matter needed to prepare for the trial (Pt. 29, PD 9.2(2)).

At least at the beginning, appeals against interlocutory decisions in multi-track cases concerning case management directions should go to the Designated Civil Judge.

The Trial

Trial periods given in multi-track cases, in lieu of a fixture, have **13.17**
to be for a period of just one week only, rather than the
possible three week period for fast track cases (Pt. 29,
r.29.8(c)(ii)).
Note Pt. 29, PD 10:

> **10.1** The trial will normally take place at the court where
> the case is being managed but it may be at another court if it
> is appropriate having regard to the needs of the parties and
> the availability of court resources.
> **10.2** The judge will generally have read the papers in the
> trial bundle and may dispense with an opening address.
> **10.3** The judge may confirm or vary any timetable given
> previously, or if none has been given set his own.
> **10.4** Attention is drawn to the provisions in Part 32 and
> the following parts of the Rules about evidence, and in
> particular:
>
> 1. to rule 32.1 (court's power to control evidence and to
>   restrict cross-examination), and
> 2. to rule 32.5(2) statements and reports to stand as
>   evidence in chief.
>
> **10.5** In an appropriate case the judge may summarily
> assess costs in accordance with rule 44.7. Attention is drawn
> to the practice directions about costs and the steps the parties
> are required to take.
> **10.6** Once the trial of a multi-track claim has begun, the
> judge will normally sit on consecutive court days until it has
> been concluded.

Costs

There are no limits on costs on multi-track matters, once they **13.18**
have been allocated to that track, as there are in small claims
and fast track cases. However, they are still subject to full
scrutiny by the court in the light of the Overriding Objective
and the principle of proportionality (see Chapter 1 — The New
Scheme). They will either be assessed summarily or by way of
detailed assessment and issues such as misconduct with regard
to the proceedings can be raised (see Chapter 21 — Costs).

Chapter 14

Interim Remedies (Part 25)

Overview

14.01
- Courts may make interim injunctions, declarations, and a variety of orders in relation to property, its preservation and its inspection, and as to goods for their delivery.

- All interim remedies are now within one Part.

General

14.02 An application for an Interim Remedy may be made at any time and if urgent, or "otherwise desirable in the interests of justice", before a claim has been made (CPR, Pt. 25, r.25.2(1)). Importantly, a draft of the order sought must be filed with the application and if possible, a disk containing the draft should be available (WordPerfect 5.1) (Pt. 25, PD 2).

Scope of the Remedy

14.03 Interim Remedies are listed in Pt. 25, r.25.1(1) under three categories, *viz.* Interim (formerly "Interlocutory") Injunctions, Declarations, and Orders. Basically, the main orders relate to the detention, custody, preservation or inspection of property (Pt. 25, r.25.1(1)(c)(i) and (ii)), for the sale or payment of income from property (Pt. 25, r.25.1(1)(c)(v) and (vi)), for entry for the purpose of those Orders (Pt. 25, r.25.1(1)(d)), and for orders for delivery up of goods under section 4 of the Torts (Interference with Goods) Act 1977.
Interim Orders may therefore be granted:

- for disclosure or inspection of property before a claim has been made;

- for interim payment which a defendant is held liable to pay, and for disputed funds to be paid into court;

- for payment into court on terms of release of property pending the outcome of proceedings relating to it;

- for accounts and inquiries.

Practical point:
The List provided by Pt. 25, r.25.1(1) is not exhaustive (Pt. 25, r.25.1(3)).

Evidence

Unless otherwise ordered, any application for an interim injunc- 14.04
tion must be supported by evidence, and this must explain why notice has not been given if made without notice (Pt. 25, r.25.3). Save that applications for "search orders" and "freezing injunctions" must be supported by affidavit, other applications, provided they are verified by a Statement of Truth, can suffice by themselves; otherwise they may be supported by evidence set out in a witness statement or in a statement of case verified by a Statement of Truth (Pt. 25, PD 3(1), (2) and (3)).

Interim Remedies before Claim Issued

These can only be granted if the matter is urgent, or "it is 14.05
otherwise desirable to do so in the interests of justice" — a defendant must seek leave if his application is to be made before filing an acknowledgement of service or a defence (Pt. 25, r.25.2).

Practical points:

14.06
- If, before issue, applicants must undertake — subject to the court otherwise ordering — to issue a Claim Form immediately, this should, where possible, be served with the Order (Pt. 25, PD 4.4(2))

- However, a Claim Form may not necessarily be directed where the application is only for pre-action disclosure.

Interim Payments

Although more than one application for an interim payment can 14.07
be made (Pt. 25, r.25.6(2)), no application can be made until the period for filing an acknowledgement of service has expired

(Pt. 25, r.25.6(1)). Where the applicant is a child or patient, permission of the court must first be obtained (Pt. 25, PD IP 1.2) The application must:

- be served at least 14 days before the hearing
- be supported by evidence (Pt. 25, r.25.6(3)).

Part 25, PD IP2.1 sets out what the evidence must deal with:

1. the sum of money sought by way of an interim payment,
2. the items or matters in respect of which the interim payment is sought,
3. the sum of money for which final judgment is likely to be given,
4. the reasons for believing that the conditions set out in rule 25.7 are satisfied,
5. any other relevant matters,
6. in claims for personal injuries, details of special damages and past and future loss, and
7. in a claim under the Fatal Accidents Act 1976, details of the person(s) on whose behalf the claim is made and the nature of the claim.

14.08 Any relevant documents should be exhibited, including, in a personal injuries case, the medical report (Pt. 25, PD IP 2.2). Any response by way of written evidence must be filed and served at least seven days before the hearing (Pt. 25, r.25.6(4))

The court will only make an interim payment order if:

- liability is admitted either in whole or in part (Pt. 25, r.25.7(1)(a)); or
- judgment has already been obtained (Pt. 25, r.25.7(1)(b)); or
- the court is satisfied that if the matter went to trial the claimant would obtain a substantial judgment (Pt. 25, r.25.7(1)(c)) (see position as to more than one defendant at para. 14.09, below); or
- it is a claim for possession and the defendant would be liable to pay for use and occupation (Pt. 25, r.25.7(1)(d)).

Where the claim is for personal injuries, an interim payment can only be ordered if:

- the defendant is insured; or
- the Motor Insurers Bureau are dealing with the claim; or
- the defendant is a public body
(Pt. 25, r.25.7(2)).

Where the claim is for possession, an interim payment can **14.09** only be ordered if the defendant would be liable to pay for use and occupation (Pt. 25, r.25.7(1)(d)).

Where there is more than one defendant in a personal injury case, the court must also be satisfied that the claimant would obtain judgment against at least one of them (Pt. 25, r.25.7(3)). Although the court can take into account contributory negligence and any set-off or counterclaim (Pt. 25, r.25.7(5)), nevertheless the amount of the interim payment should not be more than "a reasonable proportion of the likely amount of the final judgment" (Pt. 25, r.25.7(4)). The amount of the interim payments is taken into account on the final judgment and any necessary adjustments made (Pt. 25, PD IP 5). Once an interim payment has been ordered the court can make orders for repayment where necessary (Pt. 25, r.25.8).

Freezing Injunction (Formerly Called "Mareva" Injunction)

This is an order to restrain a party from removing from the **14.10** jurisdiction assets located there, or from dealing with assets wherever located.

The **High Court** alone has jurisdiction except if there is an authorised judge. The same applies to Search orders (see para. 14.12, below) (Pt. 25, PD 1.1) However, there is jurisdiction for any Master or district judge to make an order in the High Court if it is:

- by consent
- in connection with charging orders and appointments of receivers,
- In aid of execution
  (Pt. 25, PD 1.3).

Therefore, if a freezing or search order is required in a county court case, the case should be transferred to the High Court to obtain the order. The case can then, if appropriate, be transferred back to the county court.

14.11   A "Penal Notice" is required to be appended to such freezing orders. The wording is: "Penal Notice — If you the within named disobey this Order you may be held in contempt of Court and liable to imprisonment or fined or your assets seized". The applicant has to file an affidavit or affidavits on which his application is relying. Undertakings as to damages if the court later finds loss has been caused to the respondent and bank guarantees will be required. An affidavit will be called for giving the substance of what was said to the court by the applicant's counsel or solicitors. Practitioners are advised to refer to Pt. 25, PD 7 and 8 and the Annex which contains a specimen.

Search Orders (Formerly "Anton Piller" Orders)

14.12   Note that these are also the preserve of the **High Court** (see note on "freezing orders" see para. 14.10, above). The Court has been empowered, most recently by section 67 of the Civil Procedure Act 1997, to make an order to secure the preservation of evidence or of property. Such an order can only be exercised by "a supervising Solicitor" experienced in their operation.

Hearing of Applications for Search Orders

14.13   A. If after issue of a Claim Form:
        File the following:

> (i)   the Notice of Application,
> (ii) Evidence in support — see above, para. 14.04,
> (iii) draft order — see above, para. 14.02.

All the above to be filed/lodged within two hours before the hearing if this is possible (Pt. 25, PD 4.3(1)).

     B. Before issue of a claim:

All as above to be filed on the same day as the hearing, or next working day, or as ordered (Pt. 25, PD 4.3(2)).

Practical points
14.14   • In both cases, the applicant should "notify the respondent informally" of the Application (Pt. 25, PD 4.3(3)).

- In case B above — application before issue — the appellant must undertake to issue a claim form immediately, or the court will give directions for the commencement of the claim (Pt. 25, PD 4.4(1)).

Criteria for Granting Freezing (Mareva) and Search (Anton Piller) Injunctions

Practitioners should look up the criteria in any standard text **14.15** book before considering action; the established criteria may be subject to scrutiny of the "Overriding Objective" — see Chapter 1 — The New Scheme.

Practical point:
In relation to all injunctions where there is a dispute of fact, the principles laid down in *American Cyanamid v. Ethicon* [1975] A.C. 396, HL must be considered.

Hearing by Telephone

Provided the practitioner feels confident that these criteria **14.16** are satisfied, application may be made by telephone as under Pt. 25, PD 4.5:

(1) where it is not possible to arrange a hearing, application can be made between 10.00 a.m. and 5.00 p.m. weekdays by telephoning the Royal Courts of Justice on 0207 936 6000 and asking to be put in contact with a High Court Judge of the appropriate Division available to deal with an emergency application in a High Court matter. The appropriate district registry may also be contacted by telephone. In county court proceedings, the appropriate county court should be contacted;

(2) where an application is made outside those hours the applicant should either—

(a) telephone the Royal Courts of Justice on 0207 936 6000 where he will be put in contact with the clerk to the appropriate duty judge in the High Court (or the appropriate area Circuit Judge where known), or

    (b) the Urgent Court Business Officer of the appropriate Circuit who will contact the local duty judge.

(3) where the facility is available it likely that the judge will require a draft order to be faxed to him,

(4) the application notice and evidence in support must be filed with the court on the same or next working day or as ordered, together with two copies of the order for sealing,

(5) injunctions will be heard by telephone only where the applicant is acting by counsel or solicitors.

Chapter 15

Applications

Overview

Applications made during a claim, or before a claim is com- **15.01**
menced are made in accordance with CPR, Part 23. Evidence at
interlocutory hearings is dealt with in Part 32.

Certain specific applications are dealt with in the following
parts:

- to add or substitute a party — Part 19 (see para. 15.06, below)

- to make other amendments — Part 17 (see Chapter 4 — Starting a Case)

- for a consent order

- for summary judgment — Part 24 (see Chapter 9 — Summary Judgment and Disposal)

- for further information — Part 18 (see para. 15.05, below)

- to change solicitor — Part 42

- for interim remedies — Part 25 (see Chapter 14 — Interim Remedies)

All this is supplemented by the relevant practice directions.

Procedure

Applications should be made: **15.02**

- as soon as the need becomes apparent (Pt. 23, PD 2.7);

- wherever possible so that they can be considered at any other hearing whether arranged or anticipated — *e.g.*

case management conferences, allocation and listing hearings and pre-trial reviews fixed by the court (Pt. 1, r.1.4(2)(I) — the Overriding Objective) (Pt. 23, PD 2.8).

- with the knowledge that the court may wish to review the conduct of the case as a whole and give any necessary case management directions. (Pt. 23, PD 2.9)

The application is made by filing an application notice unless a rule or practice direction provides otherwise, or the court dispenses with one (Pt. 23, r.23.3)

Where a date for a hearing has been fixed and a party wishes to make an application at that hearing but he does not have sufficient time to serve an application notice he should inform the other party and the court (if possible in writing) as soon as he can of the nature of the application and the reason for it. He should then make the application orally at the hearing. (Pt. 23, PD 2.10)

15.03   An application notice must state:

- if it is intended to be made to a High Court or circuit judge but a Master or district judge may refer an application to a judge, who may deal with it or refer it back;

- what order the applicant seeks;

- brief reasons for the application;

- the title of the claim;

- the reference number of the claim;

- the full name of the applicant;

- where the applicant is not already a party, his address for service;

- a request for a hearing, or that the application be dealt with without a hearing (Pt. 23, r.23.6 and PD 1 and 2).

Generally, a copy of the application notice must be served as soon as practicable after it is filed and, in any event, at least three clear days before the hearing, unless another time limit is prescribed by a r.or practice direction (Pt. 23, PD 4).

15.04   An application may be made without serving an application notice (formerly known as *ex parte*) only:

- where there is exceptional urgency,

- where the overriding objective is best furthered by doing so,
- by consent of all parties,
- with the permission of the court,
- where paragraph 2.10 applies
- *i.e.* 2.10 Where a date for a hearing has been fixed and a party wishes to make an application at that hearing but he does not have sufficient time to serve an application notice he should inform the other party and the court (if possible in writing) as soon as he can of the nature of the application and the reason for it. He should then make the application orally at the hearing.

   or
- where a court order, rule or practice direction permits.

(Pt. 23, PD 3)

Evidence at interlocutory hearings is given in writing by witness statement, statement of case and/or application notice (if the latter is verified by a statement of truth — Pt. 32, r.32.6(2)) unless the court orders otherwise (Pt. 32, r.32.6). Affidavit evidence may be used but, unless the court has ordered it, or a rule requires it, any additional cost may not be recovered from another party (Pt. 32, r.32.15). Any evidence on which the applicant seeks to rely must be filed and served with the application notice unless it has already been filed and served (Pt. 23, PD 9.3).

Part 23, PD 10 sets out the procedure for dealing with consent orders.

Further Information (CPR, Part 18)

This replaces the previous rules on requests for further and **15.05** better particulars and interrogatories:

18.1—(1) The court may at any time order a party to —

(a) clarify any matter which is in dispute in the proceedings; or
(b) give additional information in relation to any such matter, whether or not the matter is contained or referred to in a statement of case.

The court may exercise this power either on its own initiative or on application by a party. Before seeking such an order there should have first been a request in writing to the other side who should be given a reasonable amount of time in which to respond (Pt. 18, PD 1 and 2).

Although the application must usually be made on notice, in accordance with Part 23 (Pt. 18, PD 5.1), where the respondent does not reply to the request (minimum period 14 days) the application may be made without notice (Pt. 18, PD 5.5). Consideration should carefully be given as to the efficacy of making a request before disclosure and the exchange of witness statements (*Hall v. Selvaco*, *The Times*, March 27, 1996, CA).

Adding or Substituting a Party (CPR Part 19)

15.06 The new rules are similar to the old; application is required and can be by any party, or intended party, with a hearing, or by consent.

Note Pt. 19, r.19.1:

> (2) The court may order a person to be added as a new party if —
>
>> (a) it is desirable to add the new party so that the court can resolve all the matters in dispute in the proceedings; or
>> (b) there is an issue involving the new party and an existing party which is connected to the matters in dispute in the proceedings, and it is desirable to add the new party so that the court can resolve that issue.
>
> (3) The court may order any person to cease to be a party if it is not desirable for that person to be a party to the proceedings.
> (4) The court may order a new party to be substituted for an existing one if —
>
>> (a) the existing party's interest or liability has passed to the new party; and
>> (b) it is desirable to substitute the new party so that the court can resolve the matters in dispute in the proceedings.

The court has a very wide discretion as to whether to make the order. As with amendments generally (see Part 17 and Chapter 4 — Starting a Case), it is likely that the application will be granted if it does not cause injustice to other parties which cannot otherwise be compensated by costs (*Beoco Ltd v. Alfa Laval Co. Ltd* [1994] 4 All E.R. 464, CA) and the principles of the overriding objective are upheld. The Practice Direction makes it clear that a party applying for an amendment will usually be responsible for the costs of and arising from the amendment.

Adding and substituting claimants

Applicant must file: 15.07

- the Application,
- proposed amended claim form; proposed amended particulars of claim;
- written consent of new claimant.

(Pt. 19, r.19.3 and see PD thereto)

New defendants

To be served with: 15.08

- copy order,
- the amended claim form and amended particulars of claim, and
- the "Response Pack" (see Chapter 7 — Responses to Proceedings)

(Pt. 19, PD 3.2(3)).

Special provisions about adding or substituting after the end of a period of limitation under the Limitation Act 1980 (Pt. 19, r.19.4)

An order can only be obtained if the limitation period was 15.09 current when the proceedings were "started" and the substitution or addition "is necessary" on the court being satisfied that the party previously named was by mistake for the new correct party, and unless the new party is added, or substituted the claim cannot properly be carried on by, or against the original party; or where the original party has died or had a bankruptcy order made against him.

For personal injury claims, and fatal accidents — see sections 11 and 12 of the Limitation Act 1980. For circumstances in which a new cause of action may be introduced — see section 35 of the same Act.

Chapter 16

Disclosure

Overview

- "Discovery" replaced by "Disclosure"   **16.01**
- New basis for disclosure
- "Standard disclosure" as the norm
- New duty to search
- Expanded pre-action disclosure

General

Aside from modernising the old word "Discovery" by substitut- **16.02**
ing "Disclosure", there is something of a departure from the old
culture whereby detailed notes were given in the *Supreme Court
Practice*, dealing with particular documents, and as to whether
or not those documents might be disclosable; basically, all
documents which were material, as well as relevant, which were
or had been in the possession, custody or power of the litigant
were required to be included in a list of documents, or in some
instances, affidavit. The new Civil Procedure Rules are intended
to limit or curtail discovery, and refine the procedures.

The relevant new rules are in Part 31, which applies to all
claims except a claim on the small claims track, and provide for
"Standard Disclosure".

Disclosure, as it has always been, is confined to those
documents which are or have been in a party's control, *viz.*
actually with him, or to which he has a right to possession or
inspect or take copies (Pt. 31, r.31.8). Under the new rules,
disclosure means "stating that the document exists or has
existed" and with it there is an automatic right to inspection of
such a document unless the party no longer controls the
documents or claims the right to withhold inspection (Pt. 31,
r.31.2).

"Document" means anything in which information of any description is recorded and "copy" means "anything onto which information recorded in the document has been copied by whatever means and whether directly or indirectly" (Pt. 31, r.31.4).

Standard Disclosure

16.03 There is now "Standard Disclosure" by virtue of Pt. 31, r.31.6 and this requires a party to disclose:

- all documents on which he relies;
- all documents of which he is aware which could adversely affect his own case;
- or adversely affect or support another party's case;
- and whatever may be required by any practice direction.

Thus neutral documents need not be disclosed but the rules do not restrict disclosure of adverse documents to those of which the party is aware. Instead, the concept of proportionality is introduced to the duty to disclose, and thus to the obligation to give inspection. It may be conjecture as to whether a document will support another party's case. As to what is within these areas may not always be certain, and practitioners might want to err on the side of caution and disclose if in doubt.

16.04 Part 31, r.31.5(1) provides that during proceedings "an order to give disclosure is an order to give standard disclosure unless the Court orders otherwise".

Part 31, r.31.3(2) provides:

(2) Where a party considers that it would be disproportionate to the issues in the case to permit inspection of documents within a category or class of document disclosed under Pt. 31, r.31.6(b):

(a) he is not required to permit inspection of documents within that category or class; but
(b) he must state in his disclosure statement that inspection of those documents will not be permitted on the grounds that to do so would be **disproportionate**.

However, there are still limitations on the extent to which a party must delve into records to obtain documentation for the purpose of standard disclosure and the concept of proportionality will cause controversy and, probably, more than a few appeals.

Procedure for Standard Disclosure

- The List — Form N265   16.05
- Alternative — disclose by exchange of letters
- Listing by category
- Continuing obligations

A list, identifying the documents in a convenient order and as concisely as possible — and indicating those documents which are no longer in the party's control and what has happened to such documents — must be served on every other party; the list is to be in Form N265.

Notwithstanding the stated requirement to serve a list, parties may always agree, in writing, to disclose documents without making a list or a disclosure statement, for example by referring to them in a letter, and they may also similarly agree to dispense with a "Disclosure Statement" (Pt. 31, r.31.10(8)) (see para. 16.06, below).

The party making disclosure should list the documents in date order, number them consecutively and give each a concise description (*e.g.* "letter, claimant to defendant"). Where there is a large number of documents all falling into a particular category, the disclosing party may list those documents as a category rather than individually, *e.g.* 50 bank statements relating to account number . . . at . . Bank, . 19 . . to . . 19 . .; or, 35 letters passing between . . . and . . between . . 19 . . and . . 19 . . .

Added to the list of documents is a new feature called the "disclosure statement". This is required by Pt. 31, r.31.10(5).

Part 31, r.31.10(6) provides that a disclosure statement is a 16.06
document which:

(a) sets out the extent of the search that has been made to locate documents which the party is required to disclose;

(b) certifies that the party understands the duty to disclose;

(c) certifies that the party has carried out that duty to the best of his knowledge.

Preferably this document should be signed by someone with actual knowledge of the contents. In the case of businesses, the disclosure statement must identify the person making the statement and **explain** why he is considered the appropriate person (Pt. 31, r.31.10(7)).

However, by sub-rule (8) the parties can agree in writing to waive the making of a formal list and the requirement to provide the disclosure statement.

The duty of disclosure continues during the whole of the proceedings so that any documents that come to a party's notice must immediately be disclosed (Pt. 31, r.31.11) with the duty to disclose being immediate. However, discovery may be in "stages" at the direction of the court or by agreement of the parties (Pt. 31, r.31.13).

The Duty of Search

16.07 Part 31, r.31.7 provides that when giving standard disclosure, a party is required to "make a reasonable search for documents falling within Pt. 31, r.31.6(b) or (c)". What amounts to reasonableness is defined in sub-rule (2). This involves consideration of:

(a) The number of documents involved.

(b) The nature and complexity of the proceedings.

(c) The ease and expense of retrieval of a particular document.

(d) The significance of any document likely to be located

and, it is suggested, the overriding objective under Part 1.

Again, however, disproportionality is relevant except that, this time, it is called "unreasonableness" (this is wider than disproportionality but includes it). Pt. 31, r.31.7(3) provides:

Where a party has not searched for a category or class of document on the grounds that to do so would be **unreasonable**, he must state this in his disclosure statement and identify the category or class of document.

The search can be limited by date, location or category but any limitation must be stated in the "disclosure statement" (see para. 16.06, above). This will enable the other side to be aware of the limits of the search and challenge it if necessary.

Specific Disclosure

The court may always make an Order for Specific Disclosure, 16.08
that is to disclose documents or classes of documents specified
in the Order, or to carry out a search to such extent as may be
stated in the Order, and to disclose any documents located as a
result of that search (Pt. 31, r.31.12). Whenever a party wishes
to apply for an order for specific disclosure, such application
must be supported "by evidence" and grounds must be given
(Pt. 31, PD 5.1).

Part 31, PD 5.1 gives the only ground for an application for
specific disclosure as inadequate disclosure by the other party.
As before, "fishing expeditions" are unlikely to succeed especially as the application has to be supported by evidence.

Disclosure of Documents Referred to in Other Documents

Part 31, r.31.14 states: 16.09

31.14 A party may inspect a document mentioned in —

(a) a statement of case;
(b) a witness statement;
(c) a witness summary;
(d) an affidavit; or
(e) subject to r.35.10(4), an expert's report.

If the documents are not in the possession of the respondent,
the applicant might wish to apply for non-party disclosure (Pt.
31, r.31.17) or for a deposition or a witness summons (Pt. 34,
r.34.2(4)(b)).

Inspection

Except where the document is no longer in the control of the 16.10
party who disclosed it, or that party has a right, or a duty, to
withhold inspection of it, a party to whom a document has been
disclosed has the right to inspect that document (Pt. 31, r.31.3),
but must have first given the party who disclosed the document
written notice of his wish to inspect, when inspection must be
given within seven days; if he undertakes to pay reasonable
copying charges, a party may request a copy, which again must
be supplied within seven days.

Note that under Pt. 31, r.31.15 The right to inspect includes documents mentioned in the Statement of Case, or in Witness Statements or Summaries, in Affidavits or in Experts' Reports.

Pre-proceedings Disclosure

16.11 On the application of a person who is likely to be a party in proceedings in which a claim is likely to be made, the court may order another person who is likely to be a party and to have or have had in his control documents relevant to an issue arising out of the claim to disclose whether he has such documents in his control and if so to produce them to the applicant's legal, medical or other professional advisers (but not to the applicant personally). (Supreme Court Act 1981, s.33; County Court Act 1984, s.52). Until April 26, 1999, the right to make such an application was restricted to potential proceedings for damages for personal injuries or as a result of a fatal accident. However, the Civil Procedure (Modification of Enactments) Order 1998 (S.I. 1998 No. 2940) removed this limitation so that the application can now be made in anticipation of any proceedings.

- The application is made by application notice, not by issuing a claim (Pt. 25, r.25.4).

- The application must be supported by evidence.

- The documents sought must be such as would fall to be disclosed by standard disclosure were proceedings commenced between the applicant and respondent.

- The disclosure must be desirable in order to dispose fairly of the anticipated proceedings, to assist the dispute being resolved without proceedings or to save costs.

- The order will specify the documents or classes of documents to be disclosed and require the respondent to say which (if any) of the specified documents are no longer in his control and in respect of which he claims a right or duty to withhold inspection. It may require him to say what has happened to any no longer in his control and may specify the time and place for disclosure and inspection.

- If the court makes the order, it may give directions requiring a claim to be commenced — but need not do so.

Disclosure Against Non-parties (Part 31, r.31.17)

In any proceedings, the court may on application order a person 16.12
who is not a party but is likely to have in his control documents
relevant to an issue arising out of the claim to disclose whether
he has such documents in his control and if so to produce them
to the applicant's legal, medical or other professional advisers
(but not to the applicant personally) (Supreme Court Act 1981,
s.34; County Court Act 1984, s.53). Again this right to seek
disclosure against a non-party was limited to proceedings for
personal injuries or relating to the death of a person, but the
Civil Procedure (Modification of Enactments) Order 1998 (see
para. 16.11, above) removes this limitation also.

- The application must be supported by evidence (Pt. 31, r.31.17(2)).

- The documents sought must be likely to support the case of the applicant or adversely affect that of another party (Pt. 31, r.31.17(3)(a)).

- The disclosure must be necessary in order to dispose fairly of the claim or to save costs (Pt. 31, r.31.17(3)(b)).

- The order will specify the documents or classes of documents to be disclosed and require the respondent to say which (if any) of the specified documents are no longer in his control and in respect of which he claims a right or duty to withhold inspection (Pt. 31, r.31.17(4)).

- The order may also require the respondent to say what has happened to any no longer in his control and may specify the time and place for disclosure and inspection (Pt. 31, r.31.17(5)).

Non-disclosure (Part 31, r.31.21)

"A party may not rely on any document which he fails to 16.13
disclose or in respect of which he fails to permit inspection
unless the court permits". If this is properly policed, it should
encourage early and proper disclosure. However, given that the
rules accept that the process of disclosure is a continuing one, it
is difficult to see how this rule will be effective in practice.

Subsequent Use of Disclosed Documents

16.14 Part 31, r.31.22 makes it clear that a party to whom a document has been disclosed may use the document only for the purpose of proceedings in which it is disclosed unless the document has been read to or by the court or been **referred** to during a hearing in public. Even then, the court may make an order restricting or prohibiting the use of the document.

Chapter 17

Evidence

Overview

- Expanded power for courts to control evidence
- New rules for witness statements
- Introduction of "witness summaries"
- Witness statements take over from affidavits

Court's Control of Evidence

The Court now has an expanded power to control evidence.   17.02

CPR, Pt. 32:

32.1—(1) The court may control the evidence by giving dir-
         ections as to —

      (a) the issues on which it requires evidence;
      (b) the nature of the evidence which it requires to
          decide those issues; and
      (c) the way in which the evidence is to be placed
          before the court.

   (2) The court may use its power under this rule to
      exclude evidence that would otherwise be admissible.
   (3) The court may limit cross-examination.

Directions as to the control of evidence may be given at any
stage but more usually on Allocation or at a pre-trial review.

Relevance and Admissibility

Evidence, for the purposes of civil proceedings, can be   17.03
described as information which may be properly presented to

the court to support the probability of facts being asserted before it. Evidence can only be presented if it is relevant, meaning logically probative or disprobative of the matter for which proof is required.

Evidence which is relevant is admissible, meaning receivable, by the court *unless* it is by some rule excluded from being received. Apart from public security, this comes down to "privilege", that is the exclusion of what may have passed between a party and his legal or medical advisers, or exclusion by agreement between the parties; this may arise where there has been a communication between parties where a dispute has arisen, or is likely to arise and the parties have written letters or continued negotiations in the knowledge that the courts will not order disclosure of them if a concluded agreement is not reached. That is, they are expressly or by implication, "without prejudice".

With regard to marking letters or other communications "without prejudice", the following advice is offered, namely that it is often better in the client's interests to write an open letter, so that it can be later produced. This in particular applies in respect of letters before action, setting out the claim. Note also that, in certain respects, the privilege is relation to communications between solicitors and their experts is lost if the expert is approved for use by the court (see Chapter 18 — Experts).

Hearsay Evidence

17.04 This is now always admissible but its value may be questioned.

The Civil Procedure Rules (Pt. 33, r.33.1) define hearsay as "a statement made otherwise than by a person while giving oral evidence in the proceedings, which is tendered as evidence of the matters stated" — basically, then, not the direct evidence of a witness himself, but what someone else has been heard to say. If a statement is made — other than by a witness in the course of giving his evidence — evidence of it can be given to prove that the statement was made, and that is not hearsay; but it cannot be offered as proof of its contents — that would be hearsay. For a full discussion, see *Subramaniam v. Public Prosecutor* [1956] 1 W.L.R. 965.

Section 1 of the Civil Evidence Act 1995 provides that in civil proceedings, evidence shall not be excluded on the grounds that it is hearsay. Section 2(1)(a) (*ibid.*) says that a party intending to adduce hearsay evidence "shall" give notice of that fact; such has been the requirement since the Civil Evidence Act 1968.

But now section 2(4) of the 1995 Act goes on to say that *failure* to give notice goes to costs, and weight, and not so as to make the hearsay evidence inadmissible. Thus, there is now no power to actually exclude evidence which is hearsay, assuming it is relevant, under any circumstances.

The "Hearsay Notice"

There are two circumstances under which reliance on hearsay 17.05 evidence needs to be considered — when notice is required and when it is not.

Notice required:

33.2—(1) Where a party intends to rely on hearsay evidence at trial and either —

    (a) that evidence is to be given by a witness giving oral evidence;
    or
    (b) that evidence is contained in a witness statement of a person who is not being called to give oral evidence;

that party complies with section 2(1)(a) of the Civil Evidence Act 1995 by serving a witness statement on the other parties in accordance with the court's order.

(2) Where paragraph (1)(b) applies, the party intending to rely on the hearsay evidence must, when he serves the witness statement, inform the other parties that the witness is not being called to give oral evidence.

(3) In all other cases where a party intends to rely on hearsay evidence at trial, that party complies with section 2(1)(a) of the Civil Evidence Act 1995 by serving a notice on the other parties which —

    (a) identifies the hearsay evidence; and

    (b) states that the party serving the notice proposes to rely on the hearsay evidence at trial.

(4) The party proposing to rely on the hearsay evidence must—

    (a) serve the notice no later than the latest date for serving witness statements; and

    (b) if the hearsay evidence is to be in a document, supply a copy to any party who requests him to do so.

17.06 Notice not required:

    33.3—Section 2(1) of the Civil Evidence Act 1995 (duty to give notice of intention to rely on hearsay evidence) does not apply —

    (a) to evidence at hearings other than trials;

    (b) to a statement which a party to a probate action wishes to put in evidence and which is alleged to have been made by the person whose estate is the subject of the proceedings; or

    (c) where the requirement is excluded by a practice direction.

An opposing party's application to cross examine in respect of hearsay may be made within 14 days after notice to rely on hearsay has been given; the power of the court extends to allowing the opposing party to call the maker of a hearsay statement (Pt. 33, r.33.4(1) and (2)).

Where the party relying on the hearsay statement does not himself propose to call the maker of it, the opposing party can give notice of his intention to call his evidence to attack the maker's credibility (Pt. 33, r.33.5(1)). For an expanded treatment, see Christopher Style, Charles Hollander, *Documentary Evidence*, (1997) at Chapter 16; and see *Atkin's Court Forms*, Vol. 18 (1996 issue), under "Evidence", and Forms 70 and 71 for specimens of Hearsay Notices, the procedure for which is somewhat simpler than under the early Rules.

Different Types of Evidence

17.07 Admissions (Part 14):

A fact may be admitted on the pleadings; an opponent may make use of the admittance by himself averring it with a different interpretation. Formal admissions may also be made in response to a notice to admit, or in answer to a request for further information (Part 18: see Chapter 15 — Applications). Admissions may be made at any stage, as well as at the trial itself. Formal admissions made in civil proceedings are binding only for the purpose of those proceedings.

Non-expert evidence

This is set out in Part 32. Pt. 32, r.32.1(1) states that it is for the **17.08**
court to give directions as to the issues on which evidence is
required; as to the nature of the evidence required on those
issues and the way in which the evidence is to be placed before
the court.

Part 32, r.32.1(2) states "the court may use its power as
under this rule to exclude evidence that would otherwise be
admissible".

The general principle is that evidence of witnesses is to be
proved by:

(a) At trial by oral evidence in public.

(b) At any other hearing by written evidence.

Evidence may be given by video link or by "any other means"
(r.32.3)(see para. 17.16, below).

Witness statements

The court is given the power to order a party to serve on any **17.09**
other party a witness statement of the oral evidence upon which
the party serving the statement intends to rely or in relation to
any issues of fact to be decided at trial.

A witness statement is a "written statement which contains
the evidence and only that evidence which a person will be
allowed to give orally at trial" (Pt. 32, r.32.4). It must also be
verified by a **statement of truth**: "A certificate by its maker that
he believes the statement of fact in it are true" (Pt. 32, PD 20;
see Part 22 and Chapter 4 — Starting a Case). For the format of
witness statements see Pt. 32, PD 17–24. Failure to comply with
the formalities may result in a refusal of the court to admit the
document or to allow the costs of preparation (Pt. 32, PD 25).

Practical point
A person who makes a false witness statement, being a false **17.10**
statement in a statement of case or an application containing a
statement of truth, without an honest belief in its truth is guilty
of contempt of court (Pt. 32, r.32.14). Therefore it is advisable
that the client rather than the solicitor signs the statement
unless it is a witness statement of the solicitor him/herself.

Part 32, r.32.4(2) and (3): The court can give directions as to
the order in which witness statements are to be served and

whether or not witness statements are to be filed. The normal situation will be for a witness whose statement has been served to give evidence orally in court (Pt. 32, r.32.5(1)). The written witness statement is to stand as the evidence in chief unless the court orders otherwise (Pt. 32, r.32.5(2)).

In giving oral evidence at trial, the witness may, with the permission of the court, (and if the court thinks there is good reason (Pt. 32, r.32.5(4)):

    (a) Amplify the witness statement

    (b) Give evidence in relation to new matters which have arisen since the witness statement was served on the other parties. (Pt. 32, r.32.5(3)).

If a party who has served a witness statement does not call the witness or put in the witness statement as hearsay (see para. 17.04, above), the other party may put in the witness statement as hearsay evidence (Pt. 32, r.32.5(5)).

Witness summaries as an alternative

17.11 Witness summaries may be served with the court's leave on application without notice where it is not possible to obtain a witness statement (Pt. 32, r.32.9(1)). The intention is to be able to refer to brief notes obtained and prepared which do not go quite so far as the full statement but Pt. 32, r.32.9(2)(b) provides that the document may also be a summary of "matters about which the party serving the witness summary will question the witness". This will therefore apply in the hostile witness situation. The rules as to service, amplification and form are the same as for witness statements (Pt. 32, r.32.9(4), (5)).

The idea behind witness statements is clear and is to be encouraged. However, Pt. 32, r.32.10 provides that if a witness statement for use at trial (or a witness summary) is not served in respect of an intended witness within the time specified by the court, then the witness may not be called to give oral evidence **unless the court permits.**

Attendance of Witnesses

17.12 A witness summons to secure attendance may be issued at any time except that where a party wishes to have a summons issued less than seven days before the date of the trial he must obtain permission from the court, and in certain other exceptional cases (Pt. 34, r.34.3(1), (2)). A witness summons is to be issued in the court where the case is proceedings, or where the hearing will be held (Pt. 34, r.34.3(3)).

Witness summonses are to be served by the court, unless the party on whose behalf it is issued indicates in writing when he asks the court to issue, that he wishes to serve it himself (Pt. 34, r.34.6(1)). Where the court is to serve the witness summons, the party on whose behalf it is issued must deposit in the court office the money to be paid or offered to the witness under r.34.7 (see below) (r.34.6(2)).

At the time of service, the witness must be offered or paid a sum reasonably sufficient to cover his expenses in travelling to and from the court and such sum by way of compensation for loss of time as may be specified in the relevant practice direction (Pt. 34, r.34.7) (see Pt. 34, PD Witness Attendance, para. 3). It is important to note that a witness summons may be set aside by the court which issues it, and the person served with a witness summons may apply.

The position with regard to witness summonses is not therefore much different from that which applied previously.

Affidavits

Evidence is to be given by affidavit if it is required by the court, **17.13** practice direction or any other enactment or as an alternative to witness statements or in addition to it if the court requires it (Pt. 32, r.32.15(1)). An affidavit may be used in circumstances where a statement would have sufficed but the party putting it forward may not recover any additional costs of preparing it unless the court otherwise orders (Pt. 32, r.32.15(2)). For the format of affidavits see Pt. 32, PD 2–16. Failure to comply with the formalities may have the same result as with witness statements see para. 17.09, above.

Practical point:
Apart from a few exceptions witness statements now replace affidavits as the normal way of giving evidence.

Notices to Admit Facts and/or Documents

These are available as previously under Pt. 32, rr.32.18 and **17.14** 32.19. A notice to admit facts must be served no later than 21 days before trial (Pt. 32, r.32.18(2)), while a notice to prove a document must be served by the latest date for serving witness statements or within seven days of disclosure of the document, whichever is later (Pt. 32, r.32.19(2)).

Plans, Photographs and Models

17.15 To ensure that plans etc. can be received in evidence at trial, notice of intention to make use of the plans, models etc must be given 14 days before date for serving witness statements if they are part of witness statements, or affidavits, or expert's reports, and in other cases, 21 days before the hearing (Pt. 33, r.33.6).

Video

17.16 Video is expressly referred to at Pt. 32, r.32.3:

> 32.3 The court may allow a witness to give evidence through a video link or by other means.
>
> Also in the practice direction to Part 23 at paragraph 7.

Video Conferencing:

> 7. Where the parties to a matter wish to use video conferencing facilities, and those facilities are available in the relevant court, they should apply to the Master or district judge for directions.

Video links are currently being considered by the court Service as part of their overall IT strategy. See also *Queen's Bench Masters Practice Direction No. 50 — Applications to Queen's Bench Masters by video conference.*

Chapter 18

Experts and Assessors

Overview

- No more "hired guns".   **18.01**

- Expert's duty is to the court.

- No expert evidence without leave of the court.

- Expert evidence is to be restricted to that reasonably required by the court

- Expert evidence to be in a written report only, unless otherwise directed.

- Direction may be given for one expert only.

- Typical time for exchange — within 20 weeks from Notice of Allocation.

- Fast track cases — no court attendance unless the court directs.

General

The adversarial nature of expert evidence in litigation is abol- **18.02** ished and now the expert's primary duty is to help the court, and to override any obligation to those who may have instructed or paid him. This process will begin long before the litigation stages where there are protocols, for example in the personal injury protocol. In *Baron v. Lovell* (1999) N.L.D., July 27, CA, the court held that it was proper to debar expert evidence where the expert's report was only presented on the day of the hearing and the court pointed out the necessity for early pre-trial disclosure.

The rule that expert evidence cannot be adduced without the leave of the court is re-asserted, so that no party may call an expert, or put in evidence an expert's report, without the court's permission. When permission is sought, the expert's name or else identity of the fields in which the applicant or party wishes to call evidence, must be provided (Pt. 35, r.35.4). That permission is restricted just to that expert or the area of expertise mentioned. Furthermore, the court may vary or withdraw any permission given under this rule.

Part 35, r.35.1 demands that:

"Expert evidence shall be restricted to that which is reasonably required to resolve the proceedings".

18.03   Most importantly, the duty of the expert to the court is the overriding duty. Pt. 35, r.35.3 states:

(1) It is the duty of an expert to help the court on the matters within his expertise.

(2) This duty overrides any obligation to the person from whom he has received instructions or by whom he is paid.

In *Stevens v. Gullis* (1999) N.L.D., July 27, CA, an expert who failed to comply with court orders was debarred from giving expert evidence and the Court of Appeal considered that it would also be wrong to allow him to give evidence of fact.

The court will not direct an expert to attend in fast track cases, "**unless it is necessary to do so in the interests of justice**". In "small claims", neither written nor oral expert evidence may be adduced without the permission of the court. Experts' fees, if any, in "small claims" are limited to the amount specified in Pt. 27, PD 7.3, *i.e.* 200.

Access to the Court

18.04   Perhaps more fundamentally, the expert is now given **direct access** to the court to assist him carrying out his functions as an expert to the court. An expert has the right to seek directions from the court without giving notice to either party (Pt. 35, r.35.14). However, the court may direct that a copy of the request and of the directions given be served on the parties when the directions are given.

Single Expert

18.05   The court has an overriding power to decide that evidence before it should be given by a **single joint expert** rather than the party's individual experts (Pt. 35, r.35.7). This is likely to be particularly important in fast track cases. It is certainly the thrust of the personal injury protocol and the practice direction to it.

Where two or more parties want to submit expert evidence on a particular issue, the court may direct that the evidence on that issue be given by one expert only. Where the parties cannot agree who should be the expert, the court will decide from a list prepared or identified by the parties, or may choose an expert in some other manner (Pt. 35, r.35.7(3)). Instructions for the single joint expert appointed in this manner comes from both parties. The party must exchange their respective instructions (Pt. 35, r.35.8).

The liability to pay the fees of the expert will be joint and several unless the court has ordered otherwise. The court may give directions about the arrangements of the payment of the experts fees and may limit the amount that can be paid by way of fees and expenses.

The "written questions" provision (see para. 18.08, below) is available enabling the parties to raise and clarify points with the expert. This is particularly useful in fast track cases where the single joint expert is likely to be the rule rather than the exception.

Form and Content of Reports

See Practice Direction to Part 35, 1.1–1.6 for details. The **18.06** contents reflect the new regime and remind the expert of both his duty to the court and the need to be neutral.

The report must (Pt. 35, PD 1.2):

(2) give details of any literature or other material which the expert has relied on in making the report,

(3) say who carried out any test or experiment which the has used for the report and whether or not the test or experiment has been carried out under the expert's supervision,

(4) give the qualifications of the person who carried out any such test or experiment, and

(5) where there is a range of opinion on the matters dealt with in the report—

(i) summarise the range of opinion, and

(ii) give reasons for his own opinion,

(6) contain a summary of the conclusions reached,

(7) contain a statement that the expert understands his duty to the court and has complied with that duty (r.35.10(2)), and

(8) contain a statement setting out the substance of all material instructions (whether written or oral). The statement should summarise the facts and instructions given to the expert which are material to the opinions expressed in the report or upon which those opinions are based. (rule 35.10(3)).

18.07 The report should conclude: *"I believe that the facts I have stated in this report are true and that the opinions I have expressed are correct"* and there must be a final statement in any report that the expert understands his duty to the court, and has complied with that duty.

Significantly, the report must also state the substance of all material instructions including oral instructions upon which the report was written. Instructions are therefore no longer privileged against disclosure (Pt. 35, r.35.11). However, the rules do provide that the court will not order disclosure of any specific document referred to or permit examination of the expert in relation to the instructions unless the court is satisfied that there are reasonable grounds to consider that the statement of instructions contained in the report may be incomplete. A party may use another disclosed report on which the instructing party does not rely to support their case if so desired.

Questions to Experts

18.08 Under Part 35, r.35.6 The Court may permit, or the parties may agree, to put pertinent questions, otherwise they are to be asked only to clarify.

Pt. 35, PD 4.1 and 4.2:

4.1 Questions asked for the purpose of CLARIFYING the expert's report (see Rule 35.6) should be put, in writing, to the expert not later than 28 days after receipt of the expert's report (see paragraphs 1.2 to 1.5 above as to verification).

4.2 Where a party sends a written question or questions direct to an expert and the other party is represented by solicitors, a copy of the questions should, at the same time, be sent to those solicitors.

Further detail on questions

Part 35, r.35.6   18.09

35.6—(1) A party may put to:

> (a) an expert instructed by another party, or
> (b) a single joint expert appointed under Rule 35.7, written questions about his report.

(2) Written questions under paragraph (1) —

> (a) may be put once only;
> (b) must be put within 28 days of service of the expert's report; and
> (c) must be for the purpose only of clarification of the report;

unless in any case —

> > (i) the court gives permission; or
> > (ii) the other party agrees.

(3) An expert's answers to questions put in accordance with paragraph (1) shall be treated as part of the expert's report.

(4) Where —

> (a) a party has put a written question to an expert instructed by another party in accordance with this rule; and
> (b) the expert does not answer the question,

the court may make one or both of the following orders in relation to the party who instructed the expert —

> > (i) that the party may not rely on the evidence of that expert; or
> > (ii) that the party may not recover the fees and expenses of that expert from any other party.

Discussion Between Experts and Agreement of Issues

The court may direct discussion between experts so as to   18.10
identify the issues and where possible reach an agreement, and
the court may itself specify the issues which the experts must
address when they meet, requiring the experts to prepare a

statement after they have met showing those issues on which they agree and those on which they disagree with a summary of their reasons for disagreeing. However, any agreement between the experts does not bind the parties unless the parties themselves expressly agree to be bound by it (Pt. 35, r.35.12).

Non-disclosure

18.11 Finally, perhaps the only thing which is not surprising is that non-disclosure of an expert's report means that it cannot be relied upon, nor can the party call the expert to give oral evidence. However, again, Pt. 35, r.35.13 adds "unless the court permits".

The Court's Right to Appoint Assessors

18.12 Under Pt. 35, r.35.19, the court has the right to appoint an assessor to assist the court in dealing with a matter in which the assessor has skill and experience. The assessor will take such part in the proceedings as the court directs and may at the request of the court, prepare a report which can be disclosed to the parties and which they may use at trial. The costs of the assessor will be determined by the court, which has the power to order any party to deposit a sum of money in court in respect of the assessor's fees. Where the court does so, the assessor will not be appointed until the payment has been made.

Practical points:

18.13
- Appoint a single agreed expert; if you do not the court may do it instead.

- If you and your opponent do have separate experts try and get the experts to reach agreement.

- Parties who do not recognise this new regime are liable to be penalised heavily in costs.

Thus, the previous practice of having one's own 'tame' experts must come to an end, the suggestion being that it distorts the true administration of justice. Experts by their nature will be expected to be neutral.

18.14 Even if both parties have obtained their own expert reports, the court is likely to consider a single joint expert. This is particularly so in fast track matters, where oral evidence by experts is likely to be discouraged. In such matters, the expert's report is likely to be decisive, rather like the court welfare officer's report in children matters. The judge will not be bound to follow the conclusions in the report, but will have to give good reasons for not doing so.

Further, in those cases where strict time limits have been set down, *e.g.* fast track, the "elusive" expert will be on his way out and the response by the court to a request for more time is likely to be "get another expert" (see *Matthews v. Tarmac Bricks and Tiles Ltd, The Times,* July 1, 1999, CA).

Even if the court does not permit a party to use their own expert, there is nothing to stop them from doing so in order to advise them (*i.e.* a "shadow" expert) including advising on the questions to be put to a court-approved single joint expert. However, their evidence cannot be given to the court nor can their fees be claimed as part of costs awarded against the other party.

Chapter 19

Hearings and Judgment

A. HEARINGS (CPR, PART 39)

Overview

19.01
- Mainly public hearings
- Consequences of failure to attend
- Timetables
- Trial bundles

General

19.02 Note the provisions of Pt. 39, r.39.2:

39.2—(1) **The general rule is that a hearing is to be in public.**
(2) The requirement for a hearing to be in public does not require the court to make special arrangements for accommodating members of the public.
(3) A hearing, or any part of it, may be in private if —

(a) publicity would defeat the object of the hearing;
(b) it involves matters relating to national security;
(c) it involves confidential information (including information relating to personal financial matters) and publicity would damage that confidentiality;
(d) a private hearing is necessary to protect the interests of any child or patient;
(e) it is a hearing of an application made without notice and it would be unjust to any respondent for there to be a public hearing;
(f) it involves uncontentious matters arising in the administration of trusts or in the administration of a deceased person's estate; or

162

(g) the court considers this to be necessary, in the interests of justice.

(4) The court may order that the identity of any party or witness must not be disclosed if it considers non-disclosure necessary in order to protect the interests of that party or witness.

(RSC, Ord. 52, in Schedule 1, provides that a committal hearing may be in private).

As for those cases which are to be held in private, see Pt. 39, **19.03** PD 1.5–1.14:

1.5 The hearings set out below shall in the first instance be listed by the court as hearings in private under r.39.2(3)(c), namely:

(1) a claim by a mortgagee against one or more individuals for an order for possession of land,

(2) a claim by a landlord against one or more tenants or former tenants for the repossession of a dwelling house based on the non-payment of rent,

(3) an application to suspend a warrant of execution or a warrant of possession or to stay execution where the court is being invited to consider the ability of a party to make payments to another party,

(4) a redetermination under rule 14.13 or an application to vary or suspend the payment of a judgment debt by instalments,

(5) an application for a charging order (including an application to enforce a charging order), garnishee order, attachment of earnings order, administration order, or the appointment of a receiver,

(6) an oral examination,

(7) the determination of an assisted person's liability for costs under regulation 127 of the Civil Legal Aid (General) Regulations 1989,

(8) an application for security for costs under section 726(1) of the Companies Act 1985, and

(9) proceedings brought under the Consumer Credit Act 1974, the Inheritance (Provision for Family and Dependants) Act 1975 or the Protection from Harassment Act 1997,

> (10) an application by a trustee or personal repre-
> sentative for directions as to bringing or
> defending legal proceedings.
>
> (11) an application under the Variation of Trusts
> Act 1958 where there are no facts in dispute.

1.6 Rule 39.2(3)(d) states that a hearing may be in private
where it involves the interests of a child or patient. This
includes the approval of a compromise or settlement on
behalf of a child or patient or an application for the payment
of money out of court to such a person.

1.7 Attention is drawn to paragraph 5.1 of the practice
direction which supplements Part 27 (relating to the hearing
of claims in the small claims track), which provides that the
judge may decide to hold a small claim hearing in private if
the parties agree or if a ground mentioned in rule 39.2(3)
applies. A hearing of a small claim in premises other than the
court will not be a hearing in public.

1.8 Nothing in this practice direction prevents a judge
ordering that a hearing taking place in public shall continue
in private, or vice-versa.

1.9 If the court or judge's room in which the proceedings
are taking place has a sign on the door indicating that the
proceedings are private, members of the public who are not
parties to the proceedings will not be admitted unless the
court permits.

1.10 Where there is no such sign on the door of the court
or judge's room, members of the public will be admitted
where practicable. The judge may, if he thinks it appropriate,
adjourn the proceedings to a larger room or court.

1.11 When a hearing takes place in public, members of the
public may obtain a transcript of any judgment given or a
copy of any order made, subject to payment of the appropriate fee.

1.12 When a judgment is given or an order is made in
private, if any member of the public who is not a party to the
proceedings seeks a transcript of the judgment or a copy of
the order, he must seek the leave of the judge who gave the
judgment or made the order.

1.13 A judgment or order given or made in private, when
drawn up, must have clearly marked in the title:

"Before [*title and name of judge*] sitting in Private"

1.14 References to hearings being in public or private or in a judge's room contained in the Civil Procedure Rules (including the Rules of the Supreme Court and the County Court Rules scheduled to Part 50) and the practice directions which supplement them do not restrict any existing rights of audience or confer any new rights of audience in respect of applications or proceedings which under the rules previously in force would have been heard in court or in chambers respectively.

Failure to Attend Trial (CPR, Part 39, r.39.3)

On failure of a defendant to attend, the claimant may prove his **19.04** claim and obtain judgment and, if there is a counter-claim, seek to have it struck out. Where the claimant fails to attend, the defendant may prove his counter-claim and, similarly, seek the striking out of the claim. In cases where neither party attends, the court may strike out the proceedings. This will mean that a party will be left to apply for restoration, and where appropriate for any judgment given to be set aside.

Timetables for Trial

Details of the power of the court to fix timetables and fix a date **19.05** for a trial are set out in Pt. 28, r.28.6 in relation to fast track (see Chapter 12 — Fast Track) and Pt. 29, r.29.8 for Multi-Track (see Chapter 13 — Multi-Track). The timetable will be fixed in consultation with the parties (Pt. 39, r.39.4).

Trial Bundles

Directions for preparation and lodging are likely to be given at **19.06** listing stage, but the Rules require a bundle to be lodged not more than seven and not less than three days before trial (Pt. 39, r.39.5(2)), though for fast track the directions as given in Appendix to PD 28 state that the trial bundles must be lodged at least seven days before trial. Where there is a trial window, these period would no doubt be calculated from the start of the window.

It is important to remember that a claimant will need to compile bundles for each of all other parties, and another for use of the witnesses. Originals of documents in the bundle should be available for production (Pt. 39, PD 3.3).

Format of bundles:

19.07 Pt. 39, PD 3.2 provides:

> **3.2** Unless the court orders otherwise, the trial bundle should include a copy of:
>
> (1) the claim form and all statements of case,
>
> (2) a case summary and/or chronology where appropriate,
>
> (3) requests for further information and responses to the requests,
>
> (4) all witness statements to be relied on as evidence,
>
> (5) any witness summaries,
>
> (6) any notices of intention to rely on hearsay evidence under rule 32.2,
>
> (7) any notices of intention to rely on evidence (such as a plan, photograph etc) under rule 33.6 which is not —
>
>> (a) contained in a witness statement, affidavit or experts report,
>>
>> (b) being given orally at trial,
>>
>> (c) hearsay evidence under rule 33.2,
>
> (8) any medical reports and responses to them,
>
> (9) any experts' reports and responses to them,
>
> (10) any order giving directions as to the conduct of the trial, and
>
> (11) any other necessary documents.

3.3 The originals of the documents contained in the trial bundle, together with copies of any other court orders should be available at the trial.

3.4 The preparation and production of the trial bundle, even where it is delegated to another person, is the responsibility of the legal representative (*see rule 2.3*) who has conduct of the claim on behalf of the claimant.

3.5 The trial bundle should be paginated (continuously) throughout, and indexed with a description of each document and the page number. Where the total number of pages is more than 100, numbered dividers should be placed at intervals between groups of documents.

3.6 The bundle should normally be contained in a ring binder or lever arch file. Where more than one bundle is supplied, they should be clearly distinguishable, for example, by different colours or letters. If there are numerous bundles, a core bundle should be prepared containing the core documents essential to the proceedings, with references to the supplementary documents in the other bundles.

3.7 For convenience, experts' reports may be contained in a separate bundle and cross referenced in the main bundle.

3.8 If a document to be included in the trial bundle is illegible, a typed copy should be included in the bundle next to it, suitably cross-referenced.

3.9 The contents of the trial bundle should be agreed where possible. The parties should also agree where possible:

(1) that the documents contained in the bundle are authentic even if not disclosed under Part 31, and

(2) that documents in the bundle may be treated as evidence of the facts stated in them even if a notice under the Civil Evidence Act 1995 has not been served.

Where it is not possible to agree the contents of the bundle, a summary of the points on which the parties are unable to agree should be included.

3.10 The party filing the trial bundle should supply identical bundles to all the parties to the proceedings and for the use of the witnesses.

Lever-arch files are desirable, otherwise use a ring file. A separate file is convenient for any expert evidence, and different coloured files where there are more than one, should be used.

Settlement before Trial

Note Pt. 39, PD 4:   **19.08**

4.1 Where:

(1) an offer to settle a claim is accepted,

(2) or a settlement is reached, or

(3) a claim is discontinued,

which disposes of the whole of a claim for which a date or "window" has been fixed for the trial, the parties must ensure that the listing officer for the trial court is notified immediately.

4.2 If an order is drawn up giving effect to the settlement or discontinuance, a copy of the sealed order should be filed with the listing officer.

Conduct of the Trial

19.09 Opening speeches as before, may be dispensed with whether on fast or multi-track (Pt. 28, PD 8.2 and Pt. 29, PD 10.2).

As for presentation of witness evidence, see Chapter 17 — Evidence. A company can be represented by an authorised employee provided the court gives permission (Pt. 39, r.39.6 and see Pt. 39, PD 5.2 and 5.3). Exhibits proved at the trial will be recorded by the court and kept by the court until conclusion of the trial, unless otherwise directed (Pt. 39, PD 7).

Usually the evidence will be recorded (Pt. 39, PD 6.1) and a copy of any transcript will be available on payment of a charge (Pt. 39, PD 6.3).

B. JUDGMENTS AND ORDERS (CPR, PART 40)

General

19.10 Every judgment or order, including those made at trial, will be drawn up by the court unless:

- the court orders a party to draw it up,
- a party with the permission of the court agrees to draw it up,
- the court dispenses with the need to draw it up, or
- it is a Consent Order under Pt. 40, r.40.6 (see para. 19.12, below).

(Pt. 40, r.40.3(1)

Service of Judgments or Orders

19.11 Where a judgment or order has been drawn up by a party and is to be served by the court the party who drew it up must file a copy and sufficient copies for service (Pt. 40, r.40.4). The court may also order a judgment to be served on the party, notwithstanding that he is represented by a solicitor (Pt. 40, r.40.5).

Consent Judgments and Orders

19.12 The court officer may enter and seal an agreed judgment or order if it is basically, for payment of an amount of money, delivery up of goods, dismissal of any proceedings, or their stay, or the stay of enforcement of a judgment, the setting aside of a default judgment, payment out of money which has been paid into court, the discharge from liability of any party, or the payment, assessment or waiver of costs (Pt. 40, r.40.6).

When Does a Judgment or Order Take Effect?

From the day when it is given or made, or at such later date as the court may specify (Pt. 40, r.40.7). **19.13**

Interest on Judgments

Where interest is payable on a judgment pursuant to section 17 of the Judgments Act 1838 or section 74 of the County Courts Act 1984, it shall begin to run from the date that judgment is given unless there is a rule or practice direction which makes a different provision, or the court orders otherwise, and this includes ordering interest to begin from a date before the date that judgment was given (Pt. 40, r.40.9). **19.14**

Time for Complying with a Judgment or Order

If for payment of an amount of money, including costs, compliance is required within 14 days of the date of the judgment or order unless that specifies a different date for compliance, or any of the rules specify a different date, or the court has stayed the proceedings or judgment (Pt. 40, r.40(11)). **19.15**

"Slip" Rule

The court may at any time correct an accidental slip or omission in the judgment or order and a party may apply for a correction without notice (Pt. 40, r.40.12). **19.16**

Judgment on Claim and Counterclaim

If specified amounts are awarded both to the claimant on his claim and against the claimant on a counterclaim, then whatever may be the balance in favour of the one of the parties, may be subject to an order for the net loser to pay the balance, but the court may make a separate order as to costs (Pt. 40, r.40.13). **19.17**

Chapter 20

Offers to Settle and Payments into Court (Part 36)

Overview

20.01

- A defendant's offer to settle a monetary claim must be followed by a payment into court to be effective (Pt. 36, r.36.3 and 36.4).

- An offer to settle by an actual or prospective claimant is now possible (this will be of great importance to the defendant's insurers and it will also make it necessary to quantify the claimant's losses at a much earlier date).

- If claimant does better than his Part 36 offer, the defendant may face costs on an indemnity basis plus interest on damages and costs up to 10 per cent above bank rate (Pt. 36, r.36.21).

Definitions

20.02

36.2—(1) An offer made in accordance with the requirements of this Part is called —

  (a) if made by way of a payment into court, "a Part 36 payment";
  (b) otherwise "a Part 36 offer".

(Rule 36.3 sets out when an offer has to be made by way of a payment into court)

(2) The party who makes an offer is the "offeror".
(3) The party to whom an offer is made is the "offeree".

170

General Provisions

As was the previous position, offers to settle do not apply to   20.03
small claims unless the court orders otherwise (Pt. 36, r.36.2(5))
but this, of course, only applies after allocation to track. An
offer by a defendant to settle a money claim will not have the
advantages as set out in Part 36 unless it is accompanied by a
Part 36 payment and such a payment cannot be made until
proceedings have started (Pt. 36, r.36.3). However, note Pt. 44,
costs rule 44.3(4)(c) which provides that, when dealing with the
question of costs the court can take into account an offer made
even if it does not comply with the requirements of Part 36.

The *Calderbank* principle used in family cases is now
extended to civil cases so that a claimant can make an offer to
settle (*e.g.* "I am prepared to accept to accept £x to settle my
claim") which will be binding, and, if achieved or improved
upon at trial may entitle the claimant to indemnity costs and
enhanced interest (see para. 20.10, below).

There are provisions for offers and payment in respect of
claims which have a partial monetary element. Pt. 36, r.36.4
enables a defendant to a mixed claim to make a payment in
respect of the money part and an offer in respect of the non-
money part. It provides that the claimant's acceptance of the
payment will constitute acceptance also of the offer. The
Practice Direction to Part 36 says, at para. 8.11, that the
converse is also the case — accept the offer on the non-
monetary claim and you are deemed to have accepted the
payment.

Form and Content of Part 36 *Offer*

A Part 36 payment or offer may be made at any time after the   20.04
commencement of proceedings and may be made in appeal
proceedings (Pt. 36, r.36.2(4)). The offer must be in writing and
state which part of the claim it relates to and whether any other
factors such as a counterclaim and interest have been taken into
account (Pt. 36, r.36.5(1-3)). An offer can also be made to settle
a claim for provisional damages (Pt. 36, r.36.7).

An offer is made when received by the offeree and is accepted
when notice of its acceptance is received by the offeror (Pt. 36,
r.36.8).

Notice of a Part 36 *Payment*

Similar provisions apply as with a Part 36 offer (para. 20.04,   20.05
above), but it will of course be accompanied by a payment (Pt.
36, r.36.6). Acceptance is as for offers (above). Both an offer

and a payment may be subject to clarification by the offeree (Pt. 36, r.36.9).

The defendant must file —

- the Part 36 payment notice (N242A) and copy for service if required;
- the payment (usually a cheque payable to "'Her Majesty's Paymaster General" or, in the Royal Courts of Justice, to "'the Accountant General of the Supreme Court");
- for the Royal Courts of Justice, form CFO 100 with the court Funds Office (Pt. 36, PD 4.1)

All or part of money paid into court by a defendant following an order under Pt. 3, rr.3.1(3) or 3.1(5) may be treated by him as a Part 36 payment, in which case he must file a Part 36 payment notice (Pt. 37, r.37.2).

Court to Take Account of Offer Made Before Proceedings (CPR, Part 36, r.36.10)

20.06 The court can take into account an offer to settle made **before proceedings** were begun when making any order for costs (Pt. 36, r.36.10(1)). The offer must have been expressed as being open for 21 days after the date it was made and in the case of a potential defendant include an offer to pay the costs of the offeree (Pt. 36, r.36.10(2)). If the offeror is a defendant to a money claim and proceedings are subsequently commenced, the offeror must make a Part 36 payment not less than the amount of the offer within 14 days after service of the claim form (Pt. 36, r.36.10(3)). Such an offer or payment cannot be accepted without the leave of the court (Pt. 36, r.36.10(4)).

Defence of Tender

20.07 A defendant who wishes to rely on the defence of tender before claim must pay into court the amount he says was tendered or the defence will not be available to him. The defendant may treat such a payment (or part of it) as a Part 36 payment, and if he does so, must file and serve a payment notice (Pt. 37, r.37.3).

Acceptance of Offer or Payment

20.08 Similar provisions apply as at present with the relevant period being 21 days before the date of the trial within which the court's leave will be required to accept a payment or offer provided that the parties agree the liability for costs (Pt. 36, rr.36.11 and 36.12) as it will at any time where a claim is compromised on behalf of a child or patient (Pt. 21, r.21.10)

In a claim with two or more defendants who are sued jointly or in the alternative, permission will be required unless the above conditions are satisfied and the claimant discontinues his claim against the other defendant(s) who must also give their written consent to the acceptance of the Part 36 payment or offer (Pt. 36, r.36.17(2)). The claimant may continue against other defendants whom the claimant alleges have several liability (Pt. 36, r.36.17(3)).

A notice of acceptance (N243) must be filed in court and served on the offeror. The notice must be properly headed, identify the Part 36 payment or offer to which it relates and be signed by the offeree or his legal representative (Pt. 36, PD 8.6, 8.7). Presumably the consent(s) of other defendants, where necessary, should also be filed and referred to in the notice and copies served. Where the offer relates to part of the claim, the notice of acceptance may accept the offer and abandon the remainder of the claim (Pt. 36, r.36.13(2)). Otherwise application for permission must be made, to the trial judge if the trial has started, otherwise by application notice under Part 23 (Pt. 36, rr.36.11(2) and 36.12(2)). The court will make an order for costs if it gives permission (Pt. 36, rr.36.11(3) and 36.12(3)).

Costs and Other Consequences of Acceptance

Similar provisions apply as previously, *i.e.* the claimant will be **20.09** entitled to his costs of the proceedings up to the date of service of the notice of acceptance, with costs payable on the standard basis if not agreed (Pt. 36, r.36.13). Such costs will include any costs attributable to the defendant's counterclaim if the Part 36 payment or offer states that it takes into account the counterclaim (Pt. 36, r.36.13(3)). In a similar fashion, the effect of acceptance will be to stay the proceedings (Pt. 36, r.36.15). The effect of the acceptance of an offer or payment by one of several defendants is also similar to the previous provisions (Pt. 36, r.36.17). The privilege attached to offers or payments continues to apply in as much as the trial judge will be kept ignorant of them until all questions of liability and quantum have been decided (Pt. 36, r.36.19(2)). However, this will not apply:

    (a) where the defence of tender before claim has been raised;

> (b) where the proceedings have been stayed under rule 36.15 following acceptance of a Part 36 offer or Part 36 payment; or
>
> (c) where-
>
>> (i) the issue of liability has been determined before any assessment of the money claimed; and
>>
>> (ii) the fact that there has or has not been a Part 36 payment may be relevant to the question of the costs or the issue of liability.
>
> (Part 36, r.36.19(3).)

A claimant's failure to beat a defendant's offer or payment will, as previously, result in the claimant paying the costs from the last date of possible acceptance (Pt. 36, r.36.20).

20.10 Where the claimant beats the offer or payment, not only will the claimant be entitled to his costs on an **indemnity basis** but also interest at a rate not exceeding **10 per cent above base rate** on all or part of his claim and costs unless the court considers it unjust to do so (Pt. 36, r.36.21(1–4)). In considering whether or not it would be unjust, the court will take into account all the circumstances including:

> (a) the terms of any Part 36 offer;
>
> (b) the stage in the proceedings when any Part 36 offer or Part 36 payment was made;
>
> (c) the information available to the parties at the time when the Part 36 offer or Part 36 payment was made; and
>
> (d) the conduct of the parties with regard to the giving or refusing to give information for the purposes of enabling the offer or payment into court to be made or evaluated.

(Part. 36, r.36.21(5)).

Deduction of Benefits

20.11 The deduction of benefits under the Social Security (Recovery of Benefits) Act 1997 is as previously (Pt. 36, r.36.23), *i.e.* where a payment to a claimant following acceptance of a Part 36 payment would be a recoverable benefit for the purposes of the Social Security (Recovery of Benefits) Act, 1997, section 1, if the offeror has applied for but not received a certificate of recoverable benefit when he makes the offer, he must make the payment within seven days of receipt of the certificate. The court will take into account the gross figure in the Part 36 payment notice when considering whether the claimant has bettered or obtained a more advantageous judgment than the Part 36 payment or offer (Pt. 36, PD 10.5).

Payment Out of Court (Part 36, r.36.16)

A request for payment out, following acceptance of a Part 36 **20.12** offer, is made on practice form N243 (Pt. 36, PD 8.1). This contains various details to be completed (see Pt. 36, PD 8.2). Where the request is made to the Royal Courts of Justice, CFO Form 201 will also be required (Pt. 36, PD 8.3). Instead of payment to a bank account the payee can ask for a cheque (Pt. 36, PD 8.4). As to payment out to a person who has died intestate, see Pt. 36, PD 8.5.

Chapter 21

Costs

Overview

21.01
- Scales abolished
- Summary assessment extended
- Detailed assessment replaces taxation
- Paying party encouraged to challenge costs.

General

21.02 The new Costs Rules are contained in CPR, Parts 43–48.
Note Part 44, r.44.13(1):

> Where the court makes an order which does not mention costs no party is entitled to costs in relation to that order.

In-house solicitors can now recover costs (Part 48, r.48.6). Costs draftsmen's fees can be included in the "reasonable costs of preparing and checking the bill" (Pt. 43, PD 2.16) although whether a costs draftsman is needed to prepare a summary bill of costs (see para. 21.19, below) remains to be seen, A solicitor representing himself or his firm may recover full costs and is not limited to costs as a litigant in person (Pt. 48, PD 1.7).

Definitions

21.03 Note Pt. 44, PD 2.4:

> There are certain costs orders which the court will commonly make in proceedings before trial. The following table sets out the general effect of these orders. The table is not an exhaustive list of the orders which the court may make.

Term	Effect
• Costs • Costs in any event	The party in whose favour the order is made is entitled to the costs in respect of the part of the proceedings to which the order relates, whatever other costs orders are made in the proceedings.
• Costs in the case • Costs in the application	The party in whose favour the court makes an order for costs at the end of the proceedings is entitled to his costs of the part of the proceedings to which the order relates.
• Costs reserved	The decision about costs is deferred to a later occasion, but if no later order is made the costs will be costs in the case.
• Claimant's/ Defendant's costs in the case/ application.	If the party in whose favour the costs order is made is awarded costs at the end of the proceedings, that party is entitled to his costs of the part of the proceedings to which the order relates. If any other party is awarded costs at the end of the proceedings, the party in whose favour the final costs order is made is not liable to pay the costs of any other party in respect of the part of the proceedings to which the order relates.
• Costs thrown away	Where, for example, a judgment or order is set aside, the party in whose favour the costs order is made is entitled to the costs which have been incurred as a consequence. This includes the costs of — a. preparing for and attending any hearing at which the judgment or order which has been set aside was made; b. preparing for and attending any hearing to set aside the judgment or order in question; c. preparing for and attending any hearing at which the court orders the proceedings or the part in question to be adjourned; d. any steps taken to enforce a judgment or order which has subsequently been set aside.

Term	Effect
• Costs of and caused by	Where, for example, the court makes this order on an application to amend a statement of case, the party in whose favour the costs order is made is entitled to the costs of preparing for and attending the application and the costs of any consequential amendment to his own statement of case.
• Costs here and below	The party in whose favour the costs order is made is entitled not only to his costs in respect of the proceedings in which the court makes the order but also to his costs of the proceedings in any lower court. In the case of an appeal from a Divisional Court the party is not entitled to any costs incurred in any court below the Divisional Court.
• No order as to costs • Each party to pay his own costs	Each party is to bear his own costs of the part of the proceedings to which the order relates whatever costs order the court makes at the end of the proceedings.

21.04   Further definitions are in Pt. 43, r.43.2.

43.2—(1) In Parts 44 to 48, unless the context otherwise requires —

(a) "costs" includes fees, charges, disbursements, expenses, remuneration, reimbursement allowed to a litigant in person under r.48.6 and any fee or reward charged by a lay representative for acting on behalf of a party in proceedings allocated to the small claims track;

(b) "costs judge" means a taxing master of the Supreme Court;

(c) "costs officer" means —

(i) a costs judge;

(ii) a district judge; and

(iii) an authorised court officer;

(d) "authorised court officer" means any officer
of —

   (i) a county court;
   (ii) a district registry;
   (iii) the Principal Registry of the Family
   Division; or
   (iv) the Supreme Court Costs Office;

whom the Lord Chancellor has authorised to
assess costs.

(e) "fund" includes any estate or property held for
the benefit of any person or class of person and
any fund to which a trustee or personal representative is entitled in his capacity as such;

(f) "receiving party" means a party entitled to be
paid costs;

(g) "paying party" means a party liable to pay
costs;

(h) "assisted person" means an assisted person
within the statutory provisions relating to legal
aid; and

(i) "fixed costs" means the amounts which are to
be allowed in respect of solicitors' charges in
the circumstances set out in Part 45.

(2) The costs to which Parts 44 to 48 apply include —

(a) the following costs where those costs may be
assessed by the court —

   (i) costs of proceedings before an arbitrator
   or umpire;
   (ii) costs of proceedings before a tribunal or
   other statutory body; and
   (iii) costs payable by a client to his solicitor;
   and

(b) costs which are payable by one party to
another party under the terms of a contract,
where the court makes an order for an assessment of those costs.

Meaning of Summary Assessment

43.3 "Summary assessment" means the procedure by
which the court, when making an order about

costs, orders payment of a sum of money instead of fixed costs or "detailed assessment".

Meaning of detailed assessment

> 43.4 "Detailed assessment" means the procedure by which the amount of costs is decided by a costs officer in accordance with Part 47.

Fees of Counsel

21.05 There is confusion as to whether "certificates for counsel" still need to be requested on interlocutory hearings. The sensible view would appear to be that they do not and that, indeed, Pt. 44, PD 2.6 provides a mechanism for a certificate only when the judge feels that the attention of the taxing officer needs to be drawn to it:

> 2.6(1) This paragraph applies where the court orders the detailed assessment of the costs of a hearing at which one or more counsel appeared for a party.
>
> (2) Where an order for costs states the opinion of the court as to whether or not the hearing was fit for the attendance of one or more counsel, a costs officer conducting a detailed assessment of costs to which that order relates will have regard to the opinion stated.

Solicitor's Duty to Notify Client

21.06 Under Pt. 44, r.44.2:

> 44.2—(1) Where:
>
> (a) the court makes a costs order against a legally represented party; and
> (b) the party is not present when the order is made,
>
> the party's solicitor must notify his client in writing of the costs order no later than seven days after the solicitor receives notice of the order.

Note Pt. 44, PD 1.2:

Where a solicitor notifies a client of an order under that rule, he must also explain why the order came to be made.

Practical point:
The message should be clear in that insofar as the court can penalise the solicitor they will do so Indeed, the court can always call for a copy of the letter that the solicitor sends to the client or make supply of such a letter a condition of a direction (Pt. 44, PD 1.3).

Court's Discretion and Circumstances to be Taken into Account when Exercising its Discretion as to Costs

The new Costs Rules are undoubtedly going to have a substan- **21.07** tial effect upon the principle of recoverable costs and their quantification. Hurdles for the receiving party start prior to any order for costs. Under Pt. 44, r.44.3:

44.3—(1) The court has discretion as to —

    (a) whether costs are payable by one party to another;

    (b) the amount of those costs; and

    (c) when they are to be paid.

  (2) If the court decides to make an order about costs —

    (a) the general rule is that the unsuccessful party will be ordered to pay the costs of the successful party; but

    (b) the court may make a different order.

[i.e. The "Winner takes it all" principle no longer invariably applies.]

  (3) The general rule does not apply to the following proceedings —

    (a) proceedings in the Court of Appeal on an application or appeal made in connection with proceedings in the Family Division; or

    (b) proceedings in the Court of Appeal from a judgment, direction, decision or order given or made in probate proceedings or family proceedings.

  (4) In deciding what order (if any) to make about costs, the court must have regard to all the circumstances, including —

    (a) the conduct of **all** the parties;

(b) whether a party has succeeded on **part** of his case, even if he has not been wholly successful; and

(c) any payment into court or **admissible offer to settle** made by a party which is drawn to the court's attention (whether or not made in accordance with Part 36).

(Part 36 contains further provisions about how the court's discretion is to be exercised where a payment into court or an offer to settle is made under that Part)

(5) The conduct of the parties includes —

(a) conduct before, as well as during, the proceedings, and in particular the **extent to which the parties followed any relevant pre-action protocol**;

(b) whether it was reasonable for a party to raise, pursue or contest a particular allegation or issue;

(c) the manner in which a party has pursued or defended his case or a particular allegation or issue; and

(d) whether a claimant who has succeeded in his claim, in whole or in part, **exaggerated his claim**.

(6) The orders which the court may make under this rule include an order that a party must pay —

(a) a proportion of another party's costs;

(b) a stated amount in respect of another party's costs;

(c) costs from or until a certain date only;

(d) costs incurred before proceedings have begun;

(e) costs relating to particular steps taken in the proceedings;

(f) costs relating only to a distinct part of the proceedings; and

(g) interest on costs from or until a certain date, including a date before judgment.

(7) Where the court would otherwise consider making an order under paragraph (6)(e), it must instead, if practicable, make an order under paragraph (6)(a) or (c).

(8) Where the court has ordered a party to pay costs, it
    may order an amount to be paid on account before
    the costs are assessed.

Practical point:
The general rule remains that costs should follow the event. **21.08**
However the effect of the above rules means that this is very
much a rebuttable presumption and there may well be detailed
arguments on costs where before the issue of costs may not have
been fully argued. The award of costs will now be more issue-
based. The net result of all of this is that the amount of costs
recovered is likely to be reduced.

Misconduct

The court may deal with misconduct by a party or his legal **21.09**
representative either in connection with a detailed assessment
or with regard to proceedings under Pt. 44, r.44.14. The court
may disallow all or part of the costs which are being assessed;
or order the party at fault or his legal representative to pay costs
which he has caused any other party to incur (Pt. 44,
r.44.14(2)). Note the requirement for a solicitor to notify his
client of any costs order made against the client (Pt. 44,
r.44.14(3) and see Pt. 44, r.44.2, mentioned in para. 21.06
above).
Note Pt. 44, PD 7:

7.1 Before making an order under rule 44.14 the court
must give the party or legal representative in question a
reasonable opportunity to attend a hearing to give reasons
why it should not make such an order.
7.2 Conduct before or during the proceedings which gave
rise to the assessment which is unreasonable or improper
includes steps which are calculated to prevent or inhibit the
court from furthering the overriding objective.
7.3 Although rule 44.14(3) does not specify any sanction
for breach of the obligation imposed by the rule the court
may, either in the order under paragraph (2) or in a
subsequent order, require the solicitor to produce to the
court evidence that he took reasonable steps to comply with
the obligation.

As to wasted costs generally see Part 48, r.48.7: **21.10**

48.7—(1) This rule applies where the court is considering
whether to make an order under section 51(6) of the

Supreme Court Act 1981 (court's power to disallow or (as the case may be) order a legal representative to meet, "wasted costs").

(2) The court must give the legal representative a reasonable opportunity to attend a hearing to give reasons why it should not make such an order.

(3) For the purposes of this rule, the court may direct that privileged documents are to be disclosed to the court and, if the court so directs, to the other party to the application for an order. (Note that this rule was declared *"ultra vires"* in *General Mediterranean Holdings SA v. Ransanbhai Manibhai Patel and Kumar Ransanbhai Patel, The Times,* August 12, 1999.

(4) When the court makes a wasted costs order, it must specify the amount to be disallowed or paid.

(5) The court may direct that notice must be given to the legal representative's client, in such manner as the court may direct —

   (a) of any proceedings under this rule; or
   (b) of any order made under it against his legal representative.

(6) Before making a wasted costs order, the court may direct a costs judge or a district judge to inquire into the matter and report to the court.

(7) The court may refer the question of wasted costs to a costs judge or a district judge, instead of making a wasted costs order.

21.11 The Practice Direction sets out further details of the procedure:

2.1 Rule 48.7 deals with wasted costs orders against legal representatives. Such orders can be made at any stage in the proceedings up to and including the proceedings relating to the detailed assessment of costs. In general, applications for wasted costs are best left until after the end of the trial.

2.2 The court may make a wasted costs order against a legal representative on an application under Part 23 or of its own initiative.

2.3 A party who wishes to apply for a wasted costs order must first give to the legal representative against whom the order is sought notice in writing—

   (a) of what the legal representative is alleged to have done or failed to do, and

(b) of the costs that he may be ordered to pay or which are sought against him.
The notice must be given at least three days before the hearing.

2.4 It is appropriate for the court to make a wasted costs order against a legal representative only if—

(a) he has acted improperly, unreasonably or negligently,
(b) his conduct has caused a party to incur unnecessary costs, and
(c) it is just in all the circumstances to order him to compensate that party for the whole or part of those costs.

2.5 The court will give directions about the procedure that will be followed in each case in order to ensure that the issues are dealt with in a way that is fair and as simple and summary as the circumstances permit.

2.6 As a general rule the court will consider whether to make a wasted costs order in two stages:

(a) in the first stage, the court must be satisfied —

　(i) that it has before it evidence or other material which, if unanswered, would be likely to lead to a wasted costs order being made, and
　(ii) the wasted costs proceedings are justified notwithstanding the likely costs involved.

(b) At the second stage (even if the court is satisfied under (a) above) the court will consider, after giving the legal representative an opportunity to put forward his case, whether it is appropriate to make a wasted costs order in accordance with paragraph 2.4 above.

2.7 A wasted costs order is an order that the legal representative pay a specified sum in respect of costs to a party or that costs relating to a specified sum or items of work be disallowed.

Basis of Assessment

As previously, there will be two bases of assessment set out in **21.12**
Pt. 44, r.44.4:

44.4—(1) Where the court is to assess the amount of costs (whether by summary or detailed assessment) it will assess those costs —

    (a) on the **standard basis**; or
    (b) on the **indemnity basis**,

but the court will not in either case allow costs which have been **unreasonably** incurred or are unreasonable in amount.

(Rule 48.3 sets out how the court decides the amount of costs payable under a contract)

(2) Where the amount of costs is to be assessed on the standard basis, the court will—

    (a) only allow costs which are **proportionate** to the matters in issue; and
    (b) resolve any doubt which it may have as to whether costs were **reasonably incurred or reasonable and proportionate** in amount in favour of the paying party.

(3) Where the amount of costs is to be assessed on the indemnity basis, the court will resolve any doubt which it may have as to whether costs were reasonably incurred or were reasonable in amount in favour of the receiving party.

(4) Where —

    (a) the court makes an order about costs without indicating the basis on which the costs are to be assessed; or
    (b) the court makes an order for costs to be assessed on a basis other than the standard basis or the indemnity basis, the costs will be assessed on the standard basis.

(5) This rule and Part 47 (detailed assessment of costs by a costs officer) do not apply to the extent that regulations made under the Legal Aid Act 1988 determine the amount payable.

(6) Where the amount of a solicitor's remuneration in respect of non-contentious business is regulated by any general orders made under the Solicitors Act 1974, the amount of the costs to be allowed in respect of any such business which falls to be assessed by the

court will be decided in accordance with those general
orders rather than this rule and rule 5.

The difference between standard and indemnity basis is of
vital importance. As before, the burden of proof alters between
the two; for standard it lies with the receiving party, for
indemnity — with the paying party. It is the second test in
standard which could have a dramatic effect upon quantification. That test is **proportionality**.

Proportionality in Relation to Costs

The receiving party will only be entitled to recover the costs 21.13
which are proportionate (to quote Pt. 44, r.44.4(2)(a)), ". . . to
the matters in issue". Therefore the spectacle of costs considerably exceeding the amount recovered is likely to be extremely
rare.

In this regard it is worth considering Practice Direction 3 to
Part 44:

3.1 The relationship between the total of the costs
incurred and the financial value of the claim may not be a
reliable guide. A fixed percentage cannot be applied in all
cases to the value of the claim in order to ascertain whether
or not the costs are proportionate.

3.2 In any proceedings there will be costs which will
inevitably be incurred and which are necessary for the
successful conduct of the case. Solicitors are not required to
conduct litigation at rates which are uneconomic. Thus in a
modest claim the proportion of costs is likely to be higher
than in a large claim and may even equal or possibly exceed
the amount in dispute.

3.3 Where a trial takes place, the time taken by the court
in dealing with a particular issue may not be an accurate
guide to the amount of time properly spent by the legal or
other representatives in preparation for the trial of that issue.

Practical point:
It remains to be seen how the courts will apply proportionality. 21.14
What practitioners should understand is that the question of
proportionality is an attempt by the court to drive down
recoverable costs so that eventually solicitors only incur costs in
keeping with the amount in dispute. Some guidance is provided
by the case of *Piglowska v. Piglowski, The Times*, June 25, 1999,
HL. In the judgment the following was stated — "There was

the principle of proportionality between the amount at stake
and the legal resources of the parties and the community which
it was appropriate to spend on resolving the dispute."

Factors to be Taken into Account in Deciding the Amount of Costs

21.15 The factors are:

44.5—(1)

The court is to have regard to all the circumstances in deciding
whether costs were —

> (a) if it is assessing costs on the standard basis—
>> (i) proportionately and reasonably
>> incurred; or
>> (ii) were proportionate and reasonable in
>> amount, or
>
> (b) if it is assessing costs on the indemnity basis —
>> (i) unreasonably incurred; or
>> (ii) unreasonable in amount.

(2) In particular the court must give effect to any orders
which have already been made.

(3) The court must also have regard to—

> (a) the conduct of all the parties, including in
> particular —
>> **(i) conduct before, as well as during, the**
>> **proceedings; and**
>> **(ii) the efforts made, if any, before and**
>> **during the proceedings in order to try to**
>> **resolve the dispute;**
>
> (b) the amount or value of any money or property
> involved;
>
> (c) the importance of the matter to all the parties;
>
> (d) the particular complexity of the matter or the
> difficulty or novelty of the questions raised;
>
> (e) the skill, effort, specialised knowledge and
> responsibility involved;
>
> (f) the time spent on the case; and
>
> (g) the place where and the circumstances in
> which work or any part of it was done.

Practical points:
- These factors are not in any particular order of priority. 21.16
  The most important factor to be taken into account
  would be the conduct of the parties both before and
  during the proceedings, as to which see *Mars U.K. Ltd v.
  Teknowledge Ltd (No. 2), The Times,* July 8, 1999, CA.

- Also to be taken into account in conduct are any efforts
  to try and settle the case. This is of course much wider
  than the test set by the court of trial because it includes
  any type of settlement offer and indeed the failure to
  attempt to settle.

- The question of the "value" of the amount involved to
  be taken into account smacks again of proportionality.

- The third factor is the importance of the matter to all the
  parties. This is quite a difficult concept but may be put
  up by the receiving party as a counter-argument against
  proportionality.

- The remaining factors reflect the previous position,
  namely that the court will take into account the complexity of the matter or the difficulty or novelty of the
  questions raised, the skill, effort, specialised knowledge
  and responsibility involved and, finally, the time spent on
  the case.

- The final factor to be taken into account reflects the
  place where and the circumstances under which the
  work or any part of it was done. This will allow the
  court to review the reasonableness of instructing City
  solicitors for a fast track claim in a provincial county
  court or alternatively, in combination with the other
  factors, the rate at which a solicitor outside the City of
  London should be recompensed at City rates for a
  particular type of case in which he has a specialised
  knowledge.

- Thus you win your case but you are then subjected to an
  examination at the behest of the paying party as to your
  conduct both before and during the proceedings —
  whether you have followed the protocol procedure,
  whether you have won or lost on a particular issue and,
  despite having succeeded in the case, whether you exaggerated the claim from the start.

- The other factor to be taken into account in the usual way is whether or not there has been an offer or a payment into court. This, however, is much wider than the current position because an offer may be taken into account even if it does not comply with, in the new Rules, Part 36. It includes a pre-action offer.

Fixed Costs

21.17 In the circumstances set out in Part 45, a party may recover the fixed costs specified in that rule (but the court may make a different order). Details of the amounts of costs are set out in the rule.

This is effectively the result purely of the marriage between the High Court and county court provisions — *i.e.* RSC, Ord. 62, Appendix 3 and CCR, Ord. 38, Appendix B.

It is worth noting Pt. 45, r.45.3 as to the liability of the defendant for fixed commencement costs:

45.3

(1) Where —

(a) the only claim is for a specified sum of money; and

(b) the defendant pays the money claimed within 14 days after service of particulars of claim on him, together with the fixed commencement costs stated in the claim form,

the defendant is not liable for any further costs unless the court orders otherwise.

(2) Where —

(a) the claimant gives notice of acceptance of a payment into court in satisfaction of the whole claim;

(b) the only claim is for a specified sum of money; and

(c) the defendant made the payment into court within 14 days after service of the particulars of claim on him, together with the fixed costs stated in the claim form,

the defendant is not liable for any further costs unless the court orders otherwise.

Procedure for Assessing Costs

The assessment procedure is itself subject to quite substantial 21.18
change although much of this reflects recent previous practice.
Under Pt. 44, r.44.7:

> 44.7—(1) Where the court orders a party to pay costs to
> another party (other than fixed costs) it may either —
>
> > (a) make a summary assessment of the costs; or
> > (b) order detailed assessment of the costs by a
> >   costs officer,
>
> unless any rule, practice direction or other enactment
> provides otherwise.

Summary assessment

The court has power to summarily assess costs at any hearing 21.19
where it does not order fixed costs, or where fixed costs are not
provided for (Pt. 44, PD 4.1). The courts will use this power as
often as possible where an *"inter partes"* costs order is made. It
will not be appropriate where costs are reserved or where the
order is "costs in case" (formerly "costs in cause").
Note carefully Pt. 44, PD 4.4–4.7:

> 4.4(1) The general rule is that the court will make a summary
> assessment of the costs:
>
> > (a) at the conclusion of the trial of a case which has been
> >   dealt with on the fast track, in which case the order
> >   will deal with the costs of the whole claim, and
> > (b) at the conclusion of any other hearing which has
> >   lasted less than one day, in which case the order will
> >   deal with the costs of the application or matter to
> >   which the hearing related;
>
> unless there is good reason not to do so, *e.g.* where the
> paying party shows substantial grounds for disputing the sum
> claimed for costs that cannot be dealt with summarily or
> there is insufficient time to carry out a summary assessment.
>
> 4.5(1) It is the duty of the parties and their legal repre-
> sentatives to assist the judge in making a summary assessment
> of costs in any case to which paragraph 4.4 above applies, in
> accordance with the following paragraphs.

(2) Each party who intends to claim costs must prepare a written statement of the costs he intends to claim showing separately in the form of a schedule:

(a) the number of hours to be claimed,

(b) the hourly rate to be claimed,

(c) the grade of fee earner;

(d) the amount and nature of any disbursement to be claimed, other than counsel's fee for appearing at the hearing,

(e) the amount of solicitor's costs to be claimed for attending or appearing at the hearing,

(f) the fees of counsel to be claimed in respect of the hearing, and

(g) any Value Added Tax to be claimed on these amounts.

(3) The statement of costs should follow as closely as possible Form 1 of the Schedule of Costs Forms annexed to this practice direction and must be signed by the party or his legal representative.

(4) The statement of costs must be filed at court and copies of it must be served on any party against whom an order for payment of those costs is intended to be sought. The statement of costs should be filed and the copies of it should be served as soon as possible and in any event not less than 24 hours before the date fixed for the hearing.

4.6 The failure by a party, without reasonable excuse, to comply with the foregoing paragraphs will be taken into account by the court in deciding what order to make about the costs of the claim, hearing or application, and about the costs of any further hearing or detailed assessment hearing that may be necessary as a result of that failure.

4.7 If the court makes a summary assessment of the costs the court will specify the amount payable as a single figure which will include:

(a) all sums in respect of profit costs, disbursements and VAT which is allowed, and

(b) the amount which is awarded under Part 46 (Fast Track Trial Costs).

Practical points:

21.20　　• Assessment as a procedure is well known to county court practitioners. Certainly the intention behind the Rules is that it should become much more the practice that the court dealing with the hearing makes a summary assessment of the costs immediately (Pt. 44, PD 4.4) and that costs will be collected as the case proceeds.

• This entails practitioners preparing for hearings with some detail as to the costs of the application ready for an argument about summary assessment. Indeed, the procedure requires that the parties serve summaries of costs at least 24 hours before the hearing. Failure to do so may result in the court making no order for costs or just ordering nominal costs.

• The form provided in the Appendix to the Rules and at Appendix 11 in this book is very straightforward and should not be too difficult to complete.

• It should be noted that in consent applications the **amount** of costs agreed to be paid by one party to the other should be specified otherwise the court may refuse the order for costs. On interlocutory matters summary assessment should last no longer than about three to seven minutes; after a fast track trial up to about 30 minutes.

In the absence of any other order, where the court orders payment of costs, those costs must be paid within **14 days** of a summary assessment or detailed assessment (Pt. 44, r.44.8)

Detailed assessment

Detailed assessment should be less common than the previous **21.21** taxation procedure with the encouragement to have summary assessments instead (see para. 21.19, above), especially at the end of fast track trial where it will be the rule rather than the exception.

The detailed assessment which replaces the previous taxation procedure is much as before save in one general cultural element. There is at least now one specific burden on the paying party, which is that they must now positively object to costs, failing which **all** the costs will be assessed as claimed by the receiving party. This is all set out in section II of Part 47.

The practice direction sets out full details for drawing up a bill for detailed assessment. There is a new form of bill with a single column for profit costs and disbursements, no "taxed off" column and no "legal aid only" column. The new form is computer-friendly and a disk copy must be provided free of charge to the other party if a computerised form is used. Note

that the bill should not contain costs which have been previously summarily assessed (see para. 21.19, above).

21.22   What is called the A+B basis for assessing costs is to go, *i.e.*
"care and conduct" are now included in the rates claimed. The
assessment procedure is now based on a straight hourly charge
which includes the uplift for care and conduct. Guideline hourly
rates are published by the Supreme Court Taxing Office.

Thus in the normal way the receiving party will submit a bill
for assessment. As previously the bill will have to be submitted
within three months after the date of the order for payment (Pt.
47, r.47.7). The Rules codify the current practice for sanction
for failure, *i.e.* that interest will not be allowed on the costs for
any period over and above the three months (Pt. 47, r.47.8(3)).
Further, the paying party can force the pace by making application to Court that the receiving party start the assessment,
failing which the costs will be totally disallowed (Pt. 47,
r.47.8(1) and (2)). If the procedural judge orders a detailed
assessment, he may also order an interim payment on account.

Having received the bill the paying party must within 21 days
serve points of dispute of service of the bill (Pt. 47, r.47.9(2)). A
computer-friendly form for points of dispute is set out in the
practice direction. The receiving party may serve a reply within
a further 21 days.

Default costs certificate

21.23 If no points of dispute are served the receiving party can apply
to court for a default costs certificate (Pt. 47, r.47.9(4)).
However, even if points of dispute are served late, this will
prevent any default costs certificate from being issued (Pt. 47,
r.47.9(5)). It will also mean that the paying party may not be
heard on the detailed assessment without the court's permission. Provision is made for the setting aside of a default costs
certificate if a party was not entitled to it (Pt. 47, r.47.12).

Interim costs certificate

21.24 At any time after having filed a request for detailed assessment,
the receiving party may apply to the court for an interim costs
certificate. This entitles the receiving party to receive, effectively
on account, the amount stated on the certificate. The application is made using the Part 23 procedure (see Chapter 15 —
Applications), and will be used to seek payment for those items
in the detailed bill where points in dispute are not raised. The
amount to be granted on an interim certificate should be such as

the applicant would almost certainly collect (*Mars U.K. Ltd v. Teknowledge Ltd (No. 2)*, *The Times*, July 8, 1999, CA).

Subject to having served the bill, the notice of commencement of the assessment procedure and any points of dispute, the receiving party must apply for a hearing within three months of the commencement of the detailed assessment proceedings.

When applying for the hearing, the receiving party must file **21.25** (Pt. 47, PD 4.3):

(a) a copy of the notice of commencement of detailed assessment proceedings;

(b) a copy of the bill of costs;

(c) the document giving the right to detailed assessment (see paragraph 4.5 below);

(d) a copy of the points of dispute, annotated as necessary in order to show which items have been agreed and their value and to show which items remain in dispute and their value;

(e) as many copies of the points of dispute so annotated as there are persons who have served points of dispute;

(f) a copy of any replies served;

(g) a copy of all orders made by the court relating to the costs which are to be assessed;

(h) copies of the fee notes and other written evidence as served on the paying party in accordance with paragraph (2.2) above;

(i) where there is a dispute as to the receiving party's liability to pay costs to the solicitors who acted for the receiving party, any letter or other written information provided by the solicitor to his client explaining how the solicitor's charges are to be calculated;

(j) a statement signed by the receiving party or his solicitor giving the name, address for service, reference and telephone number and fax number, if any, of —

(i) the receiving party;

(ii) the paying party;

(iii) any other person who has served points of dispute or who has given notice to the receiving party under paragraph 2.5 above;

and giving an estimate of the length of time the detailed assessment hearing will take;

> (k) where the application for a detailed assessment hearing is made by a party other than the receiving party, such of the documents set out in this paragraph as are in the possession of that party;
> (l) where the court is to assess the costs of an assisted person—
>
>> (i) the legal aid certificate, any amendment certificates, any authorities and any certificates of discharge or revocation of legal aid;
>> (ii) a certificate, in Form 4(2) of the Schedule of Costs Forms annexed to this Practice Direction;
>> (iii) if the assisted person has a financial interest in the detailed assessment hearing and wishes to attend, the postal address of that person to which the court will send notice of any hearing;
>> (iv) if the rates payable out of the legal aid fund are prescribed rates, a schedule to the bill of costs setting out all the items in the bill which are claimed against other parties calculated at the legal aid prescribed rates with or without any claim for enhancement: (further information as to this schedule is set out in Section IX (Legal aid costs at prescribed rates below));
>> (v) a copy of any default costs certificate in respect of costs claimed in the bill of costs.

21.26   Only items included in the points of dispute can be debated, unless the Court gives permission (Pt. 47, r.47.14(7)). That permission is unlikely to be forthcoming on any regular basis since it may well lead to adjournment.

As previously when the detailed assessment is completed a bill will be lodged with the balance of the taxing fee and a certificate will be forthcoming which can then be enforced. The taxing fee on a detailed assessment where the order for assessment was made on or after April 26, 1999 is £120 in the county court and £160 in the High Court. Although this is lower than the previous fees when one adds back the fact that cost draftsmen's fees can now be included (see para. 21.02, above) the cost of taxation may not be dissimilar from the former position.

Legal Aid

Legal aid taxation will take place much as the previous pro- **21.27**
cedure. The major difference will be the basis of assessment.
The basis will be standard and therefore proportionality will
also come into consideration in relation to legal aid bills.

Practical point:
As with inter partes costs the introduction of proportionality
could have a dramatic effect on payments to solicitors. It does
of course fit in well with the current agenda to try and cut the
legal aid budget.

The costs of the assessment procedure will fall in the usual
way. "Calderbank" offers to settle can be made and may have
the usual costs effect, even where no required payment into
court has been made (Pt. 47, r.47.19). However, such offers
will not be taken into account where the receiving party is
legally-aided, unless the court so orders (Pt. 47, PD 7.6).

Litigants in Person

The appropriate rule is Pt. 48, r.48.6. For the purposes of this **21.28**
rule, a litigant in person includes:

(a) a company or other corporation which is acting without
a legal representative; and

(b) a barrister, solicitor, solicitor's employee or other
authorised litigator (as defined in the Courts and Legal
Services Act 1990) who is acting for himself (r.48.6(6)).

The costs recoverable by a litigant in person must not exceed,
except in the case of a disbursement, two-thirds of the amount
which would have been allowed if the litigant in person had
been represented by a legal representative (Pt. 48, r.48.6(2)).

A litigant in person may recover:

(a) such costs which would have been allowed if the work
had been done or the disbursements made by a legal
representative on the litigant in person's behalf;

(b) the payments reasonably made by him for legal services relating to the conduct of the proceedings; and

(c) the costs of obtaining expert assistance in connection
with assessing the claim for costs. (r.48.6(3)).

Note Pt. 48.6, PD 1.3 as to who may be an expert: **21.29**

1.3 In order to qualify as an expert for the purpose of r.48.6(3)(c) (expert assistance in connection with assessing the claim for costs), the person in question must be a:

(1) barrister,
(2) solicitor,
(3) Fellow of the Institute of Legal Executives,
(4) Fellow of the Association of Law Costs Draftsmen,
(5) law costs draftsman who is a member of the Academy of Experts,
(6) law costs draftsman who is a member of the Expert Witness Institute.

Subject to the two-thirds rule in Pt. 48, r.48.6 (see para. 21.28, above), unless the litigant in person is able to prove financial loss, the amount of costs which shall be allowed to him for any item of work shall relate to the time reasonably spent by him doing the work (Pt. 48, r.48.6(4)). By Pt. 48.6, PD 1.3 the amount which may be allowed to a litigant in person under Pt. 46, r.46.3(5)(b) and Pt. 48, r.48.6(4) is £9.25 per hour. A litigant in person who recovers costs for his own attendance at court cannot, in addition, claim a witness allowance for himself (Pt. 48, r.48.6(5)).

As to evidence of financial loss note:

48.6PD   1.4 Where a litigant in person wishes to prove that he has suffered financial loss he should produce to the court any written evidence he relies on to support that claim, and serve a copy of that evidence on any party against whom he seeks costs at least 24 hours before the hearing at which the question may be decided.

1.5 Where a litigant in person commences detailed assessment proceedings under rule 47.6 he should serve copies of that written evidence with the notice of commencement.

Costs Payable Under a Contract

21.30   48.3—(1) Where the court assesses (whether by the summary or detailed procedure) costs which are payable by the paying party to the receiving party under the terms of a contract, the costs payable under those terms are, unless the contract expressly provides otherwise, to be presumed to be costs which —

(a) have been reasonably incurred; and

(b) are reasonable in amount,
and the court will assess them accordingly.
(2) This rule does not apply where the contract is between
a solicitor and his client.

Where the contract between the parties determines that any
award of costs shall be on the indemnity basis, that would
appear to be enforceable (*Gomba Holdings v. Minories Finance*
[1993] Ch. 171; *Church Commissioners for England v. Ibrahim
& Anor, The Litigation Letter*, February 9, 1996, CA). Indeed,
in mortgage possession matters, should the lender not ask for
assessment, then they are entitled to their costs as of right if the
mortgage document so provides without the court conducting
an assessment (Pt. 48.3, PD 1.2). As for the principles which
apply to costs relating to a mortgage, see Pt. 48.3, PD. 1.3.

Conditional Fee Agreements (Part 48, r.48.9)

Where a client seeks taxation of his solicitor's bill rendered **21.31**
under a conditional fee agreement, either or both of the base
cost and the conditional uplift will be subject to assessment on
the indemnity basis.
The concern that the uplift will be looked at in hindsight by
the court is allayed by the guidance in the Rule and practice
direction and the court may well take into account the risk
factors assessed by the solicitor at the commencement of the
proceedings.
See the Practice Direction to Part 48:

2.15 The factors relevant to assessing the percentage increase
include:

(a) the risk that the circumstances in which the fees or
    expenses would be payable might not occur;
(b) the disadvantages relating to the absence of payment
    on account;
(c) whether the amount which might be payable under
    the conditional fee agreement is limited to a certain
    proportion of any damages recovered by the client;
(d) whether there is a conditional fee agreement between
    the solicitor and counsel;
(e) the solicitor's liability for disbursements.

2.16 When the court is considering the factors to be taken into account, it will have regard to the circumstances **as they reasonably appeared to the solicitor or counsel when the conditional fee agreement was entered into or at the time of any variation of the agreement.**

Under the Access to Justice Act 1999, provision can be made for success fees under conditional fee arrangements to be recoverable from a losing party.

Practical points:

21.32
- Clearly a case that looks complex may become much simpler and the uplift will appear generous in hindsight. Alternatively, a simple case may become more complex or simply unwinnable. It appears that no account will be taken of the swings and roundabouts which is at the very heart of the business of managing conditional fees within the firm.

- The firm must have a spread and make up for the loss on one case by the win on another. Individually assessing cases therefore could be regarded as somewhat unfair.

Small Claims Costs and Fast Track Costs

21.33   Fixed costs for small claims and fast track are regulated by Pt. 44, r.44.9:

(1) Part 27 (Small claims) and [the fast track costs rules] contain special rules about:—

(a) liability for costs;
(b) the amount of costs which the court may award; and
(c) the procedure for assessing costs.

(2) Those special rules do not apply until a claim is allocated to a particular track.

This needs to be read in conjunction with the main Civil Procedure Rules, *i.e.* Parts 27 and 28. The general rule for small claims is that there will be no costs awards save in very particular circumstances (see Chapter 11 — Small Claims).

In fast track cases there are fixed costs for trial. The recoverable trial costs for the advocate will range between £350 and £750 depending on the size of the claim (*i.e.* the resulting judgment), not the length of the trial. The claimant's advocate's costs will depend on the amount recovered, the defendant's on the amount claimed. An attendance of £250 for an accompanying solicitor may be allowed but only in particular circumstances. Note that if a fast track trial has to go over from the one day allotted to it, no refresher fee is payable.

Court Fees

Details of these may be found in the County Court Fees Order 21.34 1999 and Supreme Court Fees order, as appropriate.

As for exemptions, reductions or remissions of fees in the county court note the following parts of the County Court Fees Order:

5.(1) No fee shall be payable under this Order by a party who, at the time when a fee would otherwise become payable:

  (a) is in receipt of any qualifying benefit, and
  (b) is not in receipt of representation under Part IV of the Legal Aid Act 1988 for the purposes of the proceedings

(2) The following are qualifying benefits for the purposes of paragraph (1)(a) above —

  (a) income support;
  (b) family credit and disability working allowance under Part VII of the Social Security Contributions and Benefits Act 1992; and
  (c) income-based jobseeker's allowance under the Jobseekers Act 1995.

(3) Paragraph (1) shall not apply to fee 4.8 (fee payable on a consolidated attachment of earnings order or an administration order).

6. Where it appears to the Lord Chancellor that the payment of any fee prescribed by this Order would, owing to the exceptional circumstances of the particular case, involve undue financial hardship, he may reduce or remit the fee in that case.

7. Where by any convention entered into by Her Majesty with any foreign power it is provided that no fee shall be required to be paid in respect of any proceedings, the fees specified in this Order shall not be taken in respect of those proceedings.

Practical point:
Under the previous Court Fees Orders litigants could only apply for reduction or remission of the fee on grounds of undue hardship once the fee had been paid. The Lord Chancellor has been urged by the Court of Appeal in *Ex parte Scarth*, *The Times*, July 8, 1999, to reconsider this requirement. It is not clear whether para. 6 above changes the position.

Appeals in Assessment Proceedings

21.35 The old system of going back to the same judge to review a taxation comes to an end. Appeals are to the next level of judge. No permission is required to appeal the decision of an authorised court officer (Pt. 47, r.47.24(1)(a)).

Permission is required to appeal a decision of a costs judge or a district judge (Pt. 47, r.47.24(2)) except a decision to impose a sanction on a legal representative for misconduct, or a wasted costs order (Pt. 47, r.47.24(1)(b)). Permission may be given by the judge who made the decision, a High Court judge or a circuit judge (Pt. 47, r.47.24(3)).

The appeals lie (Pt. 47, r.47.22):

From	To	
	High Court	county court
costs officer	costs judge or district judge	district judge
district judge	High Court judge	circuit judge
costs judge	High Court judge	n/a

21.36   Before a party may appeal a detailed assessment, he must first seek reasons for the decision and permission, unless the court orders otherwise (Pt. 47, r.47.21(1)). A receiving party must seek reasons when he files the completed bill (Pt. 47, r.47.23(2)). A paying party must seek reasons within seven days after the end of the detailed assessment proceedings (Pt. 47, r.47.23(3)). Only then will he be allowed to file notice of appeal.

The time for:

- appeal against a court officer's decision; or

- seeking permission to appeal

is 14 days after service of reasons, or seven days after the decision if reasons are not given (Pt. 47, r.47.25(2)).

The time for appealing against the decision of a costs judge or district judge is 14 days after the giving of permission (Pt. 47, r.47.25(3)).

On receipt of the notice of appeal the court will serve notice on the other parties involved together with a date for the hearing (Pt. 47, r.47.25(4)). The appeal court may sit with assessors who may be solicitors or barristers (Pt. 47, r.47.26(3), (4)). For detailed instructions as to the procedure for appeal see Section VIII of the practice direction to Part 47.

Chapter 22

Appeals

22.01 The Access to Justice Act 1999 received Royal Assent on July 27, and the provisions relating to Appeal came into force on September 27, 1999 subject to rules being made to implement them. References to sections are to this Act.

Among the provisions for appeals are the following:

- Permission to appeal to be required at all levels (s.54(1))
- Only one appeal, as a rule (s.55(1)) unless:
  - (a) the appeal would raise an important point of principle or practice, or
  - (b) there is some other compelling reason for the Court of Appeal to hear it.

22.02 Although the Act does not spell out the details, there is likely to be a new appellate ladder:

- Fast track — heard by district judge to circuit judge
- Fast track — heard by circuit judge — to High Court Judge
- Multi-track (interlocutory) — heard by district judge to circuit judge, by Master or circuit judge to High Court Judge, by High Court Judge to Court of Appeal
- Multi-track (final) — to Court of Appeal.

Appeals are not to be a re-hearing and may just be considered on the documents. The appellate court will start with the presumption that the original judge was correct.

It will be up to the trial judge to grant or refuse permission. Permission should only be granted if there is a reasonable prospect of success.

Chapter 23

Enforcement Generally: Execution, Oral Examination

General

As mentioned in Chapter 1 — The New Scheme, enforcement 23.01 was not included in the Civil Justice reforms but is likely to be in the future. For the time being, the previous County Court Rules apply, and they are in Schedule 2 to the Civil Procedure Rules. Therefore reference to "Orders" in this and the following chapters is to Orders within the County Court Rules 1981.

The general order governing enforcement is Ord. 25. Orders 26–32 each deal with a different mode of enforcement. In Ords 25–29, dealt with below, "judgment creditor" means a person who has obtained or is entitled to enforce an order, for money or otherwise, and "debtor" means the person against whom it was given or made (Ord. 25, r.1).

Orders 25 to 32 do not apply to enforcement against the Crown (Ord. 42, r.13). For the purpose of obtaining satisfaction of a judgment against the Crown, a certificate in N293, duly adapted, is issued by the court under section 25 of the Crown Proceedings Act 1947.

A county court judgment or order for the payment of a sum 23.02 in excess of £2,000 may be transferred to the High Court for enforcement (see para. 23.06, below), but in general the claimant can choose whether to enforce his court judgment in the county court or the High Court. However, if he seeks to enforce wholly or partly by execution against goods then article 8 of the High Court and County Court Jurisdiction Order 1991 (S.I. No. 724) as amended by the 1993 and 1995 Amendment Orders provides that:

(a) the High Court has exclusive enforcement jurisdiction where the sum which it is sought to enforce under a county court judgment is £5,000 or more and the judgment did not arise out of an agreement regulated under the Consumer Credit Act 1974; and

(b) the county court has exclusive enforcement jurisdiction over a county court judgment where (a) the sum is less than £1,000 or (b) the judgment arose out of a regulated Consumer Credit Act agreement irrespective of the amount involved and the method of enforcement chosen.

Where a case is required to be transferred from one county court to another for enforcement, the order for transfer may now be made by a court officer (Ord. 25, r.2).

Enforcement of High Court Judgments and Orders

23.03 High Court judgments and orders, and also judgments, orders, decrees and awards of other courts or awards of an arbitrator which are enforceable as if they were judgments of the High Court, may be enforced in the appropriate county court, usually that in whose district the debtor resides or carries on business. A transfer of the proceedings under section 40 of the 1984 Act is not required for enforcement by charging order, attachment of earnings or judgment summons but in other cases, the proceedings must first be transferred under section 40 of the 1984 Act (notes to Ord. 25). Order 25, r.1(a)–(c) applies.

The judgment creditor shall file in the appropriate court (with such documents as are required for enforcing a judgment or order of a county court, that is, a request for enforcement) the following documents:

(1) An office copy of the judgment or order or, in the case of a judgment, order, decree or award of a court other than the High Court or an arbitrator such evidence of the judgment, order, decree or award and of its enforceability as a judgment of the High Court, as the district judge may require.

(2) An affidavit (Form N321), verifying the amount due under the judgment or order.

(3) Where a writ of execution has been issued to enforce it, a copy of the sheriff's return to the writ.

There is no fee on the transfer itself although the appropriate county court fee is payable on any accompanied request for enforcement. Unlike tribunal awards (see below) no order is made by the county court. Once the application has been checked and approved it will be passed to the appropriate section to deal with any requested form of enforcement.

Enforcement of Awards of Tribunals

Order 25, r.12, as amended by rr.9, 10 and 11 of the County 23.04
Court (Amendment No. 3) Rules 1996, applies. Where, by any Act or statutory instrument other than the County Court Rules, a sum of money may be recoverable as if it were payable under an order of the county court, enforcement in the county court may be ordered (N322A).

The requirements are:

(1) An application in Form N322A which contains a certificate confirming the amount remaining due.

(2) The award, order or agreement (or duplicate thereof).

(3) Fee (see Table of Fees).

Unless otherwise provided, the application is filed in the court for the district in which the person by whom the sum is payable resides or carries on business.

The application is made without notice by filing the documents with fee, and the application is dealt with by a court officer. The award may be enforced thereafter as if it were a county court judgment.

Practical point:

In the application it would be prudent for the applicant to 23.05
confirm that the respondent has not exercised any right of appeal in respect of the award made, even though there is no provision for this on the form.

Any application to set aside the award must be made to the tribunal which made the award and not to the county court which is merely involved in enforcing the award.

Fixed costs may be claimed where solicitors are acting for the applicant. The costs that apply are those for issue of a default summons (Ord. 38, r.18, App. B). The order should provide for payment within 14 days unless the claimant specifies a particular period. Orders made under this rule are not entered in the Register of County Court Judgments.

Enforcement of County Court Judgments in the High Court

23.06   A judgment or order of a county court, other than for the payment of a sum of money in proceedings arising out of an agreement regulated by the Consumer Credit Act 1974 (see below), for the payment of a sum of money which it is sought to enforce wholly or partially by execution against goods, can be enforced only in the High Court where the sum which it is sought to enforce is £5,000 or more and only in a county court where the sum involved is less than £1,000 (article 8(1) of the High Court and County Courts Jurisdiction Order 1991 as amended by article 3, High Court and County Court Courts Jurisdiction (Amendment) Order 1996 (S.I. 1996 No. 3141), as from January 1, 1997). In any other case such a judgment or order may be enforced in either court. A relevant judgment under the Consumer Credit Act 1974 can only be enforced in a county court (article 8(1A)).

The procedure is laid down by Ord. 22, r.8(1) as amended by rr.6 and 7 of the County Court (Amendment No. 3) Rules 1994.

23.07   The practice requires that a certificate (N293) should be lodged with the county court stating that it is "for the purpose of enforcing the judgment (or order, if such be the case) in the High Court", and, if appropriate, that the intended form of enforcement is by execution against goods (fi. fa.) or, if enforcement by some other method, that an application has been made for an order under section 42 of the 1984 Act for transfer to the High Court and a copy of the application (or order) is attached to the request for a certificate. The certificate of judgment, in Form N293, may be prepared by the claimant or his solicitors. It may be signed by the court manager or any other officer of the court acting on his behalf (Ord. 22, r.8(3)). If the enforcement is intended to be by way of execution against goods then the order for transfer can be made by a court officer on granting the certificate of judgment (r.8(1)(A)). In all other cases confirmation that an application has been made for an order under section 42 together with a copy of the application will be necessary. The signed and sealed certificate of judgment, with copy, is then presented to the action department on personal attendance. The certificate is treated for enforcement purposes as a High Court judgment.

Practical point:

23.08   The advantage of enforcing in the High Court is that the High Court allows interest on the judgment debt (from the date of issue of the certificate allowing it to be transferred to the High

Court), irrespective of the amount of the judgment. There is no interest on a county court judgment debt under £5,000. Also the initial fees may be less.

Enforcement of Judgments of English and Welsh County Courts Inside and Outside the United Kingdom

Order 35 sets out the procedure for obtaining certificates of **23.09** judgments of county courts (excepting orders for maintenance) in England and Wales for enforcement, firstly, outside the United Kingdom (under the Foreign Judgments (Reciprocal Enforcement) Act 1933 as amended by the Civil Jurisdiction and Judgments Act 1982), and, secondly, in other parts of the United Kingdom (under the said 1982 Act). Note the difference in terminology under the two Acts. *The County Court Practice* sets out the relevant sections of the Act in notes under Ord. 35 and the procedure to be followed.

The form of certificate for use outside the United Kingdom is modified, see Form 110 in Appendix A to the Rules of the Supreme Court (Vol. 2 of *The Supreme Court Practice*). For use in other parts of the United Kingdom modified Forms 111 and 112 are used. A certificate of judgment in Form N293 will not be acceptable in Scotland.

Solicitor's costs for obtaining certificates are added to the balance due under Costs, Appendix B, Part III, item 9 (Ord. 35, r.5(3)(d)).

Note: **23.10**

(1) Maintenance orders of courts outside England and Wales are registered in magistrates' courts.

(2) Other judgments of courts outside England and Wales are registered in the High Court (section 18 and Sched. 6, para. 5 of the 1982 Act). After registration they may, it seems, be enforced in the county court as are High Court judgments.

In relation to enforcing the judgment in Scotland, the certificate must be lodged in the Register of Judgments of the Books of Council and Session within six months of the date of issue for which a fee is payable (tel: 0131 659 6111, ext. 3630 for further information). The Keeper of the Registers will then supply an extract of the registered certificate and an authority to enforce the judgment (warrant for execution). Once these are received a Sheriff Officer can be instructed to attempt to recover the debt (tel: 0141 420 3926 for futher information). In

Scotland the claimant is called "the pursuer" and the defendant is called "the defender".

Enforcement of County Court Maintenance Orders in Other Courts

23.11 This subject is treated at length in the latest editions of *Rayden and Jackson on Divorce and Family Matters* (Butterworths, 17th ed., 1997) and *The Family Court Practice* (Jordans, 1999) to which reference should be made.

General Limitations on the Issue of Warrants of Execution, Delivery and Possession

23.12 Permission is required where a change has occurred in the persons entitled to enforce or to those bearing liability under the order by death or otherwise. This applies where assets come after judgment into the hands of executors or administrators, or are in the hands of a receiver appointed by a court, or after the expiration of six years from the date of the judgment or order. Application for permission is usually made without notice and must be by affidavit or witness statement (Ord. 26, rr.5, 16(5) and 17(6)).

Such a warrant is valid for 12 months from the date of issue only, but may be renewed for up to 12 months on a "without notice" application by letter in the first instance (Ord. 26, rr.6, 16 and 17). An application to renew the warrant after it has expired may be allowed by the court (Ord. 26, r.6(1)). A note of the renewal is endorsed on the warrant which then retains its priority (Ord. 26, r.6(2)).

Note the exclusive jurisdiction of the county court in relation to execution against goods arising out of a money judgment which arose out of a regulated agreement under the Consumer Credit Act 1974.

Execution Against Goods

23.13 The powers and duties of the court in relation to execution against goods are set out fully in ss.85–104 of the 1984 Act.

The requirements for issue of a warrant of execution are:

    (a) request (N323) certifying the amount of money remaining due under the judgment or order; if there was an instalment order, that the whole or part of an instalment is unpaid, and the amount for which the warrant issues (Ord. 26, r.1(1));

(b) plaint note or originating process (Ord. 25, r.5);

(c) fee; see Table of Fees;

(d) addressed envelope, if by post.

In addition, if judgment or order of the High Court (or enforceable as such) see above.

When the execution is on a judgment or order of the High 23.14
Court, the warrant is issued in the court for the district in which the execution is to be levied. Notice of issue is sent by the court to the court officer of the High Court (Ord. 26, r.2(3)).

Solicitor's costs are added to the warrant (see Costs, Appendix B).

On receiving the request (whether by post or at the counter) the district judge must endorse it with the hour, day, month and year (section 85(3) of the 1984 Act. See also sections 99(3) and 103(3)), although this administrative act is usually performed by an officer of the court.

If, after issue, the district judge of the court in whose district execution takes place has reason to believe that the debtor is a farmer, he may require to be furnished with an official certificate of the result of a search of the Land Registry dated not more than three days beforehand pursuant to the Agricultural Credits Act 1928. The fee paid for the search is added to the warrant (Ord. 26, r.3).

A warrant (N42(C)) may be issued for the whole of the 23.15
unpaid balance of a money judgment and costs, when a judgment debtor can be said to be in default as to any part, though when the order is for payment by instalments it may instead be issued for part of the balance only, provided it is for an amount being not less than £50, the amount of one monthly instalment, or the amount of four weekly instalments, whichever is the greater. No warrant may be issued unless at the time when it is issued the whole or part of an instalment which has already become due remains unpaid and any earlier warrant has expired or been satisfied or abandoned (Ord. 26, r.1(2), (3)). A claimant with a judgment for £5,000 or more will be able to issue a part warrant in a county court where an instalment order and the warrant will be for under £5,000.

The judgment creditor indicates on the request the amount for which he requests a "part" warrant to issue.

Where a warrant is issued the court officer shall, unless the 23.16
district judge responsible for executing the warrant orders otherwise, send Form N326 to the debtor, allowing him seven days in which to satisfy the warrant (Ord. 26, r.1(4)). Any

payment made by a judgment debtor after issue of the warrant must be to the court unless the warrant is suspended.

Where judgment is given for a sum payable forthwith or within a certain period and costs to be taxed, the creditor may issue a warrant for the judgment only as soon as it remains unpaid and a further warrant for the costs if unpaid, 14 days after taxation (Ord. 26, r.1(5)).

The court marks the number of the warrant and the fee on the plaint note or originating process.

If the warrant is to issue against only one of two or more judgment debtors, this must be shown clearly on the request.

23.17   Where the name or address of a party differs from the name as it appeared in the judgment, and the judgment creditor satisfies the court officer that the amended name or address is applicable to the person as stated in the judgment, both names must be inserted in the warrant as follows: "CD of (name and address as given in the request) suing (or sued) as AD of (name and address in the judgment or order)" (Ord. 25, r.6).

If the debtor's name is clearly that of the original debtor, such as when the full names are given instead of initials, or additional initials are given, the request is accepted as sufficient. If there is any doubt, an accompanying letter of explanation should be written which can be referred to the district judge personally. The district judge may always require an application to be made on notice to amend the debtor's name.

Permission to issue is required where there is in force an attachment of earnings order (Attachment of Earnings Act 1971, s.8(2)(b)). Permission of the circuit judge is sometimes required where a suspended committal order has been made under a judgment summons (Ord. 28, r.7(3)).

Execution (and Enforcing a Judgment) Against a Firm

23.18   Order 25, r.9 applies where a judgment or order is against a firm (as such), it may be enforced against:

(1) any property of the firm.

(2) any person who has admitted in the action or matter that he was a partner when the cause of action arose, or who has been adjudged to be liable as a partner.

(3) any person who was individually served with the summons as a partner:

(a) if the action is a default action and judgment was entered in default of defence or on admission; or

    (b) if there was a pre-trial review (or preliminary arbitration appointment) and judgment was then entered, the defendant having entered a defence but having failed to attend; or

    (c) if there was a trial and the person so served failed to appear at the trial.

Execution may be issued against a partner who was out of England and Wales when the originating process was issued, provided that he was served with the process as a partner in England or Wales, or under Ord. 8, r.2 (Ord. 25, r.9(2)).

Where a judgment creditor wishes to issue against a partner in any of the above circumstances, the court official should refer to the court file to ensure that execution may issue under (a), (b) or (c) of the listed headings.

If the party who has obtained the judgment or order claims to be entitled to issue execution against any other person as a partner, he may apply to the district judge for permission to do so. The application must be served as if a fixed date summons under Part 8 (see Chapter 5) not less than three days before the hearing. If the alleged partner does not dispute his liability, permission to enforce may be given subject to CCR, Ord. 25, r.9(2). If he disputes liability, directions as to the trial of the issue are given (Ord. 25, r.9(3), (4)). **23.19**

The requirements are:

    (a) application and copy for service;

    (b) fee (see Table of Fees).

In the case of enforcement of a High Court judgment (or an order or arbitration award enforceable as such) against a firm Ord. 25, r.9 does not apply, but the procedure is governed by RSC, Ord. 81, r.5; CCR, Ord. 25, r.9(5).

Permission is required for enforcing a judgment between a firm and its members (Ord. 25, r.10).

Levy

If the place of levy is not within the district of the court, the warrant is sent to the court for the district in which levy is to be made. That court, known as the "foreign" court, adds its local number to the warrant. The local number appears in notices sent by the "foreign" court. When a warrant is sent to a "foreign" court, its priority is taken from the time of its receipt there, and not from the time of making an application for its **23.20** issue at the "home" court (section 103(2) of the 1984 Act), and the "foreign" district judge must endorse the warrant with the hour, day, month and year of receipt (section 103(3)). This is done administratively by the court staff.

If a warrant has not been executed within one month from the date of issue or receipt, the court officer sends notice (N317) at the end of each month to the judgment creditor, and also the "home" court if the warrant has been received from another court, giving the reason (Ord. 25, r.7(2)). According to Ord. 25, r.7(3), the responsibility for responding to any query from the judgment creditor in relation to the warrant lies with the district judge, although the reality is that this is likely to be delegated to a court officer as it would appear to be a purely administrative function.

23.21   When the warrant has been sent to another court for levy any enquiry should be made there. If the enquiry is made by letter, the number of the warrant should be quoted as well as the plaint number. The local warrant number should also be quoted, if known; otherwise an indication should be given as to when it was sent to that other court.

By internal directive within the Court Service Agency every foreign warrant is returned to the home court when:

(1) The full amount for which the warrant issued has been paid (where the payment was made into court the warrant is not returned until the money has been paid out to the creditor).

(2) The warrant is withdrawn or suspended for more than 14 days at the request of the creditor.

(3) The warrant is suspended or stayed for more than 14 days by order of the court.

(4) The bailiff has made a final return. If so the warrant should be filed and a notice of non-execution sent to the creditor then the warrant should be returned to the home court.

Foreign warrants are to be retained by the court which suspended the warrant until the time for reconsideration has passed (*i.e.* 16 days) before being returned to the home court.

23.22   Note:

(1) If a sale of the goods levied has taken place the warrant may either be retained until it is audited or returned to

the home court, in which case a photocopy is kept at the foreign court for audit purposes.

(2) Warrants are handed to the bailiff, an officer of the county court, for execution. When the bailiff levies, he hands to the execution debtor, or leaves at the place of levy, a notice of levy on N42(C) (Ord. 26, r.7).

(3) A bailiff may not force his way into a judgment debtor's house in order to gain entry to levy, such as by pushing a front door against the resistance of the debtor (*Vaughan v. McKenzie* [1968] 1 All E.R. 1154), but once the goods have been levied upon, forcible entry may be effected.

If the goods are saleable, the bailiff usually takes "walking possession", the judgment debtor signing an agreement on N42(C) to this effect. The form need not be signed by the judgment debtor personally (*National Commercial Bank of Scotland Ltd v. Arcam Demolition & Construction Ltd* [1966] 3 All E.R. 113) but it is preferable that he should do so. For a description of "walking possession", see *Lloyds & Scottish Finance Ltd v. Modern Cars & Caravans (Kingston) Ltd* [1964] 2 All E.R. 732. For effect of "walking possession" as regards third persons, see *Abingdon RDC v. O'Gorman* [1968] 3 All E.R. 79. Where the bailiffs already have walking possession of goods, they can break into premises to retrieve those goods even if the premises have not been deliberately locked against them (*McLeod v. Butterwick* [1996] 1 W.L.R. 995, ChD).

No possession fee is payable in the case of "walking posses- 23.23 sion". Appraisement is usually made after removal by the auctioneer who acts as broker for the court.

When the goods are removed, the bailiff gives or posts to the executioner debtor an inventory (Ord. 26, r.12(1)). Notice of sale must be given to the debtor not less than four days before the time fixed for the sale see above.

As to fees (and expenses), see the Table of Fees.

If a sale does not realise sufficient funds to cover the costs of levy etc, the execution creditor may be required to pay the deficiency (County Court Fees Order 1982, art. 3(3)).

Warrants of execution may be issued concurrently for execution in one or more districts, but the costs of more than one warrant may not be allowed against the execution debtor except by order of the court (Ord. 27, r.4).

Items exempt from levy

Basically, what is exempt is "necessary items". These will 23.24 include such tools, books, vehicles and other items of equipment as are necessary to the debtor for use personally in his or her job or business and such clothing, bedding, furniture, household equipment and provisions as are necessary for satisfying the basic domestic needs of the debtor and his or her family (section 89 of the 1984 Act).

The definition is worded in broad terms without any monetary limit, and allows bailiffs to exercise their discretion in ensuring a proper balance between the interests of the debtor and his family, and those of the claimant. Guidance has been given to bailiffs to help with this process.

If furniture, motor vehicles or any other goods are alleged to be subject to a hire-purchase agreement, the bailiff asks for such evidence as there may be, *e.g.* the hire-purchase agreement. If a claim is made to the goods by some other person, such as a wife, a claim in writing (see para. 23.30, below) must be given to the bailiff, unless it is obvious that the goods do not in fact belong to the debtor.

As to caravans and houseboats, there appears to be no authoritative decision to say whether they may be seized under a warrant of execution while used as a dwelling or intermittently as a dwelling, or when they are fixed to the land.

23.25 In the event of a dispute between the defendant and the bailiff in applying these definitions, the matter will be referred in the first instance to the bailiff manager. A levy should be made if at all possible.

If the bailiff manager is unable to resolve the dispute he consults with the court manager who decides whether the district judge's directions should be sought. If a district judge or bailiff refused to levy on such, a complaint might be made by way of summons (N366) to the circuit judge under section 124 of the 1984 Act and Ord. 34, r.1 when an order might be made for the trial of the issue.

If payment is likely to be made, the bailiff may allow a reasonable time for payment and no further fees are payable.

Costs of Warrants

23.26 Money paid into court between the issue of a warrant of execution and its final return is usually treated as payment under the warrant.

If costs are not recovered under execution, they may be included in a subsequent warrant of execution.

Section 15 of the Courts and Legal Services Act 1990 allows abortive warrant costs to be added to the debt where attachment of earnings, judgment summons and other enforcement proceedings are issued. This means that abortive warrant costs can be added to the judgment debt where attachment of earnings, judgment summons, etc. proceedings are issued. Abortive warrant costs cannot, however, be added to the total debt where oral examination proceedings are issued as these are not a form of enforcement.

Application to Suspend Warrant by Judgment Debtor

Unopposed applications may be determined without a hearing. 23.27

Payment

If the warrant has been sent to another court for execution, that 23.28 court remits the money to the creditor and gives notice to the home court (Ord. 25, r.7(4)).

Where "under an execution (in respect of a judgment) for a sum exceeding £500" (see below) goods are sold or money is paid in order to avoid a sale, the money, after deducting costs of executing the warrant, is retained by the court which executed the warrant for a period of 14 days pursuant to sections 183, 184 and 346 of the Insolvency Act 1986 (see section 98 of the 1984 Act). Notice (N330) is sent to the execution creditor and to the home court, if any (Ord. 26, r.8(1)).

Money will be remitted automatically (with notice in N318) after the expiration of the statutory period from a "foreign" court to the home court (Ord. 25, r.7(4)).

The amount of £500 referred to above is the amount not just of the judgment but of the total sum endorsed on the warrant (including the warrant fee, the costs allowed to the solicitor for issue and the fee for the certificate if required as to a farmer (*Re Bullen* (1872) Ch. App. 732 and notes under section 98 of the 1984 Act in the *The County Court Practice*)).

The home court is to notify the foreign court of any payment made before the final return on the warrant (Ord. 26, r.14).

Effectiveness

Where the debt is £2,000 or more it may well be worth 23.29 considering transferring the case to the High Court for enforcement. Apart from this, many warrants are returned for "insufficient goods" or are countered by applications to suspend or even set aside the judgment. Sometimes they result in the debtor actually paying up the debt. The number of occasions when goods are actually seized and sold is small in comparison with the number of warrants issued. Applying for a warrant for part only of a judgment debt may be more effective where it is felt that the debtor may not have enough goods to cover the whole of the amount outstanding.

Claims to Goods Taken in Execution

23.30 Order 33 applies. A claim in writing to the goods levied upon must be given to the bailiff or filed in the court of the district in which the goods were seized. The claim must state the grounds relied upon, and the claimant's name and address for service. Notice of the claim is then sent to the execution creditor (N358) and (except where the claim is to the proceeds or value of the goods) a notice to the claimant requiring him to give security (N359) (Ord. 33, r.1).

Within four days after receiving the notice, the execution creditor must give notice to the court that he admits or disputes the claim, or requests the bailiffs to withdraw from possession. If he admits or requests withdrawal in time, he will not be liable to the court for fees or expenses incurred after the court receives the notice (Ord. 33, r.2). Walking possession having been taken and the goods not being removed until the question of admitting the claim is settled, there are usually no further costs. Sometimes, however, it is advisable to inquire from the court whether any costs have already been incurred if a claim is to be admitted.

For claims by a landlord for rent, procedure is set out in section 102 of the 1984 Act. A landlord must give his notice of claim in the same manner as other claimants (Ord. 33, r.1).

Interpleader Proceedings Under Execution

23.31 If the execution creditor disputes the claim or does not give notice admitting the claim or requesting the court to withdraw from possession within the four days, the court shall issue interpleader proceedings unless the claim is withdrawn. An interpleader summons to the execution creditor (N88) and claimant (N88(1)) is prepared and served on them as if a fixed date summons, not less than 14 days before the return day (Ord. 33, r.4).

The summons should be served on the judgment creditor's solicitors if he is still on the record (Ord. 50, r.5(1)). Any money in court is retained pending the hearing. Thereafter the district judge directs how the money is to be disposed of, and if payment is due to the judgment creditor Ord. 25, r.7(4) then applies (Ord. 25, r.7(5)). The hearing takes place before the circuit judge on the day fixed.

Notice of a claim for damages by any party must be given to the court and the party against whom the claim is made within eight days after service of the interpleader summons on him (Ord. 33, r.5).

Warrants of Delivery

Order 26, r.16, applies.   23.32

There are two forms of warrant of delivery:

(1) Warrant of specific delivery where the person against whom the judgment or order was made is not given the alternative of paying the value of the goods. (The form is N46.)

(2) Warrant of delivery to recover the goods or their value where the option is given of paying their value (N48).

When a warrant of delivery is issued, the judgment creditor may have execution for any sum of money payable under the judgment or order (including costs) by the warrant of delivery or by a separate warrant (Ord. 26, r.16(4)). A judgment or order for specific delivery of goods may be enforced by committal (Ord. 26, r.18).

The requirements are as for a warrant of execution: see para. 23.13, above. For fee payable, see Table of Fees. The maximum fee is charged unless the value is stated in the judgment or request when the fee is calculated on that value. Where money is claimed in addition, that sum is added to the stated value to calculate the fee.

Solicitor's costs (see Table of Fixed Costs — Appendix 12) 23.33 are added to the warrant if the value of the goods plus the sum of money, if any, for which the warrant issues, exceeds 25. Order 26, rr.1–15 (which apply to warrants of execution against goods) also apply to warrants of delivery, so far as applicable (Ord. 26, r.16(5)).

The goods, the subject of the warrant, are normally delivered to the claimant or his agent at the address where the goods are. The claimant has to supply labour and transport for their removal. The method of giving an appointment varies between courts and enquiry should be made on issue as to how an appointment will be given. A preliminary visit is usually made by the bailiff before an appointment is made.

Where judgment is given for "return or value" and the goods are returned or a warrant to recover goods or value issues, money paid into court is appropriated first to any sum of money or costs awarded (Ord. 26, r.16(4A)).

Oral Examination of Debtor as to Means Judgment for Payment of Money

23.34   A judgment creditor in respect of a county court judgment or order may apply without notice for an order that the debtor (or, if a corporation, any officer thereof) be orally examined as to means and produce any books or documents relevant thereto (Ord. 25, r.3(1)). This also applies to the enforcement of an award by a tribunal (Ord. 25, r.3(1)(1A) as amended by the County Court (Amendment No. 3) Rules 1995). The examination may be ordered to take place before an officer of the court.

Where, in the case of an examination as to means, the person to be examined does not reside or carry on business within the district of the court, the judgment creditor must first apply without notice under Ord. 25, r.2 to transfer the proceedings to the court for the district in which he resides or carries on business. The application is made by letter stating the purpose of the transfer.

The requirements for application are:

(a) application (N316);

(b) plaint note or originating process;

(c) fees (see Table of Fees) and travelling expenses (optional);

(d) request for postal service if needed; and

(e) addressed envelope, if by post.

The court issues the order (N37, or N38 if against an officer of a defendant company).

23.35   Before the district judge makes an order for oral examination as to means he may give the debtor an opportunity to file a statement or affidavit as to means (Ord. 25, r.3(7)).

A copy of any statement or affidavit filed is to be sent by the court office to the creditor, who may accept it in the place of an examination.

The order for oral examination is served as if it were a Part 7 general claim (see Chapter 6) together with conduct money, that is, travelling expenses, if desired. An undertaking from the creditor's solicitor to a judgment debtor to pay the reasonable costs of his attending an oral examination made in sufficient time and on sufficient terms is an adequate alternative to cash or a cheque (*Union Bank of Finland v. Lelakis* (1996) N.L.D., June 11, QBD). If service is by solicitor, affidavit or witness statement proving service must be filed. When the order is not served, a new day will be fixed without fee. Rules as to substituted service apply.

For the examination, the court officer uses a standard questionnaire a copy of which can be obtained by the creditor. Creditors supplying their own questionnaires but not attending at the examination may find that their questionnaires are not used (see Effectiveness, para. 23.37, below).

If the person required to do so does not attend, the court may **23.36** fix a further date and issue an order (N39) containing notices that if he fails to do so, he may be committed to prison for contempt and that any payments shall thereafter be paid into court and not to the creditor. The order states, at the foot thereof, the debtor's right to require, direct from the judgment creditor, his travelling expenses, the rule itself, Ord. 25, r.3 (5A), stating "unless paid at the time of the service of the order", though the notice to the debtor is not explicit on this, and omits it. A certificate is to be filed not more than four days before the adjourned hearing that conduct money has been paid, or alternatively that none has been requested (Ord. 25, r.3(5A) and (5B).

A committal order (N40) may be made on failure to attend after service of the "N39", but the restriction on committal is that the debtor shall not be committed for failure to attend the adjourned hearing unless where he has made a request therefor, he has in fact been paid conduct money (Ord. 25, r.3(5)(C)). In practice, in most cases conduct money or travelling expenses will have been paid or tendered when the original order was served.

Where a judgment debtor attends for oral examination but refuses to co-operate by, for example, refusing to answer any questions, the court officer may refer them to the judge to consider committal for contempt.

Effectiveness

Although the threat of committal gives teeth to this method of **23.37** enforcement, the difficulty lies with the delay between the issue of the order and the eventual examination of a reluctant debtor. However, once an examination has taken place it may yield valuable information about the debtor to enable further enforcement proceedings to be taken such as garnishee, charging order or attachment of earnings, which are dealt with later in this book. Its value is much enhanced by the creditor attending by a well-instructed advocate where this is worthwhile.

Examination of Debtor Under Judgment not for Money

23.38 Order 25, r.4 states, "where any difficulty arises in . . . the enforcement of the judgment or order "the court may order" "the debtor" to attend to be examined on such questions as may be specified in the order" (Ord. 25, r.4). For "debtor" see the definition in Ord. 25, r.1.

High Court Ordering Examination in County Court

23.39 When an order for oral examination is made in the High Court, the examination may be ordered to take place before a district judge or nominated officer of a county court (RSC, Ord. 48, r.1(1)). The costs are in the discretion of the district judge in whose court the examination takes place.

Enforcement of such an order is undertaken by the High Court only.

Costs on Oral Examinations

23.40 Costs are at the discretion of the district judge. The costs may be added to the judgment, or a separate order may be made for them.

Costs allowable are court fees, travelling expenses (if paid), and solicitor's costs (see Table of Costs — Appendix 12).

Execution of Conveyance, Contract, or Other Document

23.41 If the person ordered to execute a document fails to do so, the district judge may execute it on his behalf: section 39 of the Supreme Court Act 1981, section 38 of the County Courts Act 1984 and CCR, Ord. 50, r.2.

Chapter 24

Other Methods of Enforcement

Garnishee Proceedings

Order 30 of the County Court Rules 1981 applies. Any person **24.01** who has obtained a judgment or order in a county court for the payment of money may start proceedings to obtain a payment to him of the amount of any debt owing or accruing to the judgment debtor from any other person (called the "garnishee") in England or Wales, or so much thereof as may be sufficient to satisfy the judgment or order and the costs of the garnishee proceedings (Ord. 30, r.1(1)).

The judgment or order must be for at least £50 for a garnishee order to be made (Ord. 30, r.1(1) as amended by The County Court (Amendment No. 3) Rules 1996 (S.I. 1996 No. 3218)).

A tribunal award may be so enforced, but not a High Court judgment (Ord. 30, r.1(1)), unless the proceedings are transferred (Ord. 25, rr 11, 12).

Where the debt is due from a partnership carrying on **24.02** business in England or Wales, the debt may be attached even though one or more of the partners resides outside England or Wales (Ord. 30, r.14).

Moneys in current and deposit bank accounts with any "clearing" bank, in National Savings Bank accounts and in building society accounts may be attached. No garnishee order may reduce the balance in a building society or credit union account below £1 (Ord. 30, r.1(5)). Types of debt which have been held to be not attachable are a legacy in the hands of an executor unless there has been an account from the executors which would constitute the legacy as a legal debt, money paid into court in an administration action, money in court under a judgment, a dividend distributable among creditors in the hands of an Official Receiver, a debt due to a judgment debtor and another party, money which the judgment debtor and his wife have in a joint banking account (even though he has authority to draw), officer's pay and pension, money in a wife's banking account which is housekeeping money (possibly), money held by a trustee under a strict settlement.

24.03 Trying to garnishee a solicitor's client account may be problematical because the order has the effect of freezing the whole account (see below) and it may not be possible to identify funds in relation to a particular client unless that client has a separate designated account. If in doubt, reference should be made to *The County Court Practice*, Ord. 30 and the notes to Ord. 30, rr.1 and 2 and to *The Supreme Court Practice 1999* (Sweet & Maxwell), RSC, Ord. 49, r.1 and notes thereunder.

Where money in court is due to a judgment debtor the judgment creditor may not take garnishee proceedings in respect thereof, but may apply to the district judge on notice for an order that the money, or so much thereof as may be necessary to satisfy the judgment debt and costs, may be paid to him (Ord. 30, r.12(1)).

On the filing of the application the district judge must retain the money in court pending the hearing of the application (Ord. 30, rr.12(2), 15).

Procedure

24.04 Application is made without notice by filing an affidavit in N349 or by witness statement giving the information required (Ord. 30, r.2).

Practical points:

- A creditor's bank manager can discover from a debtor's bank manager if the debtor is creditworthy, *i.e.* has some money in a current account. Such an enquiry may avoid wasting fees on a pointless application. The actual figure in the account will, of course, not be disclosed.

- A common error made by deponents to the affidavit or witness statement is to forget to state what grounds they have for believing that the proposed garnishee is holding funds for the debtor.

24.05 The requirements are:

(1) The plaint note or originating process must be produced.

(2) Fees (see Table of Fees).

(3) Addressed envelope if application by post.

The order *nisi* in N84 is drawn by the court; a return day is fixed before the district judge. A copy is served (a) on the garnishee in the same manner as a fixed date summons (see Ord. 7, r.10) at least 15 days before the return day and (b) on the judgment debtor at least seven days after service on the garnishee and at least seven days before the return day, pursuant to Ord. 7, r.1 (Ord. 30, r.3).

When served on the garnishee, the order *nisi* binds in his hands so much of the debts owing or accruing from him to the judgment debtor as will satisfy the debt due and the costs entered on the order *nisi* (Ord. 30, r.3(2)), but a "deposit-taking institution" may deduct £55 for administrative expenses before paying the judgment creditor (Attachment of Debts (Expenses) Order 1996) and sections 108 and 109 of the 1984 Act (as amended by section 55(2) of the Administration of Justice Act 1985). This is so even if it results in a reduction (or extinction) of the payment. *Rogers v. Whiteley* [1892] A.C. 118, states that the effect of a garnishee order nisi served on a banker was to bind all of the monies belonging to the debtor in the hands of the banker, who was not then liable for dishonouring cheques. This is despite what Ord. 30, r.3(2) above says. However, the usual practice is for banks to forward to the court such part of the account that amounts to the sum sought and to continue to operate the rest of the account normally.

Where a deposit-taking institution alleges it does not hold **24.06** any money to the credit of the judgment debtor's account, it should give notice to the court and to the judgment creditor. The proceedings against the garnishee are then stayed subject to Ord. 30, r.8, see below (Ord. 30, r.5), the usual procedure then being to discharge the *nisi*.

If there is a dispute, Ord. 30, rr.8, 9 apply and the court gives direction as to how the dispute may be determined. If the garnishee resides outside the district of the court and disputes the claim, he may apply *ex parte* for transfer under Ord. 30, r.10. Any costs allowed to the judgment creditor which are not ordered to be paid by the garnishee personally shall, unless otherwise ordered, be retained by the judgment creditor out of the money recovered in priority to the amount due under the judgment or order (Ord. 30, r.13).

For costs of hearing, see Table of Costs, Appendix 12. The costs may be ordered to be assessed.

If the garnishee (or judgment debtor) is bankrupted before the money is paid out of court, the trustee in bankruptcy can claim it (*George v. Thompson's Trustee* [1949] 1 All E.R. 554).

Effectiveness

24.07 Although useful, this procedure cannot be used as a "fishing expedition". To get the order *nisi* the judgment creditor has to convince the court that they know of an account being held on behalf of the debtor. However, very often it turns out that the account has no funds or is overdrawn. However, as can be seen above, the service of an order *nisi* on a bank can have a devastating effect as it can freeze the whole account if it is in credit.

Charging Orders

24.08 The Charging Orders Act 1979 enables the payment of judgment debts to be secured by a charge on land, the debtor's beneficial interest under a trust (where the debtor has an interest in land held upon trust for sale (*National Westminster Bank Ltd v. Stockman* [1981] 1 W.L.R. 67; [1981] 1 All E.R. 800)), on securities which consist of government stock, on other stock not that of a building society, on unit trusts, and on funds in court. The precise descriptions of stock given by the section should be referred to if in doubt.

Charging orders may be made under section 23 of the Partnership Act 1890 (for procedure, see notes to RSC, Ord. 81, r.10 in *The Supreme Court Practice* 1999) and charging orders may also be made under section 73 of the Solicitors Act 1974 upon property recovered or preserved through the instrumentality of the solicitor (Ord. 49, r.18 applies but such charging orders are rare). They may also be made to recover arrears of child maintenance under section 36 of the Child Support Act 1991.

The registration of a charging order over registered land does not entitle the chargee to assert the priority of his interest over a subsequent registered charge, it merely gives him a right to be notified of any proposed dealings. A charging order on land held on a trust for sale is effective to create a charge over the legal estate in the land, not merely the interests in the proceeds of sale (*Clark v. Chief Land Registrar; Chancery plc v. Ketteringham* [1993] Ch. 294; [1993] 2 All E.R. 936).

24.09 A county court may make a charging order to enforce payment of a judgment or order:

(1) to secure a High Court or county court "maintenance order" (for definitions, see Sched. 1 to the Attachment of Earnings Act 1971).

(2) to secure a High Court judgment or order or a county court judgment or order (section 1 of the Charging Orders Act 1979). A county court judgment or order here includes the award of a tribunal (Ord. 25, r.12).

The county court has exclusive jurisdiction to make a charging order on a High Court judgment less than £5,000. Note that interest still continues to run on a debt of over £5,000, even if charging order proceedings are taken (art. 4 of the County Court (Interest on Judgment Debts) Order 1991, and see Chapter 15). A charging order can carry interest even where this is not expressed in a judgment or order but not for a period more than six years before the commencement of proceedings (*Ezekiel v. Orakpo* [1997] 1 W.L.R. 340, CA).

There are frequently conflicting claims between judgment creditors and spouses where a charging order is sought on the matrimonial home. This is dealt with in some detail in the General Note to the Charging Orders Act 1979 in *The County Court Practice* to which reference should be made.

Venue

(1) If the order is sought in respect of a fund lodged in court, that court (Ord. 31, r.1(1)(a)). **24.10**

(2) Subject to (1) above, if the judgment or order was made by a county court, that court, unless the action has been transferred under Ord. 16, r.1(d) or (e), or Ord. 25, r.2 when it is the transferee court (Ord. 31, r.1(1)(b)).

(3) Subject to (1) and (2) above, the court for the district in which the debtor resides or carries on business, or, if none, in which the judgment creditor resides or carries on business (Ord. 31, r.1(1)(c)).

Procedure

Order 31, r.1 applies. It is possible to include more than one property in an application, but pay one fee only. Application is without notice on affidavit or by witness statement with a copy: **24.11**

(a) giving the debtor's name and address (the address is frequently forgotten which results in the application being returned and should be given even if it is the same as the property to be charged) and those of all known creditors;

(b) identifying the subject matter of the intended charge;

(c) verifying the debtor's beneficial interest (if the asset is held by a trustee, one of the grounds specified by section 2(1)(b) of the 1979 Act must be given and verified);

(d) where securities (other than those in court) are to be charged, giving the name and address of the person to be notified to protect the charge;

(e) where an interest under a trust is to be charged, giving the names and addresses of known trustees and beneficiaries;

(f) certifying the balance due and that the whole or any part of any instalment due remains unpaid.

If a High Court order is to be enforced, the affidavit/statement must verify the amount due and an office copy judgment and the sheriff's return (if any) to the writ must be lodged (Ord. 31, r.1(2)). Where land is registered, as the Land Register is now open for inspection, office copy entries can easily be obtained by the judgment creditor and should be exhibited to the affidavit as proof of the debtor's beneficial interest in the land to be charged. The office copy entries will also give details of other beneficial owners and registered chargees to whom notice of the order nisi and return date should be given. If it is known that the debtor is married but the property is in the debtor's name alone with no charge under the Matrimonial Homes Act 1983 having been registered by the other spouse, the court may well order that the spouse also be given notice.

24.12   Where land is vested in joint proprietors under a statutory trust for sale there is no power to make a charging order over the trust property unless the additional formalities required by Ord. 31, r.1(2)(c) are observed (*Clark v. Chief Land Registrar* [1993] Ch. 294; [1993] All E.R. 936).

In the case of a county court judgment, the plaint note or originating process must be produced (Ord. 25, r.5(d)).

- An addressed envelope is required if issued by post.

- Fee: see Table of Fees.

One charging order may be made in respect of more than one judgment (Ord. 31, r.1(3)). On issue, the court enters the matter in the records and the papers are placed before the district judge. If he is satisfied he then makes a charging order *nisi* fixing a return day. The court officer sends a copy of the order to the creditor, and the Accountant-General if funds in court are charged (Ord. 31, r.1(4) and (5)) (Form N86).

Service of the charging order nisi

Order 31, r.1(6)–(8) applies. Pursuant to Ord. 7, r.1 service 24.13 should be effected by the judgment creditor, not the court, not less than seven days before the hearing on the following:

(1) The debtor.

(2) Where funds are to be charged, the Accountant-General at the Funds Office.

(3) On the debtor's other creditors named in the affidavit, unless the district judge otherwise directs.

(4) Where a trust is involved, including where there are joint owners, one of whom is not the judgment debtor (see section 2(1)(b) Charging Orders Act 1979, on such trustees and beneficiaries and on such other trustees as may ordered by the district judge (this can include a spouse who is not a trustee).

(5) Where securities not in court are to be charged, the body or persons required by RSC, Ord. 50, r.2(1)(b).

An affidavit or witness statement proving service has to be filed (Ord. 31, r.1(9)).

Practical point:
To obtain the full value of the order *nisi* procedure, the 24.14 judgment creditor should take such additional steps before the debtor learns of the order *nisi* as will ensure that the debtor is not able on so learning to deal with the property which is the subject of the provisional charge. Thus as an example, it will be for the judgment creditor promptly to register the order *nisi* under the Land Registration Act 1925 or the Land Charges Act 1972. The creditor for such purposes should therefore arrange with the court officer to collect a copy of the order nisi as soon as it has been drawn up.

Making orders absolute

Service of the order *nisi* is required to be proved by affidavit/ 24.15 witness statement (see para. 24.13, above). Subject to proof, the order will be made absolute on the return day (N87), or else the court will discharge the order (Ord. 31, r.2(1)).

The court must consider the debtor's personal circumstances and also other creditors (section 1(5) of the 1979 Act). Conditions may be imposed (section 3(1)), including an instalment order. Where there is dispute over the beneficial ownership of any property subject to the order *nisi*, the court has the power to order that the dispute be tried first and to adjourn the application for the order absolute until it has been decided.

If an order absolute is made, the court serves it on:

(a) the debtor and creditor;

(b) (where funds in court are charged) the Accountant-General at the Funds Office; and

(c) where securities not in court are charged, the persons or body required by RSC, Ord. 50, r.2(1)(b), when a stop notice must be put in the order.

(d) unless otherwise directed any person or body on whom a copy of the order nisi was served (see above) (Ord. 31, r.2(2), (3).

For form of notice, see RSC, Ord. 50, r.5 (3); Form 76 in Appendix A to *The Supreme Court Practice 1999.*

Variation and discharge of orders

24.16 The district judge may vary or discharge his order, but if made by the circuit judge only the circuit judge may vary it. High Court procedure is followed. See note 50/1, 9/30 in *The Supreme Court Practice 1999* (Ord. 31, r 3(2), (3)). Order 13 applies.

Costs

24.17 Although fixed costs are provided for (see Table of Costs — Appendix 12) where land is registered, judgment creditors are also entitled to ask for all the incidental fees, including swearing and land registration fees, which are incurred as a result of the application (Ord. 38, r.18(1)). Creditors should bring the details of costs claimed with them to court for scrutiny by the district judge. At the time of this edition, together with the said fixed costs, they can total almost £200.

Enforcement by sale

24.18 Order 31, r.4 applies. Proceedings for a judicial sale are commenced by a claim form, and are supported by affidavit or witness statement (and copy):

(a) identifying the charging order and the property;

(b) specifying the amount for which the charge was imposed and the outstanding balance;

(c) verifying the debtor's title to the property;

(d) identifying prior incumbrances and the amounts due to them;

(e) giving an estimate of the sale price (Ord. 31, r.4(1)).

In the case of land, circumstances may favour either a sale by auction or a sale by private treaty. Time will be a factor, as also will be the clearing of the charge and prior incumbrances, with, if possible, a credit balance in hand for the debtor.

- An addressed envelope is required if issued by post.

- Fee: see Table of Fees.

The order for sale of land is provided for by Form N436, but the Judicial Studies Board considers it inadequate and, in their bench books, district judges are provided with a much fuller order based on the general format used in the Chancery Division. Also see form of order in Blackford and others, *Chancery Practice and Orders* (Longman 1991).

Venue

(1) County court charging order — the court making the order. 24.19

(2) In any other case, the court for the district in which the debtor resides or carries on business or, if none, in which the judgment creditor resides or carries on business (Ord. 31, r.4(2)).

The county court has jurisdiction only where the capital value of the land does not exceed £30,000, or in the case of a sale, the purchase money does not exceed that figure (section 23(d) of the 1984 Act and the notes thereunder in *The County Court Practice*). A copy of the affidavit witness statement is served on the debtor (Ord. 31, r.4(3)).

The district judge may determine the proceedings (Ord. 31, r.4(4)).

24.20   Note as follows:

> (1)   In the case of a charging order on land, the creditor is not thereby entitled to possession; a charging order has the effect of an equitable charge created by writing under hand (section 3(4) of the 1979 Act; *Tennant v. Trenchard* (1869) 4 Ch. 537; *The Supreme Court Practice 1999*, note 50/1 9/9).
>
> (2)   When the debtor has an interest in a property of which he is joint owner with a non-debtor, judicial sale is not appropriate and an application under section 14 of the Trusts of Land and Appointment of Trustees Act 1996 (replacing section 30 of the Law of Property Act 1925) is the alternative (see below). However, the question whether an equitable chargee, for example a bank having a charging order over the interest of one only of two or more co-owners of land, can ask the court to sell the whole of the land to realise the share over which he has the charge, has been determined in *Midland Bank plc v. Pike and Pike* (1986) 2 F.L.R. 143; [1988] 2 All E.R. 434. The chargee is entitled to apply under section 14 of the Trusts of Land and Appointment of Trustees Act 1996 for an order for the sale of all the land as "a person interested" within the meaning of that section; the chargee's rights are also to apply for an order for the sale of the co-owners' beneficial interest only, or for the appointment of a receiver of that interest, though obviously this would not enable the chargee to obtain as much as he could by sale of the property itself.
>
> (3)   The procedure following a charging order is given in the notes to RSC, Ords 50 and 88.

If a sale proceeds, a contract for sale is required, title must be proved, the costs of the proceedings and costs on sale must be provided for, a final account taken, and the proceeds distributed.

Any net proceeds received on sale must be paid into court for this purpose (Ord. 22, r.9 and Ord. 31, r.4(5)).

Effectiveness

24.21   Provided that the debtor has an effective interest in land and there is positive equity, there is no doubt that a charging order, particularly if followed by proceedings for sale, is a very effective method of enforcement. Note that charging orders are a discretionary remedy and district judges have been known to refuse them where the debt is of a small amount. Although the courts grant many charging orders, orders for sale are very much rarer. Frequently, on the application for sale the court adjourns the order to give the judgment debtor an opportunity to make realistic proposals for clearing the debt.

Judgment Summonses

Order 28 applies. Judgment summonses (N67) are issued pur- 24.22 suant to section 5 of the Debtors Act 1869. The Administration of Justice Act 1970, s.11, provides that a judgment summons may be issued in a county court in respect only of:

(1) A High Court or a county court maintenance order (Family Proceedings Rules 1991, r.7.4).

(2) A judgment or order of any court for the payment of any taxes, contributions or liabilities specified in Sched. 4 to the 1970 Act, which specifies:

    (a) income tax or any other tax or liability recoverable under section 66 of the Taxes Management Act 1970;

    (b) state scheme premiums under Part III of the Social Security Pensions Act 1975 and Class 1, 2 and 4 contributions under Part I of the Social Security Act 1975.

Judgment summonses are in practice rarely issued except in respect of judgments obtained by the Inland Revenue when the collector of taxes has their conduct and attends court, and to enforce orders for maintenance. For details of the requirements and procedure, see Ord. 28 in *The County Court Practice*.

Effectiveness

As stated above the judgment summons procedure is rarely used 24.23 except in Inland Revenue and maintenance cases. In the latter case, as the Child Support Agency is responsible for the enforcement of child-maintenance, and considering the effective power of the magistrates' courts to enforce spouse-maintenance orders registered there, its use in maintenance matters is declining considerably. Having said that, it is quite an effective procedure as it has the "bite" of committal.

Committal for Breach of Order or Undertaking

24.24 Where an "unless" or peremptory order is sought to be enforced, the order must have specified the time after service, or some other time, within which the act is to be done, and must have borne a penal notice.

Order 29 applies and provides that where a person refuses or neglects to comply with the judgment or order within the time fixed or as extended, a circuit judge may enforce it by committal. Order 29, r.1 applies also to an undertaking with certain modifications as to service (see below) (Ord. 29, r.1A).

The judgment or order must have been served (Ord. 29, r.1(2)) endorsed with a penal notice (Ord. 29, r.1(3)), save that there can be committal without service if the circuit judge is satisfied, in the case of orders to abstain from doing any act, that the person against whom the order was made was either present in court when the order was pronounced or notified whether by telephone, "telegram" or otherwise (Ord. 29, r.1(6)). Where an undertaking, rather than an order, is involved, a "proper officer" must have delivered a copy of the undertaking to the person giving it either before he left the court building, or by posting it to his place of residence or through his solicitor. If none of those methods are practical then a copy can be supplied to the other party to try and serve personally (Ord. 29, r.1A(a)).

Committal can be ordered only if the order endorsed with penal notice has been served personally (r.1(2)) or otherwise notified (r.1(6)) in sufficient time for the order to be obeyed within the time limited by the order (Ord. 29, r.1(2)(b)).

24.25 The circuit judge is empowered (Ord. 29, r.1), though possibly he may wish to exercise such power only in exceptional circumstances, to dispense with service of the judgment or order or the notice to show cause. Where service of the notice to show cause (N78) is dispensed with and a committal order made, the circuit judge may of his own motion fix a date and time when the person to be committed is to be brought before him or before the court (Ord. 29, r.1(8)). The latter is a common practice, a usual order being for committal for 14 days suspended until the adjourned hearing when, if the respondent appears, and is co-operative, the committal is usually then discharged.

Any judgment or order against a corporation which is wilfully disobeyed may be enforced by committal of the directors or its other officers (Ord. 29, r.1(1)).

For committal for non-attendance at oral examinations, see Ord. 25, r.3(5); for non-attendance on attachment of earnings hearings, see Ord. 27 and Chapter 23, for non-attendance at judgment summonses, see Ord. 28.

When an order enforceable by committal has been made, a notice (N77) will be endorsed on it by the court automatically if it is in the nature of an injunction, and in any other case on the application of the party for whose benefit the order was made (Ord. 29, r.1(3)).

A duplicate order is issued for endorsement or service by the bailiff, or to exhibit to an affidavit of service.

Fee: for service by bailiff, see Table of Fees.

Where the party is a corporation, service is to be effected on 24.26 the director or officer whose committal will be sought in default (Ord. 29, r.1(2)(a)) and the judgment creditor must give up-to-date details of officers to the court for that purpose.

If the person served fails to obey the order or see to it that it is obeyed, the court, on the application of the party entitled to enforce it, issues a notice of application (N78) to show cause why he should not be committed. The application must separately identify both the particular provision(s) of the injunction or party's undertaking alleged to have been broken and list the ways in which each breach is alleged to have happened. An affidavit in support is to be filed (Ord. 29, r.1(4A)).

The applicant or his solicitor has the responsibility for drafting the list of allegations to be relied on presenting sworn evidence to support them. It is not the responsibility of the court office to draft the specific allegations to be set out on Form N78: the court office should copy into Form N78 the list of allegations given in the request for issue of N78 (Ord. 29, r.1(4A)). If the application to commit is made in existing proceedings, it is made by an application notice (Ord. 29, PD 2.2), otherwise it is by a Part 8 claims form (Ord. 29, PD 2.1 and see Chapter 5 — Starting a case —Part 8). As to the procedure generally, see the Practice Direction to Order 29.

The application to commit must set out in the notice itself, if 24.27 need be in a schedule, sufficient information for the respondent to see the charges against him (*Harmsworth v. Harmsworth* [1987] 3 All E.R. 816). The Form (N78) must be served personally (Ord. 29, r.1(4A)), unless service is dispensed with under Ord. 29, r.1(7) (and see *Lewis v. Lewis* [1991] 3 All E.R. 251). The notice must be served at least two clear days before the hearing of the application (Ord. 13, r.1(2)). No fee is payable for service by bailiff (see Table of Fees).

The warrant is addressed in particular to the prison governor (N80). The committal order must be a Form N79 and use its precise wording. All the wording of the form should be included and particulars of the breach or contempt must be given. If service of the original order has been dispensed with under Ord. 29, r.1(6) or (7), the Form N79 must be amended accordingly. If the order to commit is suspended, then the words are: "this order will not be put into force if the said [name] complies with the following terms, namely . . . ."

24.28   The committal order may be served on a person sentenced to immediate committal within 36 hours of the execution of the warrant of committal. This is to enable the court to draw up the committal order where the findings of contempt are complex or detailed, after the contemnor is taken into custody. However, the judge must sign the warrant if the order is to be drawn up later. Technical defects will not defeat a committal order if the contemnor has suffered no prejudice or injustice (*Nicholls v. Nicholls, The Times*, January 21, 1997, CA).

Only deliberate or wilful contempt of a court order should attract imprisonment (*Guildford BC v. Valler, The Times*, May 18, 1993). Imprisonment must be ordered for a fixed term which may be up to two years (section 14 of the Contempt of Court Act 1981 and the County Courts (Penalties for Contempt) Act 1983) and a fine may be imposed on the same occasion. Persons aged over 17 but under 21 could be sentenced to be detained in a young offenders institution (section 9 of the Criminal Justice Act 1982). It was determined in *Saving and Investment Bank Limited v. Gasco Investments* (1988) 137 N.L.J. 1088, CA that the committal application is in civil proceedings, and the proceedings being interlocutory, hearsay evidence is admissible in the affidavits.

Practical point:

24.29 At least half a morning must often be allowed for the hearing, as committal applications are almost invariably contested with counsel appearing for the respondent.

For enforcing by committal in case of breach of a solicitor's undertaking, see Ord. 29, r.2, N81 and N82. A judge may initiate the process of such a committal on his own motion, but if committal is requested by the "judgment creditor" the notice to show cause issues on his application supported by affidavit.

A person arrested under a warrant of committal is imprisoned until he purges his contempt or the period of committal fixed by the court expires. He must if necessary apply for his discharge to the "home court" by written application attested by the prison governor or an officer of at least the rank of principal officer (no prescribed form). He must serve notice of the application on the party (if any) who caused him to be committed not less than one day before the application is to be heard. This procedure does not apply to applications by the Official Solicitor. If the district judge has the judge's permission the application may be made to him unless the committal order directed otherwise (Ord. 29, r.3).

Committal procedure does not apply against the Crown (Ord. 42, r.13).

A person committed to prison for contempt for breach of a court cannot be committed again if they continued to disobey the order. A further order will need to be obtained (*Kumari v. Jalal, The Times*, October 15, 1996, CA).

Committal for Contempt

Any person who assaults any officer of the court or anyone 24.30 insulting a juror, a witness, or an officer of the court, either while at the court or when going to or from the court, or for interrupting court proceedings, or misbehaving in court may either be committed to prison for up to one month or fined up to a maximum of £2,500 (see para. 24.32, below) (section 118(1) of the 1984 Act).

Any person assaulting a court officer while in the execution of his duty is liable to up to three months' imprisonment and/or a fine up to £5,000 (section 14 of the 1984 Act). The power to commit or fine under this section may be exercised by a circuit or district judge. A person rescuing or attempting to rescue goods seized under a county court execution is liable to up to one month's imprisonment and/or a fine up to £2,500 (section 92 of the 1984 Act).

The court itself may grant legal aid for representation in the county court where it appears desirable to do so in the interests of justice, whenever a person is liable to be committed or fined for either contempt in the face of the court, assaulting an officer of the court in the course of his duties, or rescuing or attempting to rescue goods seized in execution. The court does *not* have this power where someone is brought before the court under a power of arrest for breach of an injunction or for failing to attend court for a hearing.

In any contempt not covered by the above provisions, the 24.31 court may adjourn the matter and instruct the party to see a solicitor or grant ABWOR (Advice by way of Representation) under Part III of the Legal Advice and Assistance (Scope) Regulations 1989, and in particular, regulation 8. This provides for ABWOR to be given by a *solicitor* (*i.e.* not counsel) at a hearing in any proceedings in a county court to a party who is not receiving and has not been refused representation in connection with those proceedings, where the court:

   (a) is satisfied that the hearing should proceed on the same day;

   (b) is satisfied that the party would not otherwise be represented;

   (c) requests a solicitor who is within the precincts of the court for purposes other than the provision of ABWOR in accordance with this regulation, or approves a proposal from such a solicitor, that he provide a party with ABWOR.

It is important that, on committal, the respondent is given an opportunity to call witnesses, informed of his right to legally aided representation and his right to apply to the judge to purge his contempt (*King v. Read & Slack* (1996) N.L.D., November 18, CA.)

Where legal aid is granted in contempt proceedings, representation may be by solicitor or barrister for which a fixed fee is payable unless there are exceptional circumstances' which justify a greater fee.

Fines

24.32 Both the circuit judge and district judge (including a deputy) may fine any witness who having been properly summoned, fails to appear or who refuses to give evidence (section 55 of the 1984 Act — maximum fine £1,000), or any person who falsely represents a document to have been issued from the county court (section 36). The court may also fine for contempt of court under sections 14, 92 and 118 of the 1984 Act (see para. 24.30, above).

Fines may also be imposed under section 23 of the Attachment of Earnings Act 1971, for the various offences specified therein.

24.33   For breach of an injunction or undertaking to the court, the circuit judge has power to fine as well as, or in lieu of, committal: section 38 of the 1984 Act and RSC, Ord. 52, rr.1 and 9. In default of payment of a fine, CCR, Ord. 34, r.3 provides that the "proper officer" shall forthwith report the matter to the circuit judge whose powers are those contained in section 129 of the 1984 Act which provides that payment of "any fine imposed by any court under this Act" may be enforced by order of the judge either as a judgment debt, or "in like manner", as payment of a sum (payable) upon conviction by a magistrates' court which may be enforced under the Magistrates' Courts Act 1980 (see section 81(1) thereof).

The powers of the county court to fine are subject to a maximum of £5,000 as provided by section 14(2) and (4A) of the Contempt of Court Act 1981 and sections 14 and 118 of the 1984 Act. The period of imprisonment, if any, in lieu is governed by the scale in section 31(3A) of the Powers of Criminal Courts Act 1973 as amended by section 23(1) of the Criminal Justice Act 1991. A fine should not be imposed without some enquiry as to means. Apart from powers under the Attachment of Earnings Act 1971 in respect of judgment summonses, committal, contempt and insolvency, the court has, except perhaps in matrimonial proceedings, no general power to call litigants before it.

Chapter 25

Attachment of Earnings

General

25.01 The Attachment of Earnings Act 1971 and County Court Rules 1981, Ord. 27 apply.

A county court may make an attachment of earnings order to secure payments under a High Court or a county court maintenance order, payment of a judgment debt of not less than 50, or for the balance under a judgment for a sum of not less than £50 (Ord. 27, r.7(9)), or payments under a county court administration order (section 1(2) of the 1971 Act).

Maintenance orders to which the Act applies are set out in Schedule 1 to the 1971 Act, and include orders for periodical or other payments under the Matrimonial Causes Act 1973, Part II, and certain orders under the Children Act 1989 and other Acts.

The term "judgment debt" does not include a maintenance order or an administration order.

Section 24(1) and Sched. 3 to the 1971 Act define attachable earnings and section 24(2) and (3) restricts earnings that may be attached, *e.g.* the pay or allowances of members of HM Forces cannot be attached.

As part of the increased computerisation of the courts a Centralised Attachment of Earnings Payment System (CAPS) has been introduced into the county court. Where this system is in force, the relevant forms will indicate accordingly by using the prefix of "CAPS".

Members of HM Forces

25.02 Since the coming into effect of sections 59 and 61 of the Armed Forces Act 1971, deduction may be made from servicemen's pay at the discretion of the defence council or any officer authorised by them. Cases should not be referred to the Service authorities unless it has been established that the serviceman

240

will not comply with the judgment or order voluntarily. The judgment creditor or his solicitor may then refer the case to the appropriate authority, forwarding a copy of the judgment or order giving particulars of the amount already paid and the amount owing.

Inquiry should be made of the Ministry of Defence, White-hall, London SW1, in the first instance.

Index

Each county court keeps an index of debtors residing within its 25.03 district against whom there are in force attachment of earnings orders which have been made by that court, or notice of which has been received from another court, including a magistrates' court. Any person who has a judgment or order against another person believed to be residing within the district of the court may cause a search to be made in the index. Requirements for search are a request for search (N336) and an addressed envelope if search is made by post. No fee is payable.

The court issues a certificate in Form N336 as to the result of the search (Ord. 27, r.2).

The Application

Application is made to the court for the district in which the 25.04 debtor resides (Ord. 27, r.3(1)). If the debtor does not reside within England or Wales, or if the creditor does not know where he resides, the application may be made to the court in which the judgment or order was obtained (Ord. 27, r.3(2)).

Where the creditor applies for attachment of earnings orders in respect of two or more debtors jointly liable, the application is made to the court for the district in which any of the debtors resides; but if the judgment or order was given or made by any such court, the application must be made to that court (Ord. 27, r.3(3)).

In the case of a maintenance order made in a county court, the application must be made to that county court (Ord. 27, r.17(2)). A High Court maintenance order may be enforced in the county court designated in the High Court Order (Ord. 27, r.17(7)). To enforce an order for divorce costs, the application must be made to the court where the debtor resides (Ord. 27, r.3(1)).

The persons who may apply for an attachment of earnings 25.05 order are the persons to whom payment under the relevant adjudication is required to be made (whether directly or through an officer of any court); in the case of an administration order, any one of the creditors scheduled to the order may apply, or the debtor, where the application is to secure maintenance payments: he may apply on the making of the county court maintenance order or on an order varying that order (section 3(1) of the 1971 Act; Ord. 27, r.17(4)).

Where a creditor desires to make an application to a county court other than the county court in which the judgment or order was obtained, he must apply for the transfer of the proceedings to the appropriate court under Ord. 25, r.2(1)(c). A letter applying for transfer and stating the defendant's address should be written. No fee is payable. The court sends a certificate of judgment or order (see N313 for the endorsement — no longer in *The County Court Practice*) to the named court, and the district judge of that court gives the proceedings a fresh plaint number and sends notice of the transfer to both parties (N314 — no longer in *The County Court Practice*).

25.06   The requirements for the issue of an application are:

(1) Application (N337) certifying the balances due and that the whole or any part of any instalment due remains unpaid (Ord. 27, r.4(1)).

(2) Fee (see Table of Fees — Appendix 12).

In addition, if the judgment is of the High Court, or of another court or is an arbitration award enforceable as such, the requirements are also:

(3) Office copy of judgment or order or other evidence.

(4) Certificate verifying amount due.

(5) Where a writ of execution issued, office copy of sheriff's return.

(6) A certified copy of order (Ord. 25, r.11).

In addition, if to enforce a magistrates' court order, the requirements are also:

(7) Certificate verifying amount due or, if payments are required to be made to the clerk of the magistrates' court, a certificate by him to the like effect.

25.07   If the application is made against a partner in a debtor firm, see Ord. 25, r.9 (or RSC, Ord. 81, r.5 if a High Court judgment).

The name and address of the employer should be stated in 25.07 the application if known. The application issues for the balance of debt and costs in the case of a judgment debt (section 6(4) of the 1971 Act). The balance may not include the costs of an execution not recovered thereunder (Ord. 27, r.9(1)). The figures are completed by the court.

An application under section 32 of the Matrimonial Causes Act 1973 for leave to enforce the payment of arrears under a county court maintenance order, which became due more than 12 months before the application, should be made in that application (Ord. 27, r.17(3)).

Unless the debtor himself applies in respect of a maintenance order the debtor must be in default (section 3(3) of the 1971 Act). The court may make an attachment of earnings order when the maintenance order itself is made without the consent of the debtor (section 1(4)(b) of the Maintenance Enforcement Act 1991).

For fees: see Table of Fees — Appendix 12.

Service

Maintenance orders

The court prepares a notice (N55A) to the debtor and copy for 25.08 the creditor which contains a date of hearing before the district judge. Notice of the application is sent to the debtor, together with a form of reply (N56), which the debtor is required to file within eight days of receipt. The summons is served as if it were a fixed date summons (Ord. 3, r.6(6), Ord. 27, rr.5(1)), 17(3A)). The court officer may, at any stage, send an N338 (see para. 25.09, above) to the debtor's employers, if known (Ord. 27, r.6).

If the debtor attends the hearing the district judge may make such order as is appropriate (see para. 25.11, below).

Non-maintenance orders

The court prepares a notice to the debtor and makes a copy. 25.09 The form informs the debtor that unless he pays the total sum due into court, he must complete and send a reply to the court office to reach it within eight days after service. Notice of the application (N55) and a form of reply (N56) are served on the debtor as if the application were a fixed date summons (Ord. 3, r.6(6), Ord. 27, r.5(1)). If the application is not served, notice of non-service (N216 — no longer in *The County Court Practice*) is sent to the creditor.

The debtor must, within eight days after service, file in the court office the form of reply setting out particulars of his expenditure and income and the name and address of his employer, if any. The court sends a copy of the reply to the creditor (Ord. 27, r.5(3)). If the debtor does not reply in time or at any stage of the proceedings where the judgment creditor knows the employer, the court (court officer) should be asked by letter to request the employer (N 338) to give details of earnings (Ord. 27, r.6).

25.10   Where a reply is filed by a debtor in compliance with Ord. 27, r.5(2) within eight days, and he gives the name and address of his employer, the court officer can still send notice (N338) to the employer requesting him to file a statement of earnings (Ord. 27, r.6). Such a notice may be sent to an employer if the debtor gives information as to his earnings but the court doubts the debtor's statement.

If an employer does not send a statement of earnings in compliance with the request, the court may compel him to do so (sections 14(1)(b), 23(2)(c) of the Attachment of Earnings Act 1971; Ord. 27, r.15 as to enforcement).

The Order

25.11 Order 27, r.7(1) allows a court officer to make attachment of earnings orders (including consolidated orders), except on applications to secure arrears of maintenance when the order is made by the district judge (see para. 25.08, above). Applications in relation to judgment debts will not have an initial hearing and the defendant will be required either to pay the amount due to the claimant or to complete and return the form of reply which includes a statement of means (see N56). If he has sufficient information to do so, the court officer will make an order on receipt of the form, sending a copy to the parties and to the employer (Ord. 27, r.7(1)). Employers can obtain from the Publications Unit, Court Service Agency (0207 210 1700) a copy of the Employer's Handbook explaining how they should comply with any attachment of earnings order.

If the debtor fails to pay or to return the form, the court officer may and probably will order him to file a statement of means in Form N61. Failure to reply will then result in the issue of a notice to show cause which will be listed before the district judge (Ord. 27, r.7(A), 2, 3,). Order 27, r.19 provides for an application for a consolidated order to be made in any proceedings in which an attachment of earnings order (except a priority order) is in force.

Order 27, r.19(4) enables a court officer to make a consoli- 25.12
dated attachment of earnings order where a further attachment
of earnings order is applied for (see para. 25.21, below).

The judgment creditor or the debtor may, within 14 days of
service of the order on him and giving his reasons, apply on
notice for the order to be reconsidered and the court officer
shall fix a day for the hearing of the application and give to the
judgment creditor and the debtor not less than two days' notice
of the day so fixed (Ord. 27, r.7(2)).

The district judge may confirm the order or set it aside and
make such new order as he thinks fit, or instead, a day may be
fixed for hearing by the district judge (Ord. 27, r.7(5)).

No Reply Filed by Debtor; Non-attendance

If a reply has not been filed, a variety of courses are open, the 25.13
procedures differing depending on whether a maintenance
order or any other form of judgment is involved, thus:

Maintenance orders

If the debtor fails to attend then, subject to the creditor 25.14
producing sufficient evidence, the district judge may either
make an attachment of earnings order (Ord. 27, r.17) or, more
usually, adjourn the application to a specified date before the
district judge in chambers and order the debtor to attend on
threat of imprisonment (section 23(1) of the 1971 Act) (Ord.
27, r.8(1)). Notice of the adjourned hearing (N58) must be
served personally on the debtor unless an order for substituted
service is made (Ord. 27, r.8(1)). At the same time as serving
N58 the bailiff may give the debtor an opportunity of completing a form of reply (N56), a copy of which should be attached
to the order.

If the debtor attends at the adjourned hearing the district
judge can obtain the relevant information and make an appropriate order (see para. 25.18, below) (N65). If, however, he
fails to attend, the district judge may either commit the debtor
to prison (N59) for a specific period not exceeding 14 days
(section 23(1) of the 1971 Act) (Ord. 27, rr.7A(3), 17) or order
him to be arrested (N112) and brought before the court either
forthwith or on a specified date (section 23(1A)). The judge or
district judge can order that any committal order be suspended
so long as the debtor attends at the time and place specified in
the committal order. However, if he fails to attend, a certificate
to that effect given by a court officer will be sufficient authority

for the issue of a warrant of committal although the authority for such is endorsed on the attachment of earnings file by the judge or district judge (Ord. 27, r.7B).

The debtor may apply to the circuit or district judge without notice in writing for the revocation of the committal order. If in custody the debtor applies to the circuit or district judge *ex parte* in writing attested by the governor or a principal officer, otherwise by affidavit. The debtor must undertake to attend when so ordered (see Ord. 27, r.8 generally).

Other judgment debts

25.15   If it is desired to obtain from the debtor a statement of earnings, he must (a) be proved to have been served personally with N55, the form of reply and N337, or the court must be satisfied that they came to his notice in time for him to have complied with the instructions in N55 (Ord. 27, r.5(2) proviso) and (b) he must be personally served with N61(Ord. 27, r.15) which warns him of the consequences of failing to obey the order, to which he must reply within eight days with his statement of means. In default he commits an offence under sections 14(1) and 23(2)(c) of the 1971 Act and may be personally served with notice to show cause (N63) why he should not be imprisoned and a date is fixed for him to be brought before the circuit or district judge to be dealt with for that offence (Ord. 27, r.7A(2)). At any stage an N338 can be sent to the debtor's employers if they are known (see para. 25.09, above) (Ord. 27, r.6).

If the debtor does not attend, the circuit judge or district judge may commit him to prison (N59) under section 23(3) of the 1971 Act for a period not exceeding 14 days or fine him a sum up to 250 or commit him to prison for contempt under Ord. 29, r.1 (N79/80) (section 27, r.7A(3)). If the debtor attends, however, and satisfactorily completes an N56, a court officer can make an appropriate order (see para. 25.18, below). The suspended committal procedure is the same as for maintenance debts (see para. 25.14, above).

25.16   If the debtor has failed to supply sufficient information for the court officer to make an order, the papers are referred to the district judge (Ord. 27, r.7(4)) who may either make an order (N60) if he feels that there is sufficient information, or direct a hearing in which case the parties are given at least eight days' notice (Ord. 27, r.7(5)). If the debtor attends the hearing and gives sufficient information the district judge can make an appropriate order (N60). If, however, the debtor does not attend the district judge may adjourn the hearing under section 23(1) of the 1971 Act.

The court officer serves notice of the adjourned hearing (N63) (or if asked, delivers to the creditors for service) not less than five days before the hearing. If the debtor fails to attend or is unco-operative the district judge may either order him to be imprisoned for not more than 14 days (N59) (section 23(1) of the 1971 Act) or order the bailiff to arrest him and bring him to court either forthwith or on a date to be fixed (N112A).

Practical point:
There is some doubt as to this procedure as there has been no   25.17
"previous hearing". Under such circumstances it might be better to proceed by way of a suspended committal order (N118) or a warrant of committal (N59) (see *The County Court Practice 1997*, p.692).

If, however, the debtor does attend the hearing or is arrested in response to N112A, and satisfactorily completes Form N56, a court officer can make an appropriate order (N60) as above. If, on arrest under N112A, the debtor does not satisfactorily complete N56 the district judge may commit him (N59) for up to 14 days (section 23(1) of the 1971 Act).

Form of Order

The form is N60, or N65 (priority maintenance) (as amended   25.18
by the County Court (Forms) (Amendment) Rules 1996 (S.I. 1996 No. 2811) (L.9)) for maintenance. These must specify the normal deduction rate and a protected earnings rate. "Normal deduction rate" is defined in section 6(5)(a) of the 1971 Act, and is the rate at which the court thinks it reasonable for the debtor's earnings to be applied to meeting his liability. "Protected earnings rate" is defined in section 6(5)(b) and is the rate below which, having regard to the debtor's resources and needs, the court thinks it reasonable that the earnings actually paid to him should not be reduced. Protected earnings are normally calculated by reference to the rates as amended from time to time of supplementary benefits under the National Insurance Acts and to rent or mortgage payments.

An attachment of earnings order is sent by post to the debtor (or his solicitor) and to the employer unless personal service is asked for (Ord. 27, r.10(2)). If the debtor is employed by a corporation which has so requested, the order may be sent to the address given by it. If the order is to enforce a judgment or order of the High Court or a magistrates' court, a copy of the order is sent to the court officer of those courts (Ord. 27, r.10(3)). The order to the debtor states that he must inform the court of any change in employment.

25.19 An order may be made, but suspended while the debtor himself pays (N64). This is a common practice when the debtor is not anxious for his employer to know of the judgment. Should the debtor get into arrears with his payments, the creditors can apply *ex parte* to remove the suspension.

Deductions by the employer from the debtor's earnings are made in accordance with Sched. 3 to the 1971 Act. Priority as between orders is set out in this Schedule.

The employer is allowed on each deduction to deduct from the debtor's earnings, in addition, 1 towards his administrative costs (section 7(4) and Attachment of Earnings (Employer's Deductions) Order 1991 (S.I. 1991 No. 356)).

25.20 The employer is under no liability for non-compliance with the order until seven days have elapsed since the service (section 7(1)). If he does not have the debtor in his employment or if the debtor ceases to be in his employment, he must give notice of the fact to the court within ten days of service of the order or cesser (section 7(2)). If an employer ceases to have the debtor in his employment the order lapses, but the court may direct it to another employer (section 9(4)). There appears to be no provision that the court should notify the judgment creditor if a debtor leaves his employment.

The employer pays the sums deducted from the debtor's earnings to the court and the sums in court are paid out to the creditor under normal procedures. There are no rules which prescribe that the court should notify a creditor when an employer makes no payment into court. The court does not act on its own initiative to enquire from the employer any reason for payments not being received. In such cases, the creditor should write to the court requiring an enquiry to be made, and should request the court to take action where an employer refuses or neglects to give the information required. Under such circumstances the court may consider serving notice to the employer (N449), making an order to the employer for production of a statement of earnings (N61A) or issuing a summons against the employer for an offence under the 1971 Act (N62) for which a payment of a fine not exceeding £250 or committal to prison for a period up to 14 days may be ordered.

Consolidated Attachment Orders

25.21 These orders are made to secure the payment of a number of judgment debts (section 17 of the 1971 Act). Order 27, rr.18–22 apply.

They may be made by the court officer, where:

(a) two or more attachment of earnings orders are in force to secure the payment of judgment debts by the same debtor; or

(b) on an application for an attachment of earnings order to secure a judgment debt or for a consolidated attachment order, it appears that an attachment of earnings order is already in force (Ord. 27, r.18).

A consolidated attachment order in respect of maintenance orders may be made in a magistrates' court (section 17(1)) or by the district judge.
Consolidated attachment orders (N66) may be made:

(a) on an application by the judgment debtor (Ord. 27, r.19(1)(a) (see below));

(b) on an application by a judgment creditor who has obtained or is entitled to apply for an attachment of earnings order (r.19(1)(b));

(c) on the request of an employer (r.19(4)); or

(d) by the court of its own motion (see para. 25.23 below).

The judgment debtor may apply:

(a) in the proceedings in which any attachment of earnings order is in force; or

(b) on the hearing of an application for an attachment of earnings order (Ord. 27, r.19(2)).

The requirements are: 25.22

(a) application (N244) and copies for service;

(b) copies of the application are to be served by post on the judgment creditor in the proceedings and also on any other judgment creditor who has obtained an attachment of earnings order which is still in force, giving not less than two clear days' notice (Ord. 27, r.19(2); Ord. 13, r.1(2); Ord. 27, rr.3, 4, 5, do not apply).

Fees are deducted from payments into court (see Appendix 12, Table of Fees).

A judgment creditor's application must:

(a) if the judgment which he seeks to enforce was given "by the court to which the application is made", be made in accordance with Ord. 13, r.1, in the proceedings in which the judgment was obtained (Ord. 27, rr.3, 4, 5 do not apply);

(b) in any other case, the judgment is automatically transferred to the court which made the attachment of earnings order (Ord. 27, r.19(3)).

The application must certify the amount of money due under the judgment or order and that the whole or part of any instalment due remains unpaid (Ord. 27, r.19(3A)). The court officer notifies any party who may be affected by the application and requires them, within 14 days of receipt of notification, to raise any objections (r.19(3B)). If no objections are received within that time period, the court officer makes the consolidated order (r.19(3C)). If there are any objections, the matter is referred to the district judge for his consideration (r.19(3D)).

25.23   An employer to whom two or more attachment of earnings orders are directed to secure the payment of judgment debts by the same debtor may himself by a request in writing ask the court to make a consolidated attachment order. On receipt of such a request, the court must fix a hearing at which the request will be considered and give notice thereof to the debtor and the judgment creditors (Ord. 27, r.19(4)).

Where an application is made for an attachment of earnings order and there is another order already in force, the court may of its own motion make a consolidated attachment order after giving all persons concerned an opportunity of being heard (Ord. 27, r.20).

Where a consolidated attachment order is already in force, any creditor to whom another judgment debt is owed may apply to the court by whom the order was made for the consolidated attachment order to be extended to secure the payment of his judgment debt. Such an application is to be treated as an application for a consolidated attachment order (Ord. 27, r.21, applying rr.19 and 20). It would appear that the debtor need not be in arrears for the creditor to be entitled to apply.

Payment into Court

Where money is received by the court under a consolidated 25.24
attachment order, the fee is first deducted.

Fee: see Appendix 12, Table of Fees.

The remainder is distributed by way of dividends declared from
time to time (Ord. 27, r.22). Cheques from employers are
usually accepted.

Transfer of Attachment Orders

Where the court has under consideration consolidating attach- 25.25
ment orders, but has not itself made all of the orders, the court
may make request of the other courts to transfer their orders
(Ord. 27, r.14(1)).
  An attachment of earnings order may be transferred to
another county court if the matter could more conveniently
proceed there by reason of the debtor having moved his
residence, or for other reasons (Ord. 27, r.14(2)). Thereafter,
the transferee court has the same jurisdiction as if it had made
the order (Ord. 27, r.14(3)).

Cesser, Discharge and Variation

In the case of a judgment debt where the whole amount has 25.26
been paid, the court gives notice to the employer that no
further compliance is required (section 12(2) of the 1971 Act).
In the case of a maintenance order where it appears to the court
that the total payments made by the debtor (whether under the
order or otherwise) exceed the total payments required up to
that time by the maintenance order, and the normal deduction
rate (or where two or more such orders are in force, the
aggregate of such rates) exceeds the rate of payments required
by the maintenance order, and no proceedings for the variation
or discharge of the attachment of earnings order are pending,
then the "collecting officer" (the district judge) sends a notice
(N341 — no longer in *The County Court Practice*) to the
creditor and to the debtor (section 10(1) and (2); Ord. 27,
r.17(9)). The notice informs all parties that unless he applies to
the court within 14 days after the date of the notice for an
order discharging or varying the attachment of earnings order,

the court will make an order varying the attachment of earnings order by reducing the normal deduction rate to the rate of payments required by the maintenance order or a lower rate.

When an attachment of earnings order ceases to have effect on the making of an order of commitment or the issue of a warrant of commitment for the enforcement of the debt, the court gives notice of the cesser to the employer (Ord. 27, r.12).

25.27 The court may make an order discharging (N339 — no longer in *The County Court Practice*) or varying an attachment of earnings order (section 9(1) of the 1971 Act) and any party may apply on notice. An attachment of earnings order may be discharged (N339) by the court of its own motion:

(1) Where it appears that the employer or person to whom the order is directed does not have the debtor in his employment (but the court may redirect the order to another employer if known) (Ord. 27, r.13(2) and (3)).

(2) Where the court makes, or is notified of, another such order which is not to secure a judgment debt or payments under an administration order (r.13(4)).

(3) Where an administration order is made or an order made for the debtor to produce a list of his creditors with a view to the making of an administration order (r.13(5)) (but the court may vary the order to secure payment under the administration order).

(4) Where the court makes a consolidated attachment of earnings order (r.13(6)).

(5) Where the defendant has been made a bankrupt (r.13(7)).

(6) Where the court grants leave to issue execution (r.13(8)).

(7) Where the maintenance order being enforced has ceased to have effect (r.17(10)).

Notice is to be given by the court to the debtor and judgment creditor of the time and place at which the question of any discharge or variation will be considered unless the court considers it unnecessary in the circumstances to do so (Ord. 27, r.13(1)–(9)). If the debtor, at any time, satisfies the court that he is unemployed or self-employed the court may, accordingly, stay or dismiss the application for an attachment of earnings order or, where one has already been made, dismiss it.

Effectiveness

The pitfalls are fairly obvious, particularly if the debtor is 25.28
unemployed, self-employed or changes employment without
notification. However, the "teeth" attached to this method of
enforcement, including the powers to arrest (N112/A) and
commit (N59), mean that getting a response from a reluctant
debtor (and employer) is not that difficult, even though it may
take a little time and a little persistence.

Administration Orders

Order 39 applies.   25.29
    Basically, a person with multiple debts totalling not more
than £5,000 can put all of the debts in the hands of the court,
which collects a regular payment from him and distributes it
proportionally. A debtor can apply for an order provided at
least one judgment has been obtained against them. The debtor
completes a request form which includes details of his debts
(N92 or N93) (attachment of earnings) and a return date is
fixed by the court. The request also contains provision for the
debtor to ask the court to make a "composition order" (so
much in the £). The application form is N92 and notes for
guidance N270. The application form requires information
about the applicant's income and outgoings and the notes for
guidance provide information and examples to help the debtor
complete the application form. "Community Tax" arrears
should not be included nor any other debts which are enforceable in the magistrates court.
    Not less than 14 days' notice of the hearing is given to the
debtor and creditors (Ord. 39, r.5), the latter of whom have to
raise any objections at least seven days before the return date
(Ord. 39, r.6(1)).
    At the hearing the district judge decides what order should be
made. Creditors have the right to attend and, if necessary, raise
objections (Ord. 39, r.7(a)). A "reasonable period" for repayment of the debt should be calculated, usually not more than
about three years, if the court is inclined to make an administration order.
    The order is subject to review at any time on debtors and 25.30
creditors being given seven days' notice (Ord. 39, r.8), including
on a subsequent objection by a creditor who was not on the
original list (Ord. 39, r.10). Such a creditor may also ask to be
included in the order (Ord. 39, r.11). A "court officer" can
decide whether or not an administration order should be made

or revoked and the rate of payment thereunder. Any composition orders, reviews or objections to any part of the procedure are dealt with, however, by the district judge. Thus, where there is default by the debtor the court officer may require the debtor to bring payments up to date or give an explanation as to why payments are not being made (Ord. 39, r.13A(1)) If the debtor does not respond the court officer may revoke the order (r.13A(2)). If the debtor gives reasons for default in payment this will be referred to the district judge to decide whether or not to revoke or suspend the order or fix a review (r.13A(3)). On the review of an administration order the court may suspend the order on terms, vary any provision of it, revoke it or make an attachment of earnings order (r.14(1)).

An attachment of earnings order should automatically be made to secure payments under an administration order unless there are good reasons for not doing so. Administration orders are registered at the Registry of County Court Judgments.

Effectiveness

25.31 From the creditor's point of view there may not be much to be gained, other than a relatively small monthly payment. However, this may be better than nothing or the expense of bankruptcy. From the debtor's point of view, administration is known as "the poor man's bankruptcy" and there are advantages in seeking such an order where the total of the undiscounted debts does not exceed £5,000, as the court has power to make a composition order which has the effect of reducing the amount of the debts outstanding, while the debtor suffers none of the stigma and restrictions occasioned by a bankruptcy order.

Costs

25.32 Where costs are allowed, they are the same as those which would be allowed on an interim application. The costs may be fixed and allowed without a detailed assessment under Part 47 (Ord. 27, r.9(3)). For fixed costs see Table of Costs — Appendix 12.

In the case of county court maintenance orders, the district judge may refuse leave to enforce under section 32 of the Matrimonial Causes Act 1973. If both parties attend and if they agree, he may adjust the maintenance orders in the light of the evidence available.

Other Matters

In High Court maintenance orders, where an attachment of 25.33
earnings order made by the High Court designates the district
judge of a county court as the collecting officer, the district
judge sends notice (N340) to the employer (Ord. 27, r.17(7)).

If an application is required to determine whether particular
payments are earnings, such an application is made in writing to
the district judge. He thereupon fixes a date and time for the
hearing and gives notice to the employer, the debtor, the
judgment creditor and, where applicable, the collecting officer
of the magistrates' court (section 16 of the 1971 Act; Ord. 27,
r.11).

Appendices

Appendix 1

List of Rules, Practice Directions and Schedules (Civil Procedure Rules 1998)

Appendix 2

List of Forms

CPR, Pt. 4, PD.3.1

A2.01 3.1 This table lists the "N" forms that are referred to and required to be used by Practice Directions supplementing particular Parts of the CPR. A Practice Direction and its paragraphs are abbreviated by reference to the Part of the CPR which it supplements and the relevant paragraph of the Practice Direction, for example; PD 34 1.2.

No.	Title
N1	Part 7 (general) claim form (Pt 7 PD 3.1)
N1 CPC	Claim Production Centre ("CPC") claim form—rule 7.10)
N1A	Notes for claimant
N1C	Notes for defendant
N1(FD)	Notes for defendant (Consumer Credit Act cases)
N9	Acknowledgment of service/response pack (Pt 10 PD 2)
N9 CPC	CPC acknowledgment of service/response pack (Pt 10 PD 2)
N9A	Admission and statement of means (specified amount) (Pt 14 PD 2.1)
N9B	Defence and counterclaim (specified amount) (Pt 15 PD 1.3)
N9C	Admission and statement of means (unspecified amount and non money claims) (Pt 14 PD 2.1)

No.	Title
N9D	Defence and counterclaim (unspecified amount and non money claims) (Pt 15 PD 1.3)
N10	Notice that acknowledgment of service has been filed—rule 10.4
N17	Judgment for claimant (amount to be decided by court)—rules 12.5(3), 14.6(7) and 14.7(10)
N20	Witness summons (Pt 34 PD 1.2)
N21	Order for Examination for Deponent before the hearing (Pt 34 PD 4.1)
N24	Blank form of order or judgment
N30	Judgment for claimant (default HC)—rule 12.5(2)
N30	Judgment for claimant (default CC)—rule 12.5(2)
N30(1)	Judgment for claimant (acceptance HC) (Pt 14 PD 4.2)
N30(1)	Judgment for claimant (acceptance CC) (Pt 14 PD 4.2)
N30(2)	Judgment for claimant (after determination HC) (Pt 14 PD 10(4)
N30(2)	Judgment for claimant (after determination CC) (Pt 14 PD 10(4))
N30(3)	Judgment for claimant (after re-determination HC)—rule 14.13
N30(3)	Judgment for claimant (after re-determination CC)—rule 14.13
N32	Judgment for return of goods
N32(1) HP/CCA	Judgment for delivery of goods
N32(2) HP/CCA	Judgment for delivery of goods (suspended)
N32(3) HP/CCA	Judgment for delivery of goods
N32(4)	Variation order (return of goods)

No.	Title
N32(5) HP/CCA	Order for balance for purchase price
N33	Judgment for delivery of goods
N34	Judgment for claimant (after amount decided by court HC)
N34	Judgment for claimant (after amount decided by court CC)
N150	Allocation Questionnaire (Pt 26 PD 2.1)
N150A	Master/DJ's directions on allocation
N151	Allocation Questionnaire (amount to be decided by court)
N151A	Master/DJ's directions on allocation
N152	Notice that [defence] [counterclaim] has been filed (Pt 26 PD 2.5)
N153	Notice of allocation or listing hearing (Pt 26 PD 6.2)
N154	Notice of allocation to fast track (Pt 26 PD 4.2 and 9)
N155	Notice of allocation to multi track (Pt 26 PD 4.2 and 10)
N156	Order for further information (for allocation) (Pt 26 PD 4.2(2))
N157	Notice of allocation to small claims track (Pt 26 PD 4.2 and 8)
N158	Notice of allocation to small claims track (preliminary hearing) (Pt 26 PD 4.2 and 8)
N159	Notice of allocation to small claims track (no hearing) (Pt 26 PD 4.2 and 8)
N160	Notice of allocation to small claims track (with parties consent) (Pt 26 PD 4.2 and 8)
N170	Listing questionnaire (Pt 26 PD 6.1 and Pt 28 PD 8.1)
N171	Notice of date for return of listing questionnaire (Pt 26 PD 6.1 and Pt 28 PD 8.1)

No.	Title
N172	Notice of trial date
N173	Notice of non-payment of fee—rule 3.7
N205A	Notice of issue (specified amount)
N205B	Notice of issue (unspecified amount)
N205C	Notice of issue (non-money claim)
N208	Part 8 claim form (Pt 8 PD 2.2)
N208A	Part 8 notes for claimant
N208C	Part 8 notes for defendant
N209	Part 8 notice of issue
N210	Part 8 acknowledgment of service (Pt 8 PD 3.2)
N211	Part 20 claim form—rule 20.7
N211A	Part 20 notes for claimant
N211C	Part 20 notes for defendant
N212	Part 20 notice of issue
N213	Part 20 acknowledgment of service—rule 20.12
N215	Certificate of service—rule 6.10
N216	Notice of non-service—rule 6.11
N217	Order for substituted service—rule 6.8
N218	Notice of service on a partner (Pt 6 PD 4.2)
N225	Request for judgment and reply to admission (specified amount) (Pt 12 PD 3)
N225A	Notice of part admission (specified amount)—rule 15.5
N226	Notice of admission (unspecified amount)—rule 14.7
N227	Request for judgment by default (amount to be decided by the court)—rule 12.5

No.	Title
N228	Notice of admission (return of goods) (Pt 7 PD Consumer Credit Act 8.5)
N235	Certificate of suitability of litigation friend (Pt 21 PD 2.3)
N236	Notice of defence that amount claimed has been paid—rule 15.10
N242A	Notice of payment into court (in settlement)—rule 36.6(2)
N242B	Notice of payment into court (by order)
N243	Notice of acceptance of payment into court (Pt 36 PD 7.7)
N244	Application notice (Pt 23 PD 2.1)
N244A	Notice of hearing of application (Pt 23 PD 2.2)
N252	Notice of commencement of assessment (Pt 47 PD 2.3)
N253	Notice of amount allowed on provisional assessment (Pt 47 PD 6.5)
N254	Request for default costs certificate (Pt 47 PD 3.1)
N255	Default costs certificate HC (Pt 47 PD 3.3)
N255	Default costs certificate CC (Pt 47 PD 3.3)
N256	Final costs certificate HC (Pt 47 PD 5.11)
N256	Final costs certificate CC (Pt 47 PD 5.11)
N257	Interim costs certificate (Pt 47 PD 5.11)
N258	Request for assessment hearing (Pt 47 PD 4.3)
N259	Notice of appeal against a detailed assessment (Pt 47 PD 8.16)
N265	List of documents (Pt 31 PD 3.1)
N266	Notice to admit facts/admission of facts—rule 32.18

No.	Title
N268	Notice to prove documents at trial—rule 32.19
N271	Notice of transfer of proceedings—rule 30
N279	Notice of discontinuancee—rule 38.3
N292	Order on settlement on behalf of child or patient (Pt 21 PD 11.3)
N294	Claimants application for a variation order
N3677	Notice of hearing to consider why fine should not be imposed—rule 34.10
N434	Notice of change of solicitor—rule 42.2

Appendix 3

Letters of Claim

PRE-ACTION PROTOCOL FOR PERSONAL INJURY CLAIMS

Annex A

Letter of Claim

To

Defendant

Dear Sirs

Re: Claimant's full name
     Claimant's full address
     Claimant's Clock or Works Number
     Claimant's Employer (*name and address*)

We are instructed by the above named to claim damages in
connection with an *accident at work/road traffic accident/
tripping accident* on   day of   (*year*) at (*place of
accident which must be sufficiently detailed to establish
location*).

Please confirm the identity of your insurers. Please note that the
insurers will need to see this letter as soon as possible and it
may affect your insurance cover and/or the conduct of any
subsequent legal proceedings if you do not send this letter to
them.
The circumstances of the accident are:
(*brief outline*)

The reason why we are alleging fault is:
    (*simple explanation e.g. defective machine, broken ground*)

A description of our clients' injuries is as follows:
(*brief outline*)

(*In cases of road traffic accidents*)

Our client (state hospital reference number) received treatment
for the injuries at (name and address of hospital).

He is employed as (*occupation*) and has had the following time
off work (*dates of absence*). His approximate weekly income is
(*insert if known*).

*If you are our client's employers, please provide us with the
usual earnings details which will enable us to calculate his
financial loss.*

*We are obtaining a police report and will let you have a copy of
the same upon your undertaking to meet half the fee.*

We have also sent a letter of claim to (*name and address*) and a copy of that letter is attached. We understand their insurers are (*name, address and claims number if known*).

At this stage of our enquiries we would expect the documents contained in parts (*insert appropriate parts of standard disclosure list*) to be relevant to this action.

A copy of this letter is attached for you to send to your insurers. Finally we expect an acknowledgement of this letter within 21 days by yourselves or your insurers.

Yours faithfully

Pre-action Protocol for the Resolution of Clinical Disputes

Annex C

Templates for Letters of Claim and Response

C1 Letter of Claim

Essential Contents A3.02
1. **Client's name, address, date of birth, etc.**
2. **Dates of allegedly negligent treatment**

3. **Events giving rise to the claim**
   - an outline of what happened, including details of other relevant treatments to the client by other healthcare providers.

4. **Allegation of negligence and causal link with injuries**
   - an outline of the allegations or a more detailed list in a complex case an outline of the causal link between allegations and the injuries complained of.
5. **The Client's injuries, condition and future prognosis**

6. **Request for clinical records (if not previously provided)**
   - use the Law Society form if appropriate or adapt;
   - specify the records required;
   - if other records are held by other providers, and may be relevant, say so;
   - state what investigations have been carried out to date, *e.g.* information from client and witnesses, any complaint and the outcome, if any clinical records have been seen or expert's advice obtained.

7. **The likely value of the claim**
   - an outline of the main heads of damage, or in straight-forward cases the details of loss.

Optional Information
What investigations have been carried out
An offer to settle without supporting evidence
Suggestions for obtaining expert evidence
Suggestions for meetings, negotiations, discussion or mediation

Possible Enclosures
Chronology
Clinical records request form and client's authorisation
Expert report(s)
Schedules of loss and supporting evidence

Appendix 4

Letter of Response

PRE-ACTION PROTOCOL FOR THE RESOLUTION OF
CLINICAL DISPUTES

Annex C

Templates for Letters of Claim and Response

C2 *Letter of Response*

Essential Contents   A4.01
1. **Provide requested records and invoice for copying**
   - explain if records are incomplete or extensive records are held and ask for further instructions;
   - request additional records from third parties

2. **Comments on events and/or chronology**
   - if events are disputed or the healthcare provider has further information or documents on which they wish to rely, these should be provided, e.g. internal, protocol;
   - details of any further information needed from the patient or a third party should be provided.

3. **If breach of duty and causation are accepted**
   - suggestions might be made for resolving the claim and/or requests for further information;
   - a response should be made to any offer to settle.

4. **If breach of duty and/or causation are denied**
   - a bare denial will not be sufficient. If the healthcare provider has other explanations for what happened, these should be given at least in outline;
   - suggestions might be made for the next steps, *e.g.* further investigations, obtaining expert evidence, meetings/ negotiations or mediation, or an invitation to issue proceedings.

Optional Matters
An offer to settle if the patient has not made one, or a counter offer to the patient's with supporting evidence.

Possible Enclosures
    Clinical records
    Annotated chronology
    Expert reports

Appendix 5

Letter of Instruction to Medical Expert

Annex C

Letter of instruction to medical expert

Dear Sir,   A5.01

Re: (*Name and Address*)

D.O.B. —
Telephone No. —
Date of Accident —

We are acting for the above named in connection with injuries received in an accident which occurred on the above date. The main injuries appear to have been **(main injuries)**.

We should be obliged if you would examine our Client and let us have a full and detailed report dealing with any relevant pre-accident medical history, the injuries sustained, treatment received and present condition, dealing in particular with the capacity for work and giving a prognosis.

It is central to our assessment of the extent of our client's injuries to establish the extent and duration of any continuing disability. Accordingly, in the prognosis section we would ask you to specifically comment on any areas of continuing complaint or disability or impact on daily living. If there is such continuing disability you should comment upon the level of suffering or inconvenience caused and, if you are able, give your view as to when or if the complaint or disability is likely to resolve.

Please send our Client an appointment direct for this purpose. Should you be able to offer a cancellation appointment please contact our Client direct. We confirm we will be responsible for your reasonable fees.

We are obtaining the notes and records from our Client's GP and Hospitals attended and will forward them to you when they are to hand/or please request the GP and Hospital records direct and advise that any invoice for the provision of these records should be forwarded to us.

In order to comply with Court Rules we would be grateful if you would insert above your signature a statement that the contents are true to the best of your knowledge and belief.

In order to avoid further correspondence we can confirm that on the evidence we have there is no reason to suspect we may be pursuing a claim against the hospital or its staff.

We look forward to receiving your report within _____ weeks. If you will not be able to prepare your report within this period please telephone us upon receipt of these instructions.

When acknowledging these instructions it would assist if you could give an estimate as to the likely time scale for the provision of your report and also an indication as to your fee.

Yours faithfully

Appendix 6

Claim Form (N1)

A6.01

N1

Claim Form

	In the	
N1 Claim Form	**Claim No.**	

Claimant

Defendant(s)

Brief details of claim

Value

SEAL

Defendant's name and address

£

Amount claimed	
Court fee	
Solicitor's costs	
Total amount	
Issue date	

The court office at

is open between 10 am and 4 pm Monday to Friday. When corresponding with the court, please address forms or letters to the Court Manager and quote the claim number.

Claim No.	

Particulars of Claim (attached) (to follow)

Statement of Truth
* (I believe) (The Claimant believes) that the facts stated in these particulars of
claim are true.
* I am duly authorised by the claimant to sign this statement

Full name _____

Name of claimant's solicitor's firm _____

signed _____
* (Claimant) (Litigation friend) (Claimant's solicitor)

position or office held _____
(if signing on behalf of firm or company)

* delete as appropriate

Claimant's or claimant's solicitor's
address to which documents or
payments should be sent if different
from overleaf including (if appropriate)
details of DX, fax or
e-mail.

N1A

Notes for Claimant

Notes for claimant on completing a claim form

Further information may be obtained from the court in a series of free leaflets.

- Please read all of these guidance notes before you begin completing the claim form. The notes follow the order in which information is required on the form.
- Court staff can help you fill in the claim form and give information about procedure once it has been issued. But they cannot give legal advice. If you need legal advice, for example, about the likely success of your claim or the evidence you need to prove it, you should contact a solicitor or a Citizens Advice Bureau.
- If you are filling in the claim form by hand, please use black ink and write in block capitals.
- Copy the completed claim form and the defendant's notes for guidance so that you have one copy for yourself, one copy for the court and one copy for each defendant. Send or take the forms to the court office with the appropriate fee. The court will tell you how much this is.

Heading   Notes on completing the claim form

You must fill in the heading of the form to indicate whether you want the claim to be issued in a county court or in the High Court (The High Court means either a District Registry (attached to a county court) or the Royal Courts of Justice in London). There are restrictions on claims which may be issued in the High Court (see 'Value' overleaf).

Use whichever of the following is appropriate

'In the . . . . County Court'
(inserting the name of the court)

or

'In the High Court of Justice . Division'
(inserting eg. 'Queen's Bench' or 'Chancery' as appropriate)
'. . . . . District Registry'
(inserting the name of the District Registry)

or

'In the High Court of Justice . Division,
(inserting eg. 'Queen's Bench' or 'Chancery' as appropriate)
Royal Courts of Justice'

Claimant and defendant details

As the person issuing the claim, you are called the 'claimant'; the person you are suing is called the 'defendant'. Claimants who are under 18 years old (unless otherwise permitted by the court) and patients within the meaning of the Mental Health Act 1983, must have a litigation friend to issue and conduct court proceedings on their behalf. Court staff will tell you more about what you need to do if this applies to you.

You must provide the following information about yourself **and** the defendant according to the capacity in which you are suing and in which the defendant is being sued. When suing or being sued as:—

an individual:
All known forenames and surname, whether Mr, Mrs, Miss, Ms or other (e.g. Dr) and residential address (**including** postcode and telephone number) in England and Wales. Whether the defendant is a proprietor of a business, a partner in a firm or an individual sued in the name of a club or other unincorporated association, the address for service should be the usual or last known place of residence **or** principal place of business of the company, firm or club or other unincorporated association.

Where the individual is:
under 18 write '(a child by Mr Joe Bloggs his litigation friend)' after the name. If the child is conducting proceedings on their own behalf write '(a child)' after the child's name.

a patient within the meaning of the Mental Health Act 1983 write '(by Mr Joe Bloggs his litigation friend)' after the patient's name.

trading under another name you must add the words 'trading as' and the trading name e.g. 'Mr John Smith trading as Smith's Groceries'.

suing or being sued in a representative capacity you must say what that capacity is e.g. 'Mr Joe Bloggs as the representative of Mrs Sharon Bloggs (deceased)'.

suing or being sued in the name of a club or other unincorporated association add the words 'suing/sued on behalf of' followed by the name of the club or other unincorporated association.

a firm enter the name of the firm followed by the words 'a firm' e.g. 'Bandbox – a firm' and an address for service which is either a partner's residential address or the principal or last known place of business.

a corporation (other than a company) enter the full name of the corporation and the address which is either its principal office **or** any other place where the corporation carries on activities and which has a real connection with the claim.

a company registered in England and Wales enter the name of the company and an address which is either the company's registered office **or** any place of business that has a real, or the most, connection with the claim e.g. the shop where the goods were bought.

an overseas company (defined by s744 of the Companies Act 1985) enter the name of the company and either the address registered under s691 of the Act **or** the address of the place of business having a real, or the most, connection with the claim.

Brief details of claim

Note: The facts and full details about your claim and whether or not you are claiming interest, should be set out in the 'particulars of claim' (see note under 'Particulars of Claim').

You must set out under this heading:
- a concise statement of the nature of your claim
- the remedy you are seeking e.g. payment of money; an order for return of goods or their value; an order to prevent a person doing an act; damages for personal injuries.

Value

If you are claiming a **fixed amount of money** (a 'specified amount') write the amount in the box at the bottom right-hand corner of the claim form against 'amount claimed'.

If you are *not* claiming a fixed amount of money (an 'unspecified amount') under 'Value' write "I expect to recover" followed by whichever of the following applies to your claim:
- "not more than £5,000" **or**
- "more than £5,000 but not more than £15,000" **or**
- "more than £15,000"

If you are **not able** to put a value on your claim, write "I cannot say how much I expect to recover".

Personal injuries
If your claim is for 'not more than £5,000' and includes a claim for personal injuries, you must also write "My claim includes a claim for personal injuries and the amount I expect to recover as damages for pain, suffering and loss of amenity is" followed by either:
- "not more than £1,000" **or**
- "more than £1,000"

Housing disrepair
If your claim is for 'not more than £5,000' and includes a claim for housing disrepair relating to residential premises, you must also write "My claim includes a claim against my landlord for housing disrepair relating to residential premises. The cost of the repairs or other work is estimated to be" followed by either:
- "not more than £1,000" **or**
- "more than £1,000"

If within this claim, you are making a claim for other damages, you must also write:
"I expect to recover as damages" followed by either:
- "not more than £1,000" **or**
- "more than £1,000"

Issuing in the High Court

You may only issue in the High Court if one of the following statements applies to your claim:–
"By law, my claim must be issued in the High Court.
The Act which provides this is ......(specify Act)"
or
"I expect to recover more than £15,000"
or
"My claim includes a claim for personal injuries and the value of the claim is £50,000 or more"

or
"My claim needs to be in a specialist High Court list, namely.....(state which list)".

If one of the statements does not apply and you wish to, or must by law, issue your claim in the High Court, write the words "I wish my claim to issue in the High Court because" followed by the relevant statement e.g. "I wish my claim to issue in the High Court because my claim includes a claim for personal injuries and the value of my claim is £50,000 or more."

Defendant's name and address

Enter in this box the full names and address of the defendant receiving the claim form (i.e. one claim form for each defendant). If the defendant is to be served outside England and Wales, you may need to obtain the court's permission.

Particulars of claim

You may include your particulars of claim on the claim form in the space provided or in a separate document which you should head 'Particulars of Claim'. It should include the names of the parties, the court, the claim number and your address for service and also contain a statement of truth. You should keep a copy for yourself, provide one for the court and one for each defendant. Separate particulars of claim can either be served
- with the claim form **or**
- within 14 days after the date on which the claim form was served.

If your particulars of claim are served separately from the claim form, they must be served with the forms on which the defendant may reply to your claim.

Your particulars of claim must include
- a concise statement of the facts on which you rely
- a statement (if applicable) to the effect that you are seeking aggravated damages or exemplary damages
- details of any interest which you are claiming
- any other matters required for your type of claim as set out in the relevant practice direction

Address for documents

Insert in this box the address at which you wish to receive documens and/or payments, if different from the address you have already given under the heading 'Claimant'. The address must be in England or Wales. If you are willing to accept service by DX, fax or e-mail, add details.

Statement of truth

This must be signed by you, by your solicitor or your litigation friend, as appropriate.
Where the claimant is a registered company or a corporation the claim must be signed by either the director, treasurer, secretary, chief executive, manager or other officer of the company or (in the case of a corporation) the mayor, chairman, president or town clerk.

N1C

Notes for Defendant

Notes for defendant on replying to the claim form

Please read these notes carefully – they will help you decide what to do about this claim. Further information may be obtained from the court in a series of free leaflets

- If this claim form was received with the particulars of claim completed or attached, you must reply within 14 days of the date it was served on you. If the words 'particulars of claim to follow' are written in the particulars of claim box, you should not reply until after you are served with the particulars of claim (which should be no more than 14 days after you received the claim form). If the claim was sent by post, the date of service is taken as the second day after posting (see post mark). If the claim form was delivered or left at your address, the date of service will be the day after it was delivered.
- You may either
  - pay the amount claimed
  - admit that you owe all or part of the claim and ask for time to pay or
  - dispute the claim
- If you do not reply, judgment may be entered against you.
- The notes below tell you what to do.
- The response pack will tell you which forms to use for your reply. (The pack will accompany the particulars of claim if they are served after the claim form).
- Court staff can help you complete the forms of reply and tell you about court procedures. But they cannot give legal advice. If you need legal advice, for example about the likely success of disputing the claim, you should contact a solicitor or a Citizens Advice Bureau immediately.

Registration of Judgments: If the claim results in a judgment being made against you in a **county court**, your name and address may be entered in the Register of County Court Judgments. This may make it difficult for you to obtain credit.

Costs and Interest: Additional costs and interest may be added to the amount claimed on the front of the claim form if judgment is entered against you. In a county court, if judgment is for £5,000 or more, or is in respect of a debt which attracts contractual or statutory interest for late payment, the claimant may be entitled to further interest.

Your response and what happens next

How to pay

Do not bring any payments to the court – they will not be accepted.

When making payments to the claimant, quote the claimant's reference (if any) and the claim number.

Make sure that you keep records and can account for any payments made. Proof may be required if there is any disagreement. It is not safe to send cash unless you use registered post.

Admitting the Claim

Claim for specified amount

If you admit all the claim, take or send the money, including any interest and costs, to the claimant at the address given for payment on the claim form, within 14 days.

If you admit all the claim and you are asking for time to pay, complete Form N9A and send it to the claimant at the address given for payment on the claim form, within 14 days. The claimant will decide whether to accept your proposal for payment. If it is accepted, the claimant may request the court to enter judgment against you and you will be sent an order to pay. If your offer is not accepted, the court will decide how you should pay.

If you admit only part of the claim, complete Form N9A and Form N9B (see 'Disputing the Claim' overleaf) and send

them to the court within 14 days. The claimant will decide whether to accept your part admission. If it is accepted, the claimant may request the court to enter judgment against you and the court will send you an order to pay. If your part admission is not accepted, the case will proceed as a defended claim.

Claim for unspecified amount

If you admit liability for the whole claim but do not make an offer to satisfy the claim, complete Form N9C and send it to the court within 14 days. A copy will be sent to the claimant who may request the court to enter judgment against you for an amount to be decided by the court, and costs. The court will enter judgment and refer the court file to a judge for directions for management of the case. You and the claimant will be sent a copy of the court's order.

If you admit liability for the claim and offer an amount of money to satisfy the claim, complete Form N9C and send it to the court within 14 days. The claimant will be sent a copy and asked if the offer is acceptable. The claimant must reply to the court within 14 days and send you a copy. If a reply is not received, the claim will be stayed. If the amount you have offered is **accepted** –

- the claimant may request the court to enter judgment against you for that amount.
- if you have requested time to pay which is not accepted by the claimant, the rate of payment will be decided by the court.

If your offer in satisfaction is **not accepted** –

- the claimant may request the court to enter judgment against you for an amount to be decided by the court, and costs; and
- the court will enter judgment and refer the court file to a judge for directions for management of the case. You and the claimant will be sent a copy of the court's order.

Disputing the claim

If you are being sued as an individual for a specified amount of money and you dispute the claim, the claim may be transferred to your home court i.e. the one nearest your home or your solicitor's practice if different from the court where the claim was issued.
If you need longer than 14 days to prepare your defence or to contest the court's jurisdiction to try the claim, complete the Acknowledgement of Service form and send it to the court within 14 days. This will allow you 28 days from the date of service of the particulars of claim to file your defence or make an application to contest the court's jurisdiction. The court will tell the claimant that your Acknowledgment of Service has been received.
If the case proceeds as a defended claim, you and the claimant will be sent an Allocation Questionnaire. You will be told the date by which it must be returned to the court. The information you give on the form will help a judge decide whether your case should be dealt with in the small claims track, fast track or multi-track. After a judge has considered the completed questionnaires, you will be sent a notice of allocation setting out the judge's decision. The notice will tell you the track to which the claim has been allocated and what you have to do to prepare for the hearing or trial. **Leaflets telling you more about the tracks are available from the court office.**

Claim for specified amount
If you wish to dispute the full amount claimed or wish to claim against the claimant (a counterclaim), complete Form N9B and send it to the court within 14 days.
If you admit part of the claim, complete the Defence Form N9B <u>and</u> the Admission Form N9A and send them both to the court within 14 days. The

claimant will decide whether to accept your part admission in satisfaction of the claim (see under 'Admitting the Claim – specified amount'). If the claimant does not accept the amount you have admitted, the case will proceed as a defended claim.
If you dispute the claim because you have already paid it, complete Form N9B and send it to the court within 14 days. The claimant will have to decide whether to proceed with the claim or withdraw it and notify the court and you within 28 days. If the claimant wishes to proceed, the case will proceed as a defended claim.

Claim for unspecified amount/return of goods/non-money claims
If you dispute the claim or wish to claim against the claimant (counterclaim), complete Form N9D and send it to the court within 14 days.
Personal injuries claims:
If the claim is for personal injuries and the claimant has attached a medical report to the particulars of claim, in your defence you should state whether you:
- agree with the report **or**
- dispute all or part of the report **and** give your reasons for doing so **or**
- nether agree nor dispute the report **or** have no knowledge of the report

Where you have obtained your own medical report, you should attach it to your defence.
If the claim is for personal injuries and the claimant has attached a schedule of past and future expenses and losses, in your defence you must state which of the items you:
- agree **or**
- dispute **and** supply alternative figures where appropriate **or**
- neither agree nor dispute or have no knowledge of

Address where notices can be sent
This must be either your solicitor's address, your own residential or business address in England and Wales or (if you live elsewhere) some other address within England and Wales.

Statement of truth
This must be signed by you, by your solicitor or your litigation friend, as appropriate.
Where the defendant is **a registered company or a corporation** the response must be signed by either the director, treasurer, secretary, chief executive, manager or other officer of the company **or** (in the case of a corporation) the mayor, chairman, president or town clerk.

Notes for defendant on replying to the claim form (Consumer Credit Act claim)

Please read these notes carefully – they will help you decide what to do about this claim. You will have received a notice of hearing telling you when and where to come to court with the claim form. A leaflet is available from the court office about what happens when you come to a court hearing.

- You must reply to the claim form within 14 days of the date it was served on you. If the claim form was
  - sent by post, the date of service is taken as the second day after posting (see post mark)
  - delivered or left at your address, the date of service will be the day after it was delivered
  - handed to you personally, the date of service will be the day it was given to you
- You may either
  - pay the amount claimed
  - admit liability for the claim and offer to make payments to keep the goods
  - dispute the claim
- If you do not reply or attend the hearing, judgment may be entered against you.
- The notes below tell you what to do.
- Court staff can help you complete the forms of reply and tell you about court procedure. But they cannot give legal advice. If you need legal advice, for example about the likely success of disputing the claim, you should contact a solicitor or a Citizens Advice Bureau immediately.

Registration of Judgments: If the claim results in a judgment being made against you in a **county court**, your name and address may be entered in the Register of County Court Judgments. This may make it difficult for you to obtain credit.

Costs and Interest: Additional costs and interest may be added to the amount claimed on the front of the claim form if judgment is entered against you. In a county court, if judgment is for £5,000 or more, or is in respect of a debt which attracts contractual or statutory interest for late payment, the claimant may be entitled to further interest.

Your response and what happens next

How to pay

Do not bring any payments to the court – they will not be accepted.

When making payments to the claimant, quote the claimant's reference (if any) and the claim number.

Make sure that you keep records and can account for any payments made. Proof may be required if there is any disagreement. It is not safe to send cash unless you use registered post.

Admitting the Claim

If you admit liability for the claim and offer to make payments in order to keep the goods. Complete Form N9C and send it to the court within 14 days. **Remember** to keep a copy for yourself. The court will send a copy of your admission to the claimant and ask if your offer is acceptable.

If the claimant **accepts your offer** and asks the court to enter judgment before the date of the hearing, you will be sent a copy of the judgment and need not come to the hearing. If you do not hear from the court it is in your interests to attend the hearing.

If your offer is **not accepted**, you should attend the hearing. The court will treat your admission as evidence so remember to bring a copy of your admission with you to the hearing.

Disputing the claim

If you dispute the claim or wish to claim against the claimant (counterclaim), complete Form N9D and send it to the court within 14 days. **Remember** to keep a copy for yourself and to bring it with you to the hearing. The court will send a copy of your defence to the claimant. At the hearing the court may make a final order or judgment in the claim. If the court agrees that you have a valid defence (or counterclaim), it will tell you and the claimant what to do to prepare for a future hearing. If you send your defence to the court after the 14 days has expired, and you want to rely on it at the hearing, the court may take your failure to file it on time into account when deciding what order to make in respect of costs.

Statement of truth

This must be signed by you, by your solicitor or your litigation friend, as appropriate. Where the defendant is **a registered company or a corporation** the response must be signed by either the director, treasurer, secretary, chief executive, manager or other officer of the company **or** (in the case of a corporation) the mayor, chairman, president or town clerk.

Appendix 7

Part 8 Claim Form (N208)

THE COUNTY COURT PRACTITIONER 2000
N208
Claim Form (CPR Part 8)

	In the
Claim Form (CPR Part 8)	**Claim No.**

Claimant

Defendant(s)

SEAL

Details of claim (see also overleaf)

Defendant's name and address   £

Court fee	
Solicitor's costs	
Issue date	

The court office at

is open between 10 am and 4 pm Monday to Friday. When corresponding with the court, please address forms or letters to the Court Manager and quote the claim number.

Claim No.	

Details of claim (continued)

Statement of Truth
* (I believe)(The Claimant believes) that the facts stated in these particulars of
  claim are true.
* I am duly authorised by the claimant to sign this statement

Full name _____

Name of claimant's solicitor's firm _____

signed _____ position or office held _____
*(Claimant)(Litigation friend)(Claimant's solicitor) (if signing on behalf of firm
or company)

* delete as appropriate

Claimant's or claimant's solicitor's address
to which documents should be sent if
different from overleaf. If you are
prepared to accept service by DX, fax or
e-mail, please add details.

Notes for Claimant (CPR Part 8)

Notes for claimant on completing a Part 8 claim form

- Please read all of these guidance notes before you begin completing the claim form. The notes follow the order in which information is required on the form.
- Court staff can help you fill in the claim form and give information about procedure once it has been issued. But they cannot give legal advice. If you need legal advice, for example, about the likely success of your claim or the evidence you need to prove it, you should contact a solicitor or a Citizens Advice Bureau.
- If you are filling in the claim form by hand, please use black ink and write in block capitals.
- You must file any written evidence to support your claim either in or with the claim form. Your written evidence must be verified by a statement of truth.
- Copy the completed claim form, the defendant's notes for guidance and your written evidence so that you have one copy for yourself, one copy for the court and one copy for each defendant. Send or take the forms and evidence to the court office with the appropriate fee. The court will tell you how much this is.

Notes on completing the claim form

Heading

You must fill in the heading of the form to indicate whether you want the claim to be issued in a county court or in the High Court (The High Court means either a District Registry (attached to a county court) or the Royal Courts of Justice in London).
Use whichever of the following is appropriate:

'In the . . . . County Court'
(inserting the name of the court)
or
'In the High Court of Justice . Division'
(inserting eg. 'Queen's Bench' or 'Chancery' as appropriate)
'. . . . . District Registry'
(inserting the name of the District Registry)
or
'In the High Court of Justice . Division,
(inserting eg. 'Queen's Bench' or 'Chancery' as appropriate)
Royal Courts of Justice'

Claimant and defendant details

As the person issuing the claim, you are called the 'claimant'; the person you are suing is called the 'defendant'. Claimants who are under 18 years old (unless otherwise permitted by the court) and patients within the meaning of the Mental Health Act 1983 must have a litigation friend to issue and conduct court proceedings on their behalf. Court staff will tell you more about what you need to do if this applies to you.

You must provide the following information about yourself **and** the defendant according to the capacity in which you are suing and in which the defendant is being sued. When suing or being sued as:—

an individual:
All known forenames and surname, whether Mr, Mrs, Miss, Ms or Other (e.g. Dr) and residential address (including postcode and telephone and any fax or e-mail number) in England and Wales. Where the defendant is a proprietor of a business, a partner in a firm or an individual sued in the name of a club or other unincorporated association, the address for service should be the usual or last known place of residence or principal place of business of the company,

firm or club or other unincorporated association.

Where the individual is:
under 18 write '(a child by Mr Joe Bloggs his litigation friend)' after the child's name.

a patient within the meaning of the Mental Health Act 1983 write '(by Mr Joe Bloggs his litigation friend)' after the patient's name.

trading under another name you must add the words 'trading as' and the trading name e.g. 'Mr John Smith trading as Smith's Groceries'.

suing or being sued in a representative capacity you must say what that capacity is e.g. 'Mr Joe Bloggs as the representative of Mrs Sharon Bloggs (deceased)'.

suing or being sued in the name of a club or other unincorporated association add the words 'suing/sued on behalf of' followed by the name of the club or other unincorported association.

a firm enter the name of the firm followed by the words 'a firm' e.g. 'Bandbox – a firm' and an address for service which is either a partner's residential address or the principal or last known place of business.

a corporation (other than a company) enter the full name of the corporation and the address which is either its principal office or any other place where the corporation carries on activities and which has a real connection with the claim.

a company registered in England and Wales enter the name of the company and an address which is either the company's registered office or any place of business that has a real, or the most, connection with the claim e.g. the shop where the goods were bought.

an overseas company (defined by s744 of the Companies Act 1985) enter the name of the company and either the address registered under s691 of the Act or the address of the place of business having a real, or the most, connection with the claim.

Brief details of claim

Note: The facts and full details about your claim and whether or not you are claiming interest, should be set out in the 'particulars of claim' (see note under 'Particulars of Claim').

You must set out under this heading:
- a concise statement of the nature of your claim
- the remedy you are seeking e.g. payment of money; an order for return of goods or their value; an order to prevent a person doing an act; damages for personal injuries.

Value

If you are claiming a fixed amount of money (a 'specified amount') write the amount in the box at the bottom right-hand corner of the claim form against 'amount claimed'.

If you are not claiming a fixed amount of money (an 'unspecified amount') under 'Value' write "I expect to recover" followed by whichever of the following applies to your claim:
- "not more than £5,000" or
- "more than £5,000 but not more than £15,000" or
- "more than £15,000"

If you are not able to put a value on your claim, write "I cannot say how much I expect to recover".

Personal injuries

If your claim is for 'not more than £5,000' and includes a claim for personal injuries, you must also write "My claim includes a claim for personal injuries and the amount I expect to recover as damages for pain, suffering and loss of amenity is" followed by either:
- "not more than £1,000" or
- "more than £1,000"

Housing disrepair

If your claim is for 'not more than £5,000' and includes a claim for housing disrepair relating to residential premises, you must also write "My claim includes a claim against my landlord for housing disrepair relating to residential premises. The cost of the repairs or other work is estimated to be" followed by either:
- "not more than £1,000" or
- "more than £1,000"

If within this claim, you are making a claim for other damages, you must also write:
"I expect to recover as damages" followed by either:
- "not more than £1,000" or
- "more than £1,000"

Issuing in the High Court

You may only issue in the High Court if one of the following statements applies to your claim:-
"By law, my claim must be issued in the High Court.
The Act which provides this is ......(specify Act)"
or
"I expect to recover more than £15,000"
or
"My claim includes a claim for personal injuries and the value of the claim is £50,000 or more"

or
"My claim needs to be in a specialist High Court list, namely.....(state which list)".

If one of the statements does not apply and you wish to, or must by law, issue your claim in the High Court, write the words "I wish my claim to issue in the High Court because" followed by the relevant statement e.g. "I wish my claim to issue in the High Court because my claim includes a claim for personal injuries and the value of my claim is £50,000 or more."

Defendant's name and address

Enter in this box the full names and address of the defendant receiving the claim form (i.e. one claim form for each defendant). If the defendant is to be served outside England and Wales, you may need to obtain the court's permission.

Particulars of claim

You may include your particulars of claim on the claim form in the space provided or in a separate document which you should head 'Particulars of Claim'. It should include the names of the parties, the court, the claim number and your address for service and also contain a statement of truth. You should keep a copy for yourself, provide one for the court and one for each defendant. Separate particulars of claim can either be served
- with the claim form or
- within 14 days after the date on which the claim form was served.

If your particulars of claim are served separately from the claim form, they must be served with the forms on which the defendant may reply to your claim.

Your particulars of claim must include
- a concise statement of the facts on which you rely
- a statement (if applicable) to the effect that you are seeking aggravated damages or exemplary damages
- details of any interest which you are claiming
- any other matters required for your type of claim as set out in the relevant practice direction

Address for documents

Insert in this box the address at which you wish to receive documents and/or payments, if different from the address you have already given under the heading 'Claimant'. The address must be in England or Wales. If you are willing to accept service by DX, fax or e-mail, add details.

Statement of truth

This must be signed by you, by your solicitor or your litigation friend, as appropriate.

Where the claimant is a registered company or a corporation the claim must be signed by either the director, treasurer, secretary, chief executive, manager or other officer of the company or (in the case of a corporation) the mayor, chairman, president or town clerk.

N208C

Notes for Defendant (CPR Part 8)

Notes for defendant (Part 8 claim form)

Please read these notes carefully – they will help you decide what to do about this claim.

- You have 14 days from the date on which you were served with the claim form (see below) in which to respond to the claim by completing and returning the acknowledgment of service enclosed with this claim form.
- If you **do not return** the acknowledgment of service, you will be allowed to attend any hearing of this claim but you will **not** be allowed to take part in the hearing unless the court gives you permission to do so.

Court staff can tell you about procedures but they cannot give legal advice. If you need legal advice, you should contact a solicitor or Citizens Advice Bureau immediately

Responding to this claim

Time for responding

The completed acknowledgment of service must be returned to the court office within 14 days of the date on which the claim form was served on you. If the claim form was

- sent by post, the 14 days begins 2 days from the date of the postmark on the envelope.
- delivered or left at your address, the 14 days begins the day after it was delivered.
- handed to you personally, the 14 days begins on the day it was given to you.

Completing the acknowledgment of service

You should complete section A, B, or C as appropriate **and all** of section D.

Section A – contesting the claim
If you wish to contest the remedy sought by the claimant in the claim form, you should complete section A. If you seek a remedy different from that sought by the claimant, you should give full details in the space provided.

Section B – disputing the court's jurisdiction
You should indicate your intention by completing section B and filing an application disputing the court's jurisdiction within 14 days of filing of your acknowledgment of service at the court. The court will arrange a hearing date for the application and tell you and the claimant when and where to attend.

Section C – objecting to use of procedure
If you believe that the claimant should not have issued the claim under Part 8 because:

- there is a substantial dispute of fact involved and
- you do not agree that the rule or practice direction, stated does provide for the claimant to use this procedure

you should complete section C setting out your reasons in the space provided.

Written evidence

If you wish to file written evidence in reply to the claimant's written evidence, you must send it to the court with your acknowledgment of service. Your written evidence must be verified by a statement of truth or the court may disallow it.

Serving other parties

At the same time as you file your completed acknowledgment of service (and any written evidence) with the court, you must also send copies of both the form and any written evidence to any other party named on the claim form.

What happens next

The claimant may, within 14 days of receiving any written evidence from you, file further evidence in reply. On receipt of your acknowledgment of service and any evidence from the claimant in reply, the court file will be referred to the judge for directions for the disposal of the claim. The court will contact you and tell you what to do next.
Note: The court may already have given directions or arranged a hearing. If so, you will have received a copy with the claim form. You should comply with any directions and attend any hearing in addition to completing, filing and serving your acknowledgment of service.

Statement of truth

This must be signed by you, by your solicitor or your litigation friend, as appropriate. Where the claimant is a registered company or a corporation the claim must be signed by either the director, treasurer, secretary, chief executive, manager or other officer of the company or (in the case of a corporation) the mayor, chairman, president or town clerk.

Appendix 8

Defence and Counterclaim Forms (N9B/N9D)

THE COUNTY COURT PRACTITIONER 2000
N9B
Defence and Counterclaim (specified amount)

Defence and Counterclaim (specified amount)

- Fill in this form if you wish to dispute all or part of the claim and/or make a claim against the claimant (counterclaim).
- You have a limited number of days to complete and return this form to the court.
- Before completing this form, please read the notes for guidance attached to the claim form.
- Please ensure that all boxes at the top right of this form are completed. You can obtain the correct names and number from the claim form. The court cannot trace your case without this information.

How to fill in this form

- Complete sections 1 and 2. Tick the correct boxes and give the other detail asked for.
- Set out your defence in section 3. If necessary continue on a separate piece of paper making sure that the claim number is clearly shown on it. In your defence you must state which allegations in the particulars of claim you deny and your reasons for doing so. **If you fail to deny an allegation it may be taken that you admit it.**
- If you dispute only some of the allegations you must
  - specify which you admit and which you deny; and
  - give your own version of events if different from the claimant's.

In the

Claim No.

Claimant (including ref.)

Defendant

□ I paid the amount admitted on (*date*)
or
□ I enclose the completed form of admission (*go to section 2*)

- If you wish to make a claim against the claimant (a counterclaim) complete section 4.
- Complete and sign section 5 before sending this form to the court. Keep a copy of the claim form and this form.

Legal Aid

- You may be entitled to legal aid. Ask about the legal aid scheme at any county court office, Citizens Advice Bureau, legal advice centre or firm of solicitors displaying the legal aid sign.

1. How much of the claim do you dispute?

□ I dispute the full amount claimed as shown on the claim form
or
□ I admit the amount of £

If you dispute only part of the claim you must **either:**

- pay the amount admitted to the person named at the address for payment on the claim form (see How to Pay in the notes on the back of, or attached to, the claim form). Then send this defence to the court
or
- complete the admission form **and** this defence form and send them to the court.

2. Do you dispute this claim because you have already paid it? *Tick which ever applies*

□ **No** (*go to section 3*)

□ **Yes** I paid £ to the claimant

on (*before the claim form was issued*)

Give details of where and how you paid it in the box below (*then go to section 5*)

3. Defence

Defence (continued)   Claim No. [   ]

4. If you wish to make a claim against the claimant (a counterclaim)

If your claim is for a specific sum of money, how much are you claiming? £ [   ]

- To start your counterclaim, you will have to pay a fee. Court staff will tell you how much you have to pay.

My claim is for (*please specify nature of claim*)

[   ]

- You may not be able to make a counterclaim where the claimant is the Crown (e.g. a Government Department). Ask your local county court office for further information.

What are you reasons for making the counterclaim?
If you need to continue on a separate sheet put the claim number in the top right hand corner.

[   ]

5. Signed
(To be signed by you or by your solicitor or litigation friend)

delete as appropriate

| *(I believe) (The defendant believes) that the facts stated in this form are true. *I am duly authorised by the defendant to sign this statement | Position or office held (if signing on behalf of firm or company) |

Date [   ]

Give an address to which notices about this case can be sent

Postcode

Tel. no. [   ]

	if applicable
fax no.	
DX no.	
e-mail	

A8.02   **N9D**

Defence and Counterclaim (unspecified amount and non-money claims)

Defence and Counterclaim (unspecified amount, non-money and return of goods claims)	In the	

- Fill in this form if you wish to dispute all or part of the claim and/or make a claim against the claimant (counterclaim)

	Claim No.	
	Claimant (including ref.)	

- You have a limited number of days to complete and return this form to the court.
- Before completing this form, please read the notes for guidance attached to the claim form.

	Defendant	

- Please ensure that all the boxes at the top right of this form are completed. You can obtain the correct names and number from the claim form. The court cannot trace your case without this information.

How to fill in this form
- Set out your defence in section 1. If necessary continue on a separate piece of paper making sure that the claim number is clearly shown on it. In your defence you must state which allegations in the particulars of claim you deny and your reasons for doing so. **If you fail to deny an allegation it may be taken that you admit it.**
- If you dispute only some of the allegations you must
  - specify which you admit and which you deny; and
  - give your own version of events if different from the claimant's.
- If the claim is for money and you dispute the claimant's statement of value, you must say why and if possible give your own statement of value.

- If you wish to make a claim against the claimant (a counterclaim) complete section 2.
- Complete and sign section 3 before returning this form.

Where to send this form
- send or take this form immediately to the court at the address given on the claim form.
- Keep a copy of the claim form and the defence form.

Legal Aid
- You may be entitled to legal aid. Ask about the legal aid scheme at any county court office, Citizens Advice Bureau, legal advice centre or firm of solicitors displaying the legal aid sign.

1. Defence

Defence (continued)

Claim No. [   ]

---

2. If you wish to make a claim against the claimant (a counterclaim)

If your claim is for a specific sum of money, how much are you claiming? £ [   ]

My claim is for (*please specify*)

[   ]

- To start your counterclaim, you will have to pay a fee. Court staff will tell you how much you have to pay.

- You may not be able to make a counterclaim where the claimant is the Crown (e.g. a Government Department). Ask at your local county court office for further information.

What are you reasons for making the counterclaim?
If you need to continue on a separate sheet put the claim number in the top right hand corner

---

3. Signed
(To be signed by you or by your solicitor or litigation friend)

* delete as appropriate

*(I believe)(The defendant believes) that the facts stated in this form are true. *I am duly authorised by the defendant to sign this statement

Position or office held
(if signing on behalf of firm or company)

Date [   ]

Give an address to which notices about this case can be sent to you

Postcode

Tel. no.

	if applicable
fax no.	
DX no.	
e-mail	

Appendix 9

Allocation Questionnaire (N150)

N150   A9.01

Allocation Questionnaire

Allocation questionnaire

In the

To

Claim No.

Last date for filing with court office

(SEAL)

Please read the notes on page five before completing the questionnaire.

Please note the date by which it must be returned and the name of the court it should be returned to since this may be different from the court where proceedings were issued.

If you have settled this case (or if you settle it on a future date) and do not need to have it heard or tried, you must let the court know immediately.

A Settlement

Do you wish there to be a one month stay to attempt to settle the case?   ☐ Yes   ☐ No

B Track

Which track do you consider is most suitable for your case? *(Tick one box)*   ☐ small claims   ☐ fast track   ☐ multi-track

If you think your case is suitable for a specialist list, say which:

If you have indicted a track which would not be the normal track for the case, please give brief reasons for you choice:

C   Pre-action protocols

Have you complied with any pre-action protocol applicable to your claim?

☐ None applicable to this claim   ☐ Yes   ☐ No

If Yes, please say which protocol:

If No, please explain to what extent and for what reason it has no been complied with:

D   Applications

If you have not already sent the court an application for summary judgment, do you intend to do so?

☐ Yes   ☐ No

If you have not already issued a claim in the case against someone not yet a party, do you intend to apply for the court's permission to do so?

☐ Yes   ☐ No

In either case, if Yes, please give details:

E   Witnesses of fact

So far a you know at this stage, what witnesses of fact do you intend to call at the hearing?

Witness name	Witness to which facts

F Experts' evidence

Do you wish to use expert evidence at the hearing? ☐ Yes ☐ No

Have you already copied any experts' report(s) to   ☐ None ☐ Yes ☐ No
the other party(ies)?   obtained
                                                        as yet

Please list the experts whose evidence you think you will use:

Expert's name	Field of expertise (eg. orthopaedic surgeon, mechanical engineer)

Will you and the other party use the same expert(s)? ☐ Yes ☐ No

If No, please explain why not:

Do you want your expert(s) to give evidence orally at ☐ Yes ☐ No
the hearing or trial?

If Yes, give the reasons why you think oral evidence is
necessary:

G Location of trial

Is there any reason why your case needs to be heard ☐ Yes ☐ No
at a particular court?

If Yes, give reasons (eg. particular facilities required,
convenience of witnesses, etc.)

and specify the court:

H Representation and estimate of hearing/trial time

Do you expect to be represented by a solicitor
or counsel at the hearing/trial?   No   Solicitor   Counsel

How long do you estimate it will take to put
your case to the court at the hearing/trial?   days   hours   minutes

If there are days when you, your representative,
expert or an essential witness will not be able
to attend court, give details:

Name   Dates not available

I Costs (only relates to costs incurred by legal representatives)

What is your estimate of costs incurred to date,
excluding disbursements, VAT and court fees?   £

What do you estimate the overall costs are likely to be,
excluding disbursements, VAT and court fees?   £

J Other information

Have you attached documents you wish the judge to
take into account when allocating the case?   Yes   No

Have they been served on the other parties?   Yes   No

If Yes, say when

Have the other parties agreed their content?   Yes   No

Have you attached a list of the directions you think
appropriate for the management of your case?   Yes   No

Are they agreed with the other parties?   Yes   No

Are there any other facts which might affect the
timetable the court will set? If so, please state

Signed   Date

[Counsel] [Solicitor] [for the] [Claimant] [Defendant]

APPENDIX 9

A9.01

Notes for completing an allocation questionnaire

- If the case is not settled, a judge must allocate it to an appropriate case management track. To help the judge choose the most just and cost-effective track, you must now complete the attached questionnaire.
- If you fail to return the allocation questionnaire by the date given, the judge may make an order which leads to your claim or defence being struck out, or hold an allocation hearing. If there is an allocation hearing the judge may order any party who has not filed their questionnaire to pay, immediately, the costs of that hearing.
- If you wish to make an application, for example, for special directions, for summary judgment on the grounds that the other party has no reasonable chance of success in their claim or defence, or for permission to add another party to the claim, you should send it and any required fee with the completed allocation questionnaire. If a hearing is fixed for your application, it may also be used as an allocation hearing.
- Any other documents you wish the judge to take into account should be filed with the questionnaire. But you must confirm that the documents have been sent to the other party, or parties, saying when they would have received them and whether they agreed their contents.
- Use a separate sheet if you need more speace for your answers marking clearly which section the information refers to. Write the case number on it, sign and date it and attach it securely to the questionnaire.
- The letters below refer to the secitons of the questionnaire and tell you what information is needed.

A Settlement
If you think that you and the other party may be able to negotiate a settlement you should tick the 'Yes' box. The court may order a stay, whether or not all the other parties to the case agree. You need not complete the rest of the questionnaire, even if you are requesting a stay. Where a stay is granted it will be for an initial period of one month.

B Track
The basic guide by which cases are normally allocated to a track depends on the money value of the claim, although other factors such as the complexity of the case will also be considered:

Small Claims track	Claims values at £5,00 or less unless they include a claim for personal injuries worth over £1,000; or a claim for housing disrepair where the costs of the repairs or other work is more than £1,000 and any other claim for damages is more than £1,000
Fast track	Claims valued at more than £5,000 but not more than £15,000
Multi-track	Claims over £15,000

A leaflet available from the court office explains these limits in greater detail.

C Pre-action protocols
For certain kinds of claim, there are protocols which set out what ought to be done before court proceedings are issued. As at April 1999 there are protocols for clinical negligence and personal injury claims.

D Applications
If you intend to apply for summary judgment or for permission to add another party to the claim or make any other application you should, if you have not already done so, file the application with your completed allocation questionnaire.

E Witnesses of fact
Remember to include yourself, if you will be giving evidence; but not experts, who should be included in section F.

F Experts' evidence
Oral or written expert evidence will only be allowed at the trial with the court's permission. The judge will decide what permission it seems appropriate to give when the case is allocated to track.

G Location of trial
High Court cases are usually heard at the Royal Courts of Justice or certain Civil Trial Centres. Other multi-track cases are heard at the Civil Trial Centre for the court where they are proceeding. Fast track cases are usually heard either at the court in which they are proceeding or its Civil Trial Centre. The court office will tell you which is the Civil Trial Centre for any particular county court. Small claims cases are usually heard at the court in which they are proceeding.

H Representation and estimate of hearing time
If the case is allocated to the fast track, no more than one day will be allowed for the trial of the whole case.

Appendix 10

Listing Questionnaire (N170)

Listing Questionnaire

Listing questionnaire	In the
	Claim No.
	Last date for filing with court office
To	

- The court will use the information which you and the other party(ies) provide to fix a date for trial (or to confirm the date and time if one has already been fixed), to confirm the estimated length of trial and to set a timetable for the trial itself. In multi-track cases the court will also decide whether to hold a pre-trial review.

- If you do not complete and return the questionnaire the procedural judge may
  - make an order which leads to your statement of case (claim or defence) being struck out.
  - decide to hold a listing hearing. You may be ordered to pay (immediately) the other parties' costs of attending.
  - if there is sufficient information, list the case for trial and give any appropriate directions.

A Directions complied with

1. Have you complied with all the previous directions given by the court?   ☐ Yes ☐ No

2. If no please explain which directions are outstanding and why

Directions outstanding	Reasons directions outstanding

3. Are any further directions required to prepare the case for trial?   ☐ Yes ☐ No
   (If no go to section B)

4. If yes, please explain directions required and give reasons

Directions required	Reasons required

B Experts

1. Has the court already given permission for you to use written expert evidence?　　　Yes　　　No
           (If no go to section B6)

2. If yes, please give name and field of expertise.

Name of expert	Whether joint expert *(please tick, if appropriate)*	Field of expertise

3. Have the expert(s)' report(s) been agreed with the other parties?　　　Yes　　　No

4. Have the experts met to discuss their reports?　　　Yes　　　No

5. Has the court already given permission for the expert(s) to give oral evidence at the trial?　　　Yes　　　No
           (If yes go to Q7)

6. If no, are you seeking that permission?　　　Yes　　　No
           (If no go to section C)

7. If yes, give your reasons for seeking permission.

8. If yes, what are the names, addresses and fields of expertise of your experts?

Expert 1	Expert 2	Expert 3	Expert 4

9. Please give details of any dates within the trial period when your expert(s) will not be available

Name of expert	Dates not available

C Other witnesses

(*If you are not calling other witnesses go to section D*)

1. How many other witnesses (including yourself) will be giving evidence on your behalf at the trial? (*do not include experts – see section B above*)

(*Give number*)

2. What are the names and addresses of your witnesses?

Witness 1	Witness 2	Witness 3	Witness 4

3. Please give details of any dates within the trial period when you or your witnesses will not be available?

Name of witness	Dates not available

4. Are any of the witness statements agreed?   Yes   No

(*If no go to question C6*)

5. If yes, give the name of the witness and the date of his or her statement

Name of witness	Date of statement

6. Do you or any of your witnesses need any special facilities?   Yes   No

(*If no go to question C8*)

7. If yes, what are they?

8. Will any of your witnesses be provided with an interpreter?   Yes   No

(*If no go to section D*)

9. If yes, say what type of interpreter e.g. language (stating which), deaf/blind etc.

305

D Legal representation

1. Who will be presenting your case at the hearing or trial? ☐ You ☐ Solicitor ☐ Counsel

2. Please give details of any dates within the trial period when the person presenting your case will not be available.

Name	Dates not available

E Other matters

1. How long do you estimate the trial will take, including cross-examination and closing arguments?

Minutes	Hours	Days

If your case is allocated to the fast track the maximum time allowed for the whole case will be no more than one day.

2. What is the estimated number of pages of evidence to be included in the trial bundle?

(please give number)

Fast track cases only

3. The court will normally give you 3 weeks notice in the fast track of the date fixed for a fast track trial unless, in exceptional circumstances, the court directs that shorter notice will be given. Would you be prepared to accept shorter notice of the date fixed for trial?   ☐ Yes   ☐ No

Signed

Claimant/defendant or Counsel/Solicitor for the claimant/defendant

Date

Appendix 11

Schedule of Costs for Summary Assessment

A11.01

SCHEDULE OF COSTS FORMS: FORM 1

COURT   CASE REFERENCE
JUDGE/MASTER
CASE TITLE

      [Party]'s Statement of Costs for the hearing on [date]
Description of fee earners*
(1)   [name]   [grade]   [hourly rate claimed]
(2)   [name]   [grade]   [hourly rate claimed]

Attendances on [Party]
[number] hours at £   £

Attendances on opponents
[number] hours at £   £

Attendances on others
(1) [number] hours at £   £
(2) [number] hours at £   £

Work done on documents
[number] hours at £   £

Attendance at hearing
[number] hours at £   £
[number] hours travel and waiting at £   £

Counsel's fees [name] [year of call]
Fee for [advice/conference/documents]   £
Fee for hearing   £

Other expenses
[court fees]   £
Others [give brief description]   £

TOTAL
Amount of VAT claimed
       on solicitor's and counsel's fees £
       on other expenses   £

GRAND TOTAL   £

The costs estimated above do not exceed the costs which the [party] is
liable to pay in respect of the work which this estimate covers.
Dated   Signed
                          Name of firm of solicitors
                          [partner] for the [party]

* 4 grades of fee earner are suggested: (1) partners and solicitors with over 4 years PQE
(2) solicitors with up to 4 years PQE, and senior legal executives (3) legal executives
and senior para-legals (4) trainee solicitors and junior para-legals. In respect of each fee
earner communications should be treated as attendances and routine communications
should be claimed at one tenth of the hourly rate.

Appendix 12

Table of Fixed Costs (CPR, Part 45) and Fees (County Court Fees Order 1999)

A12.01   FIXED COSTS ON COMMENCEMENT OF A CLAIM

Relevant Band	Where the claim form is served by the court or by any method other than personal service by the claimant	Where • the claim form is served personally by the claimant; and • there is only one defendant	Where there is more than one defendant, for each additional defendant personally served at separate addresses by the claimant
Where— • the value of the claim exceeds £25 but does not exceed £500	£50	£60	£15
Where— • the value of the claim exceeds £500 but does not exceed £1000	£70	£80	£15
Where— • the value of the claim exceeds £1000 but does not exceed £5000; or • the only claim is for delivery of goods and no value is specified or stated on the claim form	£80	£90	£15

Where— • the value of the claim exceeds £5000	£100	£110	£15

Comment—The table provides different levels of fees depending upon the value of the claim, the method of service and the number of defendants. The relevant band is ascertained by reference to the amount claimed and the value of the goods in the claim form.

TABLE 2

A12.02

FIXED COSTS ON ENTRY OF JUDGMENT

	Where the amount of the judgment exceeds £25 but does not exceed £5000	Where the amount of the judgment exceeds £5000
Where judgment in default of an acknowledgment of service is entered under rule 12.4(1) (entry of judgment by request on claim for money only)	£22	£30
Where judgment in default of a defence is entered under rule 12.4(1) (entry of judgment by request on claim for money only)	£25	£35
Where judgment is entered under rule 14.4 (judgment on admission), or rule 14.5 (judgment on admission of part of claim), and claimant accepts the defendant's proposal as to the manner of payment.	£40	£55
Where judgment is entered under rule 14.4 (judgment on admission), or rule 14.5 (judgment on admission on part of claim) and court decides the date or times of payment	£55	£70
Where summary judgment is given under Part 24 or the court strikes out a defence under rule 3.4(2)(a), in either case, on application by a party	£175	£210

Where judgment is given on a claim for delivery of goods under a regulated agreement within the meaning of the Consumer Credit Act 1974 and no other entry in this table applies	£60	£85

Comment—The table sets out the fixed costs on entry of judgment. Different costs are payable in respect of cases above and below £5,000 and in different circumstances. The amount which is included in the judgment is the aggregate of the fixed commencement costs (see Table 1, r.45.2) and the relevant figure in Table 2.

TABLE 3

MISCELLANEOUS FIXED COSTS

For service by a party of any document required to be served personally including preparing and copying a certificate of service for each individual served	£15
Where service by an alternative method is permitted by an order under rule 6.8 for each individual served	£25
Where a document is served out of the jurisdiction— (a) in Scotland, Northern Ireland, the Isle of Man or the Channel Islands (b) in any other place	£65 £65

(Other rules which provide for situations where fixed costs may be allowed can be found in Schedule 1 in RSC Order 62 and in Schedule 2 in CCR Order 38, Appendix B.)

Comment—As to fixed costs on the issue of a Default Costs Certificate see Directions relating to Pt 45, paras 2.1—2.2 (see para. 45PD—001).

COUNTY COURT FEES ORDER 1999

SCHEDULE 1

FEES TO BE TAKEN

Number & description of fee	Amount of fee
1. Commencement of proceedings 1.1 On the commencement of originating proceedings (including originating proceedings issued after leave to issue is granted) to recover a sum of money, except in CPC cases, where the sum claimed:	(a) does not exceed £200 . . . £20 (b) exceeds £200 but not £300 . . . £30 (c) exceeds £300 but not £400 . . . £40 (d) exceeds £400 but not £500 . . . £50 (e) exceeds £500 but not £1,000 . . . £70 (f) exceeds £1,000 but not £5,000 . . . £100 (g) exceeds £5,000 but not £15,000 . . . £200 (h) exceeds £15,000 but not £50,000 . . . £300 (i) exceeds £50,000 or not limited . . . £400
1.2 On the commencement of originating proceedings to recover a sum of money in CPC cases, where the sum claimed:	(a) does not exceed £200 . . . £15 (b) exceeds £200 but not £300 . . . £25 (c) exceeds £300 but not £400 . . . £35 (d) exceeds £400 but not £500 . . . £45 (e) exceeds £500 but not £1,000 . . . £65 (f) exceeds £1,000 but not £5,000 . . . £95 (g) exceeds £5,000 but not £15,000 . . . £195 (h) exceeds £15,000 but not £50,000 . . . £295 (i) exceeds £50,000 or not limited . . . £395

Number & description of fee	Amount of fee
1.3 On the commencement of originating proceedings for any other remedy or relief (including originating proceedings issued after leave to issue is granted)	£120
Fees 1.1 and 1.3 Recovery of land or goods Where a claim for money is additional or alternative to a claim for recovery of land or goods, only fee 1.3 shall be payable.	
Fees 1.1 and 1.3 Claims other than recovery of land or goods Where a claim for money is additional to a non-money claim (other than a claim for recovery of land or goods) then fee 1.1 shall be payable in addition to fee 1.3. Where a claim for money is alternative to a non-money claim (other than a claim for recovery of land or goods) then fee 1.1 or fee 1.3 shall be payable, whichever is the greater.	
Fees 1.1 and 1.3 Generally Where more than one non-money claim is made in the same proceedings, fee 1.3 shall be payable once only, in addition to any fee which may be payable under fee 1.1.	
Fees 1.1 and 1.3 shall not be payable where fee 1.6(b) or fee 8 apply.	

Number & description of fee	Amount of fee
Fees 1.1 and 1.3 Amendment of claim or counterclaim Where the claim or counterclaim is amended, and the fee paid before amendment is less than that which would have been payable if the document, as amended, has been so drawn in the first instance, the party amending the document shall pay the difference.	
1.4 On the filing of proceedings against a party or parties not named in the originating proceedings	£30
Fee 1.4 shall be payable by a defendant who adds or substitutes a party or parties to the proceedings or by a claimant who adds or substitutes a defendant or defendants.	
1.5 On the filing or a counterclaim	The same fee as if the relief or remedy sought were the subject of separate proceedings
1.6 (a) On an application for leave to issue originating proceedings	£30
(b) On an application for an order under Part III of the Solicitors Act 1974 for the assessment of costs payable to a solicitor by his client	£30
2. General Fees 2.1 On the claimant filing an allocation questionnaire; or	£80

Number & description of fee	Amount of fee
where the court dispenses with the need for an allocation questionnaire, within 14 days of the date of despatch of the notice of allocation to track; or	
where the CPR or a Practice Direction provide for automatic allocation or provide that the rules on allocation shall not apply, within 28 days of the filing of the defence (or the filing of the last defence if there is more than one defendant), or within 28 days of the expiry of the time permitted for filing all defences if sooner	
Fee 2.1 shall be payable by the claimant except where the action is proceeding on the counterclaim alone, when it shall be payable by the defendant —	
on the defendant filing an allocation questionnaire; or	
where the court dispenses with the need for an allocation questionnaire, within 14 days of the date of despatch of the notice of allocation to track; or	
where the CPR or a Practice Direction provide for automatic allocation or provide that the rules on allocation shall not apply, within 28 days of the filing of the defence to the counterclaim (or the filing of the last defence to the counterclaim if there is more than one party	

Number & description of fee	Amount of fee
entitled to file a defence to a counterclaim), or within 28 days of the expiry of the time permitted for filing all defences to the counterclaim if sooner	
2.2 On the claimant filing a listing questionnaire; or where the court fixes the trial date or trial week without the need for a listing questionnaire, within 14 days of the date of despatch of the notice (or the date when oral notice is given if no written notice is given) of the trial week or the trial date if no trial week is fixed	
(a) if the case is on the multi-track	£300
(b) in any other case	£200
Fee 2.2 shall be payable by the claimant except where the action is proceeding on the counterclaim alone, when it shall be payable by the defendant — on the defendant filing a listing questionnaire; or where the court fixes the trial date or trial week without the need for a listing questionnaire, within 14 days of the date of despatch of the notice (or the date when oral notice is given if no written notice is given) of the trial week or the trial date if no trial week is fixed.	

Number & description of fee	Amount of fee
Where the court receives notice in writing — before the trial date has been fixed or, where a trial date has been fixed, at least 7 days before the trial date, from the party who paid fee 2.2 that the case is settled or discountinued, fee 2.2 shall be refunded.	
Fees 2.1 and 2.2 Generally Fees 2.1 and 2.2 shall be payable once only in the same proceedings.	
Fees 2.1 and 2.2 shall be payable as appropriate where the court allocates a case to a track for a trial of the assessment of damages.	
Fee 2.1 shall not be payable where the procedure in Part 8 of the CPR is used.	
Fee 2.2 shall not be payable in respect of a small claims hearing.	
2.3 On filing notice of appeal including an appeal against an allocation decision where no other fee is specified	£100
2.4 On an application on notice other than an application to fix the rate of payment before judgment where no other fee is specified	£50
2.5 On an application by consent or without notice for a judgment or order where no other fee is specified	£25

Number & description of fee	Amount of fee
For the purpose of fee 2.5 a request for a judgment or order on admission or in default shall not constitute an application and no fee shall be payable.	
2.6 On an application for a summons or order for a witness to attend court to be examined on oath, other than an application for which fee 4.3 is payable	£30
2.7 On an application to vary a judgment or suspend enforcement (where more than one remedy is sought in the same application only one fee shall be payable)	£25
3. Determination of costs **Transitional provision** Where a bill of costs or a request for detailed assessment or a request for a detailed assessment hearing is filed pursuant to an order made by the court before the coming into operation of this Order, or an application is made to the judge to review a taxation made before the coming into operation of this Order, the fees payable shall be those which applied immediately before this Order came into force.	
3.1 On the filing of a request for detailed assessment where the party filing the request is legally aided and no other party is ordered to pay the costs of the proceedings.	£80

Number & description of fee	Amount of fee
3.2 On the filing of a request for a detailed assessment hearing in any case where fee 3.1 does not apply; or on the filing of a request for a hearing date for the assessment of costs payable to a solicitor by his client pursuant to an order under Part III of the Solicitors Act 1974	£120
Where there is a combined party and party and legal aid determination of costs, fee 3.2 shall be attributed proportionately to the party and party and legal aid portions of the bill on the basis of the amount allowed.	
3.3 On an application for the issue of a default costs certificate	£40
3.4 On an appeal against a decision made in detailed assessment proceedings or on an application to set aside a default costs certificate	£50
3.5 On applying for the court's approval of a Legal Aid Assessment Certificate	£20
Fee 3.5 is payable at the time of applying for approval and is recoverable only against the Legal Aid Fund.	
4. Enforcement 4.1 On an application for or in relation to enforcement of a judgment or order of a county court or through a county court;	

Number & description of fee	Amount of fee
in cases other than CCBC cases, by the issue of a warrant of execution against goods except a warrant to enforce payment of a fine;	(a) Where the amount for which the warrant issues does not exceed £125 . . . £25 (b) Where the amount for which the warrant issues exceeds £125 . . . £45
In CCBC cases, by the issue of a warrant of execution against goods except a warrant to enforce payment of a fine	(c) Where the amount for which the warrant issues does not exceed £125 . . . £20 (d) Where the amount for which the warrant issues exceeds £125 . . . £40
4.2 On a request for a further attempt at execution of a warrant at a new address following a notice of the reason for non-execution (except a further attempt following suspension and CCBC cases)	£20
4.3 On an application to question a judgment debtor or other person on oath in connection with enforcement of a judgment	£40
4.4 On an application for a garnishee order nisi or a charging order nisi, or the appointment of a receiver by way of equitable execution	£50
Fee 4.4 shall be payable in respect of each party against whom the order is sought.	
4.5 On an application for a judgment summons	£80
4.6 On the issue of a warrant of possession or a warrant of delivery	£80

Number & description of fee	Amount of fee
Where the recovery of a sum of money is sought in addition, no further fee is payable.	
4.7 On an application for an attachment of earnings order (other than a consolidated attachment of earnings order) to secure payment of a judgment debt	£50
Fee 4.7 is payable for each defendant against whom an order is sought. Fee 4.7 is not payable where the attachment of earnings order is made on the hearing of a judgment summons.	
4.8 On a consolidated attachment of earnings order or on an administration order	for every £1 or part of a £1 of the money paid into court in respect of debts due to creditors 10p
Fee 4.8 shall be calculated on any money paid into court under any order at the rate in force at the time when the order was made (or, where the order has been amended, at the time of the last amendment before the date of payment).	
4.9 On the application for the recovery of a tribunal award	£30
4.10 On a request for an order to recover an increased penalty charge provided for in a parking charge certificate issued under paragraph 6 of Schedule 6 to the Road	£5

Number & description of fee	Amount of fee
Traffic Act 1991 or on a request for an order to recover amounts payable by a person other than a London authority under an adjudication of a parking adjudicator pursuant to section 73 of the Road Traffic Act 1991; on a request to issue a warrant of execution to enforce such an order	
Fee 4.10 is payable on a request for an order but no further fee is payable on a request to issue a warrant of execution.	
5. Sale **5.1** For removing or taking steps to remove goods to a place of deposit	The reasonable expenses incurred
Fee 5.1 is to include the reasonable expenses of feeding and caring for any animals.	
5.2 For advertising a sale by public auction pursuant to section 97 of the County Courts Act 1984	The reasonable expenses incurred
5.3 For the appraisement of goods	5p in the £1 or part of a £1 of the appraised value
5.4 For the sale of goods (including advertisements, catalogues, sale and commission and delivery of goods)	15p in the £1 or part of a £1 on the amount realised by the sale or such other sum as the district judge may consider to be justified in the circumstances

Number & description of fee	Amount of fee
5.5 Where no sale takes place by reason of an execution being withdrawn, satisfied or stopped	(a) 10p in the £1 or part of a £1 on the value of the goods seized, the value to be the appraised value where the goods have been appraised or such other sum as the district judge may consider to be justified in the circumstances; and in addition (b) any sum payable under fee 5.1, 5.2 or 5.3
6. Copy documents 6.1 On a request for a copy of any document (including a faxed copy where requested) or for examining a plain copy and marking it as an office copy; (a) per page for the first five pages of each document	£1
(b) per page for subsequent pages	25p
Fee 6.1 is pyable whether or not the copy is issued as an office copy.	
6.2 Where copies of any document are made available on a computer disk or in other electronic form, for each such copy	£3
7. Registry of County Court Judgments 7.1 On a request for the issue of a certificate of satisfaction	£10
8. Companies Act 1985 and Insolvency Act 1986 8.1 On entering a bankruptcy petition:	£120

Number & description of fee	Amount of fee
(a) if presented by a debtor or the personal representative of a deceased debtor	
(b) if presented by a creditor or other person	£150
8.2 On entering a petition for an administration order	£100
8.3 On entering any other petition	£150
One fee only is payable where more than one petition is presented in relation to a partnership.	
8.4 (a) On a request for a certificate of discharge from bankruptcy	£50
(b) and after the first certificate, for each copy	£1
Requests and applications with no fee No fee is payable on a request or on an application to the court by the Official Receiver when applying only in the capacity of Official Receiver to the case (and not as trustee or liquidator), or on an application to set aside a statutory demand.	

Index

Accelerated possession orders,
applications for
starting proceedings, 5.06
Access to Justice (Woolf Report,
1996), 1.01
Accounts and inquiries
generally, 9.05
interim order, 14.03
practical point, 9.11
principles, 9.09–9.10
procedure,
application, 9.06–9.07
hearing, 9.08
Acknowledgment of service
failure to file, and,
and see Default judgment
forms, 7.11
generally, 7.05–7.07
procedure, 7.08–7.09
special cases, 7.10
generally, 7.04
Addition of parties
claimant, by, 15.07–15.08
expiry of limitation period,
after, 15.09
generally, 15.06
Address for service
claim form, on,
children, 4.31
firms, 4.32
generally, 4.30, 6.17
patients, 4.31
represented party, 6.07
unincorporated bodies, 4.32
unrepresented party, 6.08
defence, on, 7.19

Administration orders
costs, 25.32
effectiveness, 25.31
generally, 25.29–25.30
Admiralty proceedings, 1.04
Admissions
costs, 7.17
admissibility,
generally, 17.03
hearsay evidence,
17.04–17.06
evidence, and, 17.07
generally, 7.12
request for time to pay, 7.18
specified sums,
part of claim, 7.14
whole of claim, 7.13
unspecified sums,
generally, 7.15
offer in satisfaction, with,
7.16
Adoption proceedings, 1.03
Affidavits, 17.13
Allocation
fast track, 10.09, 12.04
generally, 10.06
multi-track, 10.09, 13.03
possession proceedings, 10.12
questionnaire, 10.07–10.08
generally, 10.07–10.08
precedent, A9.01
rules, 10.10–10.11
small claims track, 10.09
Allocation questionnaire
generally, 10.07–10.08
precedent, A9.01

INDEX

INDEX

INDEX

INDEX

INDEX

INDEX

INDEX

INDEX

INDEX

INDEX

INDEX

INDEX

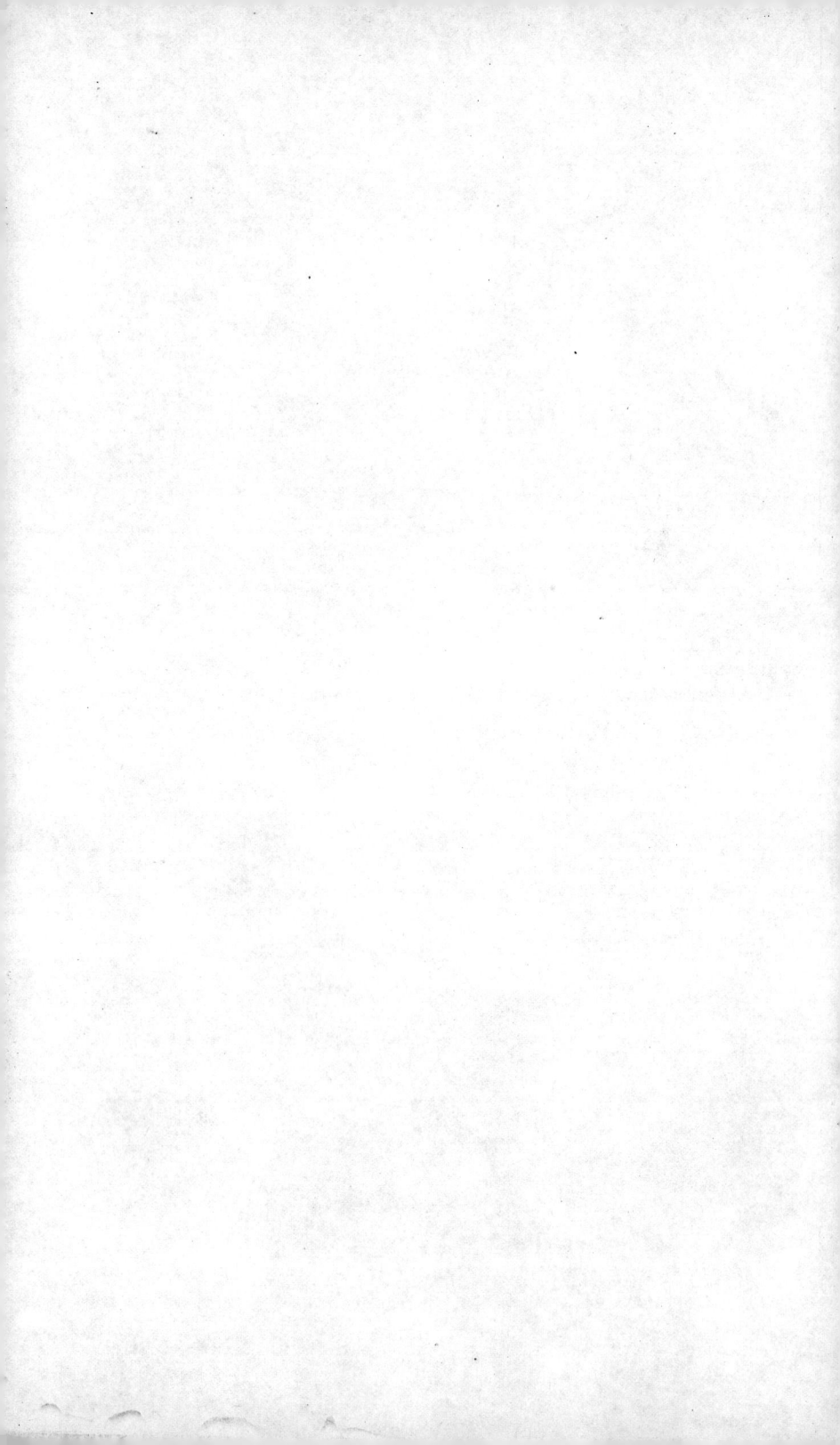